RE-INVENTING

Japan in the Modern World

Series Editor: Mark Selden

RE-INVENTING Japan

TIME, SPACE, NATION

Tessa Morris-Suzuki

An East Gate Book

M.E. Sharpe
Armonk, New York
London, England

An East Gate Book

Copyright © 1998 by M. E. Sharpe, Inc.

All rights reserved. No part of this book may be reproduced in any form
without written permission from the publisher, M. E. Sharpe, Inc.,
80 Business Park Drive, Armonk, New York 10504.

Chapter 1 is a revised version of a chapter first published in S.Tønnesson and H. Antlöv, eds.,
Asian Forms of the Nation (London: Curzon Press, 1996). I am grateful to Curzon Press for
permission to reprint this chapter in revised form. Chapter 2 is a substantially revised version of
an article originally published in *East Asian History*, no. 1 (June 1991); Chapter 3 is a revised
version of an article originally published in *The Journal of Asian Studies*, 54, no. 3 (1995); and
Chapter 7 is a substantially revised version of an article originally published in *Positions: East
Asia Cultures Critique*, 1, no. 2 (1993). I am grateful to the editors of *East Asian History*, the
Asian Studies Association, Inc., and Duke University Press for their permission to reprint these
articles in revised forms. Chapter 8 was originally presented as the annual Asia Lecture at the
Flinders University of South Australia in October 1996. An earlier version of some sections of
Chapter 9 appeared as an article in *Shisō* (September 1996). My thanks to Iwanami Shoten
Publishers for permission to reproduce these sections in substantially revised form.

The author and publishers wish to thank the following individuals and organizations for
permission to use copyrighted illustrations: Iwanami Shoten, for illustrations from
Kinsei kagaku shisō and *Shizuka na taichi*; Meichō Kankōkai for the illustrations from
Kita Ezo Zusetsu; Ryūkei Shoten for the reprinted illustrations from *Tokyo Puck;* Nippon
Hosō Shuppan Kyōkai for the cover illustration from *NHK dorama gaido Oshin;* Kodansha
Ltd. for the illustration from *Tate shakai no ningen kankei;* and Ms. K. Moriki for the
illustration from *Kokusai kekkon handobukku*, published by Akashi Shoten.

Library of Congress Cataloging-in-Publication Data

Morris-Suzuki, Tessa.
Reinventing Japan: time, space, nation / Tessa Morris-Suzuki.
p. cm.—(Japan in the modern world)
Includes bibliographical references and index.
ISBN 0-7656-0081-1 (cloth : alk. paper).— ISBN 0-7656-0082-X (pbk. : alk. paper)
1. Japan. I. Title. II. Series
DS806.M367 1998
952—dc21   97-41873
CIP

Printed in the United States of America

| BM (c) | 10 | 9 | 8 | 7 | 6 | 5 | 4 | 3 | 2 | 1 |
| BM (p) | 10 | 9 | 8 | 7 | 6 | 5 | 4 | 3 | 2 | 1 |

Contents

Author's Note

Asian names are given in the normal order of family name followed by surname, except in the listing of authors of English language works in the bibliography. Macrons are included on long Japanese vowels except in the cases of place names and other words which are familiarly used in English (e.g., Tokyo, not Tōkyō; Shinto, not Shintō).

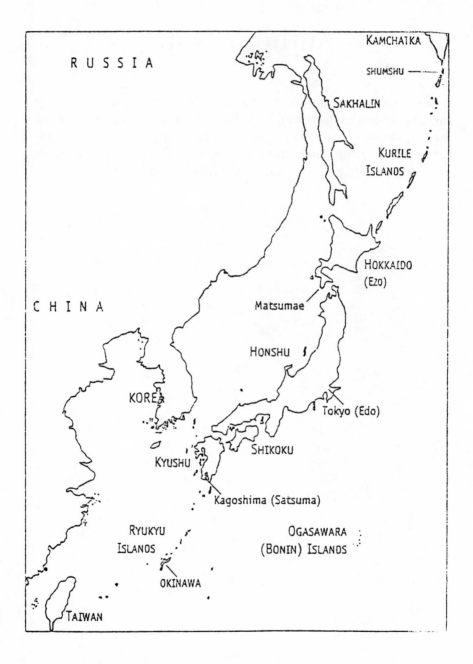

RUSSIA

KAMCHATKA

SHUMSHU ——

SAKHALIN

KURILE
ISLANDS

HOKKAIDO
(Ezo)

CHINA

Matsumae

HONSHU

KOREA

Tokyo (Edo)

KYUSHU

SHIKOKU

Kagoshima (Satsuma)

RYUKYU
ISLANDS

OGASAWARA
(BONIN) ISLANDS

OKINAWA

TAIWAN

RE-INVENTING

Japan

— 1 —

Introduction

Samuel Johnson defined a nation as "people distinguished from other people" (quoted in Fried 1975, 9). His definition is a particularly pleasing one because it exposes the enormous questions concealed inside this self-assertive little word. How do we distinguish between people? Where do we draw the lines? What gives us the confidence not simply to sum up 124 million "Japanese," 80 million "Germans," 1.1 billion "Chinese," or 250 million "Americans" in a single word, but actually to turn these words into actors in the stories we tell: The Japanese are group conscious; the Germans are worried about Russian nationalism; the Chinese mistrust the Japanese; the Americans disapprove of the Chinese attitude to human rights, and so on.

These questions have nagged at me over twenty years of researching and teaching about Japan. In order to say anything at all it is necessary to generalize. So we use conceptual categories which will never be able to capture the fluid, iridescent stuff of reality in all its complexity. But the categories that we commonly use to study a phenomenon like "Japan"—nation, national culture, Japanese society, Japanese people— beg so many questions that they deserve closer scrutiny than they have received so far. Of course, the dividing lines between national, ethnic, and other identity groups have become the subjects of intense debate in the past few years; so much so that I can almost hear the sighs of readers or of casual browsers in bookshops—"Not *another* book on national identity!" But in the midst of this debate, key terms such as "culture," "ethnicity," and "identity" are often tossed around with such abandon that they themselves have become obstacles rather than aids to better understanding.

This book, then, is not an attempt to sketch a new model of Japanese culture or to say something novel about the origins and makeup of the Japanese race (*jinshu*) or ethnic group (*minzoku*). Instead, it is an attempt to delve into the categories of thought which underlie concepts of nationhood—the notions of culture, race, ethnicity, civilization, and Japan itself—and discover how these categories have been used in the Japanese context. In the process, I hope to tease out some of the shifting meanings of these dividing lines between people and to consider the political and social implications of their use. It would be possible, of course, to write a whole book about the evolution of each concept in Japan, for all have long, complex, and fascinating histories. In the confines of a single volume, it is not possible to cover more than a small fraction of the historical and contemporary debates surrounding each. But the advantage of looking at several conceptual categories in a single study, however briefly, is that it helps us see the connections between them and to observe the ways in which imagery and concepts flow back and forth between the rhetoric of culture, natural environment, race, and civilization.

A theme running through the book is the relationship between time and space. In defining the boundaries of the nation and creating images of national belonging, governments, academics, and the popular media make use of both spatial and temporal dimensions. The nation is seen as a bounded geographic entity, whose shape is imprinted on the minds of children by maps on the walls of countless classrooms. It is also an environmental space, understood in terms of familiar imagery of climate and landscape. This sense of the nation as a spatially bounded natural entity is often closely connected with ideas of ethnicity: of citizens as sharing a genetic and cultural heritage adapted to the natural environment of the spatial realm in which they live. But nations can also be seen as "time zones," separated from others by chronology rather than geography. From this point of view, the relationship between "our nation" and others may be understood as a relationship between a more advanced form of social system and more primitive forms. "Our nation" is often assumed to represent the present or future, while "foreigners" represent the past, though sometimes this imaginative relationship is reversed. Jawaharlal Nehru once remarked: "We in India do not have to go abroad in search of the Past and the Distant. We have them here in abundance. If we go to foreign countries, it is in search of the Present" (quoted in Chatterjee 1986, 138; see also Fabian 1983; Wallerstein 1991a). One aim of this study is to explore the varied and often closely interconnected ways in which the dimensions of space and time have been deployed in Japanese debates on nationhood.

The book begins with the notion of Japan itself. Although Japan, unlike some continental countries with constantly shifting borders, appears a readily defined "natural nation," its frontiers are recent, and in places still disputed, inventions. In exploring the drawing of those frontiers, I try to show how ideas of time and space were used to create an image of the nation and to deal with the relationship between frontier regions, such as the Ainu and Okinawan communities, and the center. The creation of nationhood involves not only the drawing of political frontiers but the development of an image of the nation as a single natural environment or habitat—what the philosopher Watsuji Tetsurō called *fūdo*—which comes to be symbolized in the minds of citizens by mountains or deserts, shifting seasons, flowers, mammals, or birds (even though these wild creatures may be ones which most citizens have never seen). Chapter 3 looks at some emerging ideas about Japan as natural environment and about the relationship between Japanese people and that environment.

During the twentieth century, notions of culture, race, and ethnicity—based partly on newly emerging anthropological and archaeological approaches—became key concepts in the understanding of nationhood. The notions were used to define an image of Japan in relation to images of other powerful nation-states (such as the United States, Britain, and France). They were also mobilized to deal with the complex social intersections created by imperial expansion into Taiwan, Korea, Karafuto, and parts of China and Micronesia and by flows of migration into and out of "Japan proper" (*naichi*). Chapters 4 and 5 consider how these new ideas were adopted and developed in Japan and how early twentieth-century understandings of "culture" (*bunka*), "race" (*jinshu*), and "ethnic group" (*minzoku*) continue to color contemporary interpretations of Japanese society. The depictions of the Japanese nation presented both in official writings and in academic and popular debates, although they made frequent use of terms such as "culture" and "ethnicity," seldom explicitly incorporated discussions of gender. But, as argued in Chapter 6, the images which they embodied were often profoundly gendered and conveyed important implicit messages about the relationship between masculinity, femininity, and national identity. Chapter 7 examines how some of these enduring themes in national identity debates survive and are reworked in contemporary Japanese theories of civilization.

What I am developing here is a criticism of ideas like "culture," "ethnicity," and "civilization." But this raises an obvious question. If we abandon notions of an integrated "Japanese culture" or "Japanese civilization," or of a homogeneous "Japanese ethnic group," how can we deal with Japan as a subject of discussion at all? One idea which I use in an attempt to answer this question is the idea of "traditions" in the plural. By "traditions," I mean words, phrases, and bodies of thought which are passed on from one generation to the next and are in the process constantly reinterpreted, reworked, and interwoven. Although I do not think that it is meaningful to talk about a single thing called "Japanese culture," I do think that we can define a multitude of traditions that form the intellectual repertoire of large groups of people in Japan, although they may be interpreted in very different ways by different individuals. These traditions include not only ideas which are readily recognized as "Japanese"—Shinto mythology or the techniques of haiku poetry, for example—but also others whose roots may be traced to societies more recently incorporated into the Japanese state (to Ainu or Okinawan society, for example) or to China, Europe, North America, or elsewhere. A host of such traditions have gradually been assimilated into the domestic repertoire of thought and have become important raw material for contemporary Japanese debates: Confucian notions of the just ruler, ideas about the rise and fall of civilizations, German hermeneutic philosophies and Weberian sociology, among many others.

The particular ways in which these multiple traditions are combined and developed depends not just on political and social developments in Japan itself but also on Japan's relationship with the wider world order. Chapter 8 traces changes in the structure of the twentieth-century world order and relates these changes to shifting formulations of identity in Japan. The final chapter of the book brings the story to the present, when questions of citizenship and political rights are becoming inseparably intertwined with questions of ethnic, cultural, and gender identities. Here I sketch out an alternative way of looking at nationality in a world of global knowledge flows and multiple identities.

Although this is a book about Japan, the issues which I am trying to resolve, in my own mind as well as on the page, are ones with much wider resonances. This problem of distinguishing people lies at the heart of debates about nationhood, citizenship, ethnicity, and multiculturalism in many parts of the world. The concerns of this study are driven by my own experience of a life across frontiers, as a woman

born in Britain, living in Australia, married to a Japanese man, and researching Japanese history; as the mother of a half-English, half-Japanese
son brought up in Australia and living in the United States. It could be
argued that I have let personal experience shape my intellectual agenda
too much: that the problems I speak of here have little relevance to the
large numbers of people who are born, grow up, and die in the same
regional or national community. But the crossing of frontiers seems to
be an inevitable part of present-day society, for in this age of global
information flows you do not need to migrate from place to place to be
confronted by the ideas, fashions, and values of the wider world. Stay
at home and the world—refracted through a host of invisible lenses—
will come to you. So the problem of boundaries, frontiers, and dividing
lines exists not just "out there" at the geographic limits of the nation's
territory: It exists also in our own homes and in our own minds.

While I was writing this book, Australia was in the midst of a
particularly harrowing debate about issues of national identity. The
image of the nation as a multicultural society, which, it was generally
felt, had been gaining ground over the past fifteen years or so, was
opened up to new questioning by a number of public figures, who
suggested a need for a "return" to something closer to the images of
"British heritage" which had dominated the discourse of national identity in the 1940s and 1950s. Although this revisionism was strongly
opposed by supporters of multiculturalism, it made me aware more
than ever of the real power of words like "culture" and "ethnicity" to
fuel political debate and define the practical lines of social inclusion
and exclusion. In countless political speeches, television interviews,
and letters to the editor, I noticed how these seemingly simple words
carry explosive charges of hidden meanings, historical memories, and
implicit stereotypes.

The Australian debate on multiculturalism also reflected in other
ways on my attempts to consider the makings of Japanese national
identity. One common theme of the debate was that, although racism
may be a problem in Australia, "Asians" (or sometimes specifically
"Japanese") are even more racist than "we" are. This glibly repeated
statement encouraged me to look more closely at the (undeniably serious) issue of racism in Japan and at the ideas which underpin that
racism. But it also led me to wonder whether the people who make
such statements are not precisely replicating the mental imagery of the
people they claim to criticize. In other words, when Australians (or

Europeans, Americans, etc.) accuse "the Japanese" of racism, does their category of "Japanese" include people involved in the movement for Okinawan autonomy, Ainu indigenous rights activists and their non-Ainu supporters, Japanese citizens of Korean or Filipino origin who are seeking to gain full acceptance as nationals, or those other Japanese citizens who support their struggles? I suspect that the answer would generally be no—after all, they're not *real* Japanese, are they?

My point is that categories of exclusion—the lines we use to divide people—do not exist only within the boundaries of each nation, but replicate themselves across frontiers like a chain reaction. Exclusivist images of "culture" or "ethnicity" in one nation feed off and reinforce exclusivist images in neighboring nations. At a time when the international mobility of people, goods, ideas, and capital is challenging conventional boundaries of identity, and when notions of nationalism, ethnocentrism, multiculturalism, religious fundamentalism, and cultural relativism are contending with one another, it is more important than ever to go back to Samuel Johnson's image of the nation and to re-examine the lines which divide. Although dividing lines, categories, and simplifications are necessary to make sense of the world we live in, we can try to erase the rigid lines laid down by fossilized dogmas and to sketch out new boundaries which allow room for intersection, multiplicity, mobility, and change. The process is not an easy one, but a journey through the origins and evolution of ideas like "culture," "race," and "civilization" may be the beginning of this process of rediscovery.

2

Japan

Historians of Japan become accustomed to dealing with slippery concepts. They wrestle with definitions of development, modernization, and Westernization; they worry over the application to the Japanese experience of concepts like feudalism, fascism, and democracy. But in all this the one term which seldom appears to need discussion is the word "Japan." Japan seems real and self-explanatory: as Delmer Brown once put it, a "natural region" whose isolation and climatic uniformity accounted for the early rise of national consciousness (Brown 1955, 6–7). In the words of a more recent study, "the surrounding ocean serves as a protective moat" shielding Japan both from invasion and migration, so that since the third or fourth century A.D. there has been "very little infusion of other ethnic groups, resulting in a contemporary population that is fundamentally homogeneous" (Hayes 1992, 4–6).

It is only recently that some Japanese historians have started to pull at the threads holding together this vision of a cohesive national fabric and have shown how readily those threads, when teased, unravel. The purpose of this chapter is to take the process of unraveling a little further by focusing on the problem of Japan's frontiers. I begin with the rather obvious observation that Japan in its present form is a modern artifact, whose frontiers were drawn in the middle of the nineteenth century and have been a source of contention for much of the twentieth. The "moat" surrounding Japan is in fact dotted with lines of stepping stones: small islands which have acted as zones of continuous economic and cultural interchange. The drawing of modern frontiers cuts across these zones and enclosed within the Japanese state a number of groups whose language and history had very little in common with those of (say) Tokyo or Osaka: among them were some 20,000–30,000 Ainu who inhabited Hokkaidō, southern Sakhalin, and the Kur-

ile Archipelago and, to the south, a quarter of a million Okinawans
who inhabited the Ryūkyū Archipelago.

I have chosen to start by looking at the story of these groups—societies
which suddenly found themselves stranded on the margins of a modern
state—because it can tell us a good deal about the nature of the nation
itself. The policies of assimilation used to turn the people of the frontier into Japanese citizens involved a sharpening of the official definition of what it meant to be Japanese. But that definition itself was not
constant or stable. Instead, as we shall see, it was contextual and
changing, shaped both by circumstances within Japan and by the nature of relations between the Japanese state and the societies of the
periphery.

At the core of this changing definition of the nation lay notions of
space and time. The modern nation-state has commonly been presented, by governments and by many social theorists, not just as a
clearly bounded geographic space, but also as the bearer of historical
progress. The nation, as they depicted it, lay at the top of an evolutionary scale which ascended from scattered bands and tribes, through
chiefdoms, ancient empires, and feudal states. Its triumphal march into
the future dominated visions of history, and all too often the small
nonstate societies or microstates which existed and evolved in the in-
terstices between emergent nations were banished from the narratives
of history, consigned to the remote realms of prehistory or to the
timeless world of anthropology.

The formation of "Japan" as a modern nation within its contemporary boundaries involved an important reworking of the relationship
between the Japanese state, on the one hand, and, on the other, regional
communities whose ties to the central government had often been extremely tenuous and the frontier societies of the Ainu and the Ryūkyū
Archipelago. Until the early nineteenth century the Japanese state had,
by and large, perceived the frontier regions in geographical terms as
"foreign" or "exotic." But during the nineteenth century new ideas of
historical progress, imported from Europe and North America, allowed
officials and scholars to reinterpret the unfamiliar features of the outerlying societies in terms of time rather than space: to see them, in
other words, as symptoms of "backwardness" rather than "foreignness." This reconceptualization of difference was a crucial step in the
formation of the image of Japan as a single, clearly bounded modern
nation and of the Japanese as a single "ethnic group." It is therefore

worth tracing the passage of the periphery from space to time in some detail.

Three Views of the World

Let us begin with three views of the world as it appeared from various perspectives in the period which, in European history, is labeled the "early modern" age. One is a view from the north: that is, from the perspective of Ainu society. The Ainu did not keep written records, but some fragments of their world view can be recaptured from their treasury of legends and from the language they used to describe themselves and others. In the eighteenth and nineteenth centuries, a number of Ainu-Japanese vocabularies were compiled for trade and diplomatic purposes and, as Kikuchi Isao has shown, we can use these to draw interesting conclusions about the Ainu sense of place. Like many identity groups, the Ainu saw themselves simply as ordinary people: the word "Ainu" is the word for "human being." Ainu society was structured around small self-organizing communities called *kotan*, often situated along a river or by the seashore. Each *kotan* had defined areas where its members hunted and fished. Women of the *kotan* grew crops of millet and vegetables in riverside gardens which would be used for a year or two and then left to return to wilderness and regain their productive forces. Particular areas of land were therefore identified with particular communities, but not "owned" by individuals or groups in the modern legal sense (Uemura 1990).

Kotan in turn participated in a variety of wider regional and kinship groups, of which the largest, often made up of settlements based along the same river, came together for important religious ceremonies. These regional groups were known as *kur* or *utar*, which might loosely be translated as "clan," and the same words were used to describe small neighboring societies like the Uilta and Nivkh of Sakhalin (who were designated *Rebunkur*, "Clans of Beyond the Sea," as opposed to the Ainu *Yaunkur* or "Clans of the Land"). But there was also another category of society—the large social groups which the Ainu called *shisam*. Initially applied to the Japanese (also referred to as *Yaunshisam*, "Neighbors of the Land") this word also came to be used as the name for Russians and, in the nineteenth century, for American whalers (*Fuureshisam* or "Red Neighbors," presumably because of the color of their hair) (Kikuchi 1991, 90–96).

The term "Japanese," in this context, needs some further examination. The north of the Japanese archipelago was an area of continuing interaction between language groups and social formations. During the period from the thirteenth to the fifteenth centuries, the northern tip of Honshū and the southern part of Hokkaidō had been under the control of the Andō warrior family, who treated the region essentially as their own independent realm. By the beginning of the Tokugawa period (1603–1867), this realm had been brought under the control of the Japanese state, and its territory was divided up among various domain lords (although the Matsumae family, who were recognized as lords of the northernmost domain, located in Hokkaidō, persisted in viewing themselves as somewhat distinct from the rest of Japan). As borders were redefined, the chief dividing line came to be one between those who were incorporated into the control systems of the domain and the Japanese state, referred to as *Shisam* in Ainu and as *Wajin* in Japanese, and those who were largely outside the control systems of the state, called *Ainu* in Ainu and *Ezo* in Japanese. The distinction was first and foremost "political" rather than "racial," and the word *Nihonjin,* though used to distinguish Japanese from Chinese and Europeans, was hardly ever used to distinguish "Japanese" from "Ainu."

The Ainu expression *Shisam* is a word with neutral or even perhaps positive overtones, literally meaning "great and nearby" (Kikuchi 1991, 94). This reflects the open attitude of the Ainu to strangers—an attitude not uncommon in small societies which, like that of the Ainu, rely heavily on trade. The Russian explorer von Krusenstern was echoing a much repeated sentiment when he described the Ainu as showing "neither fear nor backwardness" in their encounters with strangers but as having a hospitality and courtesy which "make me consider the Ainos [*sic*] as the best of all the people that I have hitherto been acquainted with" (von Krusenstern 1968, 76, 83).

Until the middle of the seventeenth century, the Ainu had some reason to welcome Japanese traders. Although contacts with the Neighbors of the Land were always turbulent and sometimes violent, trade relations flourished during the fifteenth and sixteenth centuries with Ainu exchanging furs, fish, hunting hawks, and a variety of goods from the Asian continent for Japanese swords, cooking vessels, and lacquerware. Many Ainu households acquired collections of Japanese metal and lacquer goods which were important sources of prestige and were passed down as family heirlooms from generation to generation.

After the establishment of the Tokugawa Shogunate in 1603, however, trade came under new forms of control. The domain of Matsumae (in southern Hokkaidō) tightened its grip over commerce with the Ainu, creating a monopoly which enabled its representatives to demand exorbitant prices for Japanese goods. In the eighteenth century, merchants licensed by Matsumae started to establish more permanent bases in Ainu territory, setting up fisheries in which they often employed Ainu as semi-slave labor.

The changing relationship looked, from the Ainu perspective, like an increasing Japanese disregard for the basic human etiquette of commercial exchange. In Ainu oral tradition, this seems to be expressed in a sense of betrayal by people who had once been trusted. A famous ballad, for example, tells how a Japanese merchant tried to steal the wife of the god Oina, in the process killing her infant son. The ensuing revenge by Oina on the Japanese is seen by some as an allegorical description of the Shakushain War, the large-scale Ainu uprising against Japanese incursions into their territory which occurred in 1669. But the cry of Oina's wife to her captors suggests a wider consciousness of a souring in the relationship between the Ainu and the neighbors of the Land: "I had heard the Japanese called honorable people, people with truly good hearts, but how evil your hearts must be!" (Shinya 1977, 242).

Next, a view from "the metropolis," or at least from the standpoint of the relatively educated urban section of the Japanese population. Until the middle of the eighteenth century most ordinary people in Japan would have had little cause to reflect on their identity as *Nihonjin* (or as *Wajin*). The word *kuni* (country), when it was used, more often referred to the local region or domain than to Japan as a whole. Even in the early nineteenth century, travelers were warned that once outside their own region they were in "enemy territory," and guidebooks found it necessary to advise the visitor to strange provinces not to laugh at local customs or accents (Vaporis 1989).

Among intellectuals, however, the sudden expansion of contacts with the outside world in the sixteenth century stimulated curiosity about Japan's place in the world—a curiosity which was not extinguished by the tight controls on foreign trade imposed from the mid-seventeenth century onward; and, as the social commentator Tokutomi Sohō was later to argue: "the concept 'foreign nations' brought forth the concept 'Japanese nation' " (Myers and Peattie 1984, 64). A fascinating expression of this gradually emerging sense of nationality can be found in the illustrated guides to the "Peoples of the World" which appeared in Japan from the late sixteenth century onward. The first examples were incorporated into decorative screens which included maps of the world copied from imported Western sources. Intriguingly, these screens faithfully reproduced the Western schema by which nations are presented as contiguous blocks of bold primary colors, separated by clearly defined borders. Yet their designers do not seem to have made a clear association between political nationhood and the colors represented on the map: Japan is typically partitioned into several differently colored blocks, representing the long-vanished provinces of the Nara period (A.D. 645–794) (Muroga 1978).

The ethnic groups presented on these screens were at first depicted in a style which suggests meticulous copying of a European prototype, but as time went on the iconography became "Japanized" and the imagery vividly inventive. One *Bankoku Sōzu* (Chart of All the Nations), produced in 1640, depicts forty different ethnic groups, each illustrated by a man and woman wearing national dress. Japan, represented by a splendidly armored samurai and his wife, occupies pride of place in the top righthand corner and is followed by China, Tartary, Taiwan and a variety of Southeast Asian countries such as Java, Sumatra, Annam, and Tonkin. Further down the chart come India and several European countries, ending with some rather speculative depictions of "Americans" and "Africans" (Torii 1926, 122–124). As Ronald Toby has pointed out, these representations were related to a wider fascination with the "other," stimulated by the arrival of the exotic Europeans, which was also expressed in drama and pageants where participants appeared dressed as "foreigners" of various shapes and forms (Toby 1994, 332–335).

Before the late eighteenth century, however, most Japanese visions of the world outside were still more powerfully influenced by China than by the West. The widely circulated *Wakan Sansai Zue* (Illustrated Japanese-Chinese Encyclopedia) of 1712 borrowed much of its information from a Chinese prototype, the Illustrated Encyclopedia of 1609, but supplemented this with knowledge gathered by Japanese scholars from Dutch merchants and other sources. The Encyclopedia divided the world beyond Japan into two parts: "foreign countries" (*ikoku*) populated by those who used Chinese characters and chopsticks and "outer barbarians" (*gai-i*), peopled by those who wrote horizontally and ate with their hands (Terajima 1929, 217). In the first category comes China, Korea, Chinra (Cheju Island, in fact long since absorbed by the Korean kingdom), Mongolia, the Ryūkyū Kingdom, Ezo (the land of the Ainu), Tartary, the land of the Jurchens, Taiwan, Cochin, and Tonkin (Terajima 1929, 202–216). The second group includes some readily recognizable regions such as Malacca, Siam, Luzon, Spain, Java, Jakarta (*Jagatara*—treated separately from Java), Bengal, and Holland. Interspersed among them are less familiar places, including the Land of the Pygmies, the Land of the Giants, and the Land of the Bird People (Terajima 1929, 217–246). Each country is both illustrated and described, sometimes in considerable detail. The sections on Korea, Ezo, and the Ryūkyū Kingdom, for example, not only provide several paragraphs on national history and customs but also include a sample vocabulary of the local language. The feeling conveyed by this work is of a world made up of concentric circles of increasing strangeness, stretching almost infinitely outward from a familiar center. Holland's position as one of the last countries to be described—just before the Land of the Dragons and the place inhabited by creatures with six legs and four wings—indicates, perhaps, that it represented the most distant and strangest people of whom the Japanese were clearly aware.

This vision of the world as a series of concentric circles was drawn from the Chinese *Hua-yi* (in Japanese, *ka-i*) model of the world, in which barbarism (*i*) increases the farther one moves away from the settled and civilized center (*ka*). In the Illustrated Japanese-Chinese Encyclopedia there seems still to be some ambiguity as to whether Japan or China is to be regarded as the center. It is true that China is listed as a "Foreign Country," while Japan does not appear at all in the description of the peoples of the world. Other sections of the Encyclopedia, however, contain much more information about Chinese geography than they do about the geography of Japan.

By the end of the eighteenth century, however, Japan's place in the order of things had become more confident. The *Chinsetsu kidan ehon bankokushi* (Illustrated Strange Tales and Wonderful Accounts of the Countries of the World) of 1772 (revised in 1826) begins with Japan, before working its way gradually outward to such places as the Land of People with One Eye and the Land of People with One Leg. Japan, while still illustrated by a picture of a samurai, is now represented by a distinctly urbanized samurai encountering a group of geisha in a city street. The author, without undue modesty, lists nobility and instinctive moral rectitude as being among the defining characteristics of the Japanese: "even if they do not know the five [Confucian] virtues, they still keep to the true path." The most important characteristic of Japaneseness, however, and the one discussed at greatest length, is a sensitive appreciation of the beauties of poetry (Torii 1926, 139). This description seems to reflect the influence of the emerging ideas of the Nativism, propagated by scholars like Motoori Norinaga (1730–1801), in which Japanese identity was defined in terms of spontaneous virtue and creativity, as opposed to the rigidity and sterility attributed to Chinese learning (see Chapter 3).

Lastly, a view from the south. The intellectual life of the Ryūkyū Kingdom, like the intellectual life of Japan, was deeply influenced by China and absorbed the same *ka-i* model of the global order. Indeed, as its power expanded in the fifteenth and sixteenth centuries, the kingdom constructed its own miniature version of the Chinese system, exacting tribute from outlying islands such as Yaeyama, to the south of the main Okinawan Island. Within this order, however, Ryūkyūan scholars of the fifteenth and sixteenth centuries were conscious of their kingdom as a small country poised in the most delicate of strategic locations between the powerful presences of Chinese, Koreans, and Japanese (whom they called *Yamatonchu*). On the one hand, Ryūkyūan writings reveal familiarity with and respect for the power of their larger neighbors. The songs of the classical *Omoro sōshi* (including material dating from the twelfth to early seventeenth centuries) praise local cities by comparing them to the splendors of the Japanese cities of Kyoto and Kamakura, and the sixteenth-century king Shō Shin's achievements are listed as including the "emulation of the system of the imperial palaces of China, [in which] blue stones have been carved to make the balustrades which span the lower section of the palace. This is a sign of prosperity which was not seen in ancient times." Better still, Shō Shin had succeeded in having Ryūkyū's tribute missions to China increased from triennial to annual events: an achievement which not only brought increased trading profits into the kingdom but also marked a satisfying recognition by the great Ming empire of the Ryūkyūs' significance (Sakihara 1987, 166).

At the same time, however, the kingdom's social elite were aware and proud of their special place as a crossroads of East Asian trade. A fifteenth-century inscription commissioned by King Shō Taikyū describes his realm as "the anchorage of all the nations," an archipelago whose small size is made up for by its position on the intersecting sea-roads from north (Japan and Korea), west (the Ming empire), and south (the many lands of Southeast Asia). The Ryūkyūs "gather together all that is best from the three kingdoms of Korea, they serve as a balancing wheel to the Great Empire of Ming, and stand at the mouth of the Region of the Sun [Japan]" (Higashionna 1966, 68–70). Although it might lack military or political power, the kingdom could still envisage itself as possessing a special commercial hold over a vast geographical area: "Kyoto and Kamakura,/ Java and the South Seas [literally 'southern barbarians']/ China and Miyako [a small archipelago to the south of the Ryūkyū islands]/ Let them all serve our king," ran one verse from the *Omoro sōshi* (quoted in Sakihara 1987, 177).

This sense of strategic importance—of balancing the competing pressures and demands of larger neighbors—was a source both of pride and of considerable unease. After the invasion of the Ryūkyūs by the Japanese domain of Satsuma in 1609, the kingdom was forced into the particularly invidious position of maintaining its traditional tributary relationship with China while at the same time trying to satisfy the injunctions of a new and more assertive tributary overlord, Satsuma, and through it indirectly the Japanese Shogunate.

The *Ka-I* Order and the Logic of Difference

The path which led to the redefinition of Ainu and Ryūkyūans as "Japanese" was shaped by two forces. The first was the force of Japan's changing relationship with China; the second, the force of the encounter with the European powers from the late eighteenth century onward. Although the relationships with China and with Europe were in many ways interconnected, the logic of these forces often pulled in different directions.

The consolidation of power in the hands of the Tokuagawa Shogunate, after centuries of intermittent civil war, encouraged Japan's elite to attempt to redraw the traditional *ka-i* view of the world so that Japan itself would be the pre-eminent *ka,* the civilized center of its own miniature world order (Toby 1984, 217–219). This required a restructuring of relations between inside and outside, placing the societies of the Japanese periphery in a subordinate, tributary relationship modeled after the relationship between the Chinese empire and its "barbarian" periphery. The foundations of the new order were laid down at the beginning of the Tokugawa period, when the domain of Matsumae was granted a monopoly over trade with the Ainu and Satsuma's invasion subordinated the Ryūkyū Kingdom to its control.

The symmetry between north and south was not perfect. In the south, Satsuma posted its officials in the Ryūkyū capital, Shuri, and claimed the right to regulate the kingdom's trade and taxation system. Part of the tax in kind levied on Ryūkyū agriculture was transferred to Satsuma, becoming an important source of the domain's income, and regular tribute missions from the Ryūkyūs were sent, not simply to Satsuma but to the shogun's seat of government in Edo. Until the early eighteenth century, the Shogunate itself took little interest in these visits, but from about 1708 onward the central government began to recognize them as a crucial legitimating symbol of its claim to stand at the pinnacle of a hierarchical world order whose focal point was Edo (Kamiya 1990, 249–251). In the north, meanwhile, the domain of Matsumae showed little desire to intervene in the life of the Ainu and allowed its appointed officials (and, later, licensed merchants) to trade and exploit as they wished. Matsumae levied no official tax on the Ainu, but creamed off a substantial portion of the profits of trade. Although Ainu elders made annual ceremonial visits to the Lord of Matsumae's castle—visits which the domain interpreted as tribute missions—they did not make the long journey to the shogunal capital.

The common cornerstone of the *ka-i* edifice, however, was the logic of difference. The relationships with the Ainu and the Ryūkyū Kingdom were important precisely because they represented the subordination of foreign people to Japanese dominion. Everything about the relationship, therefore, had to be structured in such as way as to magnify the exotic character of the peripheral societies. In Matsumae domain, the Ainu families who had lived side by side with *Wajin* settlers in the southern tip of modern Hokkaidō were gradually driven out into "Ezochi"—Ainu territory. Ainu were forbidden to learn Japanese or wear characteristically Japanese articles of clothing such as straw sandals and straw raincoats and were discouraged from engaging in farming. (The Ainu economy was based largely on hunting, fishing, and gathering, but Ainu women also cultivated small plots of millet and vegetables. Among the measures used by Matsumae to suppress this was a prohibition on the sale of seeds to the Ainu) (Mogami 1972, 315). A similar policy of separation was applied, until the early eighteenth century, to the very small communities of a few hundred Ainu who still lived in the northern Honshū domains of Tsugaru and Nambu. Here too Ainu lived in separate villages, were subject to distinct rules and regulations, and were from time to time required to make ceremonial missions to the domain lord (Namikawa 1992, 48–63).

In the relationship between Satsuma and the Ryūkyū Kingdom, the most important celebration of difference was the tribute mission to Edo. Each mission was an extravagant and elaborately staged dramatization of the logic of *ka-i*. The large Ryūkyū contingent, including merchants, scholars, and craftspeople, as well as government officials, traveled in procession from Satsuma to Edo, flanked by an armed guard of Satsuma warriors. Ryūkyū officials were given precise instructions about their dress and conduct for these occasions. A decree of 1709, for example, stated that they were to carry long swords, dress in brocade, and bring with them "Chinese-style" weaponry. Their equipment, above all, must be "of the sort used in a foreign court, so that they cannot be mistaken for Japanese" (Kamiya 1990, 255).

The sense of difference was inscribed in the Japanese popular imagination not just by ceremonial events like the tribute missions to Edo, but also by travelers' accounts of the exotic "world outside" published from the early eighteenth century onward. Images of difference presented by early travelers were often copied word for word by other writers, creating a stock repertoire of distinctions between center and periphery. Descriptions of the Ainu almost always began with comments about hairstyle, clothing, jewelry, and the facial tattooing common among Ainu women. As David Howell observes, in Tokugawa society differing hairstyles were one of the most obvious marks of status, and the only people who did not bind or shave their hair were members of certain outcaste groups. The flowing locks and beards of the Ainu were therefore the visible sign of a people beyond the realms of the existing social order (Howell 1994, 88; Kikuchi 1988, 206–229). After detailed discussions of clothing and footwear, the accounts generally went on to discuss the Ainu diet. To *Wajin* observers it was striking that the Ainu grew no rice (although they bought it in considerable quantities from Japanese merchants), that they took their meals at irregular times, and that they ate deer and bear as well as salmon and a variety of other fish (a practice uncommon except in the remote mountain regions of Japan itself).

Japanese travelers' tales, as much as those of their eighteenth-century European counterparts, are often supercilious in their descriptions of the "barbarians." The illiteracy of the Ainu and their "ignorance" of the Confucian sages aroused particular contempt. On the other hand, Ainu skill at diving for shellfish was remarked upon, as was their use of poisoned arrows for hunting. Matsumae domain, in fact, made strenuous efforts to discover the secrets of Ainu arrow poisons, and several Japanese visitors to the region seem to have studied Ainu herbal medicine in the hope of finding new cures to familiar maladies (Sakakura 1979, 73; Mogami 1972; Arai 1979).

In accounts of Okinawa, the narrative often began with a retelling of the legend (apparently propagated from the early seventeenth century onward) which identified the kings of Ryūkyū as descendants of the Japanese warrior Minamoto no Tametomo, thus offering an official justification of the view that the archipelago owed allegiance to Japan. They then described the ranks of Ryūkyū nobility, commenting particularly on the clothes and headgear which distinguished each rank. (The unusual hats worn by the Ryūkyū nobility figured prominently in the iconography of difference.) As in the case of the Ainu, the hairstyles, jewelry, and tattoos of Ryūkūan women attracted comment. The many ceremonies marking the seasons of the year and the stages of human life in the Ryūkyū kingdom were recorded in detail. Descriptions of events like the celebration of the new year, when children played special ball games and demonstrated their agility on homemade seesaws, give a picturesque flavor to accounts of life in the "South Seas." The songs and dances of the archipelago were often discussed at length, as were the local cremation practices, including the Ryūkyūan practices of washing and arranging the bones of the deceased after cremation. Although some similarities with Japan were noted—houses looked similar, and the literate sections of the Ryūkyū population used the Japanese phonetic syllabary—the overall impression is very much of "different country," though not of a place whose exoticism would put it in the outer circles of barbarism (for example, Anon. 1981).

The Nation-State and the Logic of Assimilation

Japan's growing contact with the European powers from the late eighteenth century onward, on the other hand, exposed the country to the pressures of a quite different world order: an order based upon European notions of nationhood. The imperial nations of Europe, of course, had their "barbarian peripheries," but these were not arranged in concentric circles around the metropolis: They were far-flung maritime empires, linked to the mother country by the invisible webs of worldwide shipping routes. From the Japanese point of view, what was new about this was not the notion of a frontier itself: Japan was full of frontiers, well-marked and well-guarded lines separating domain from domain, or (in the case of Matsumae) separating the Japanese-settled area from Ainu territory. Rather, it was the idea of the frontier as a single, unequivocal line marking the boundary between one nation and another, instead of the idea (inherited from the Chinese worldview) of a series of frontiers marking gradually increasing degrees of difference.

Japan's first truly alarming encounter with this European order occurred in the north, as Russian traders, soldiers, and missionaries extended their influence from Kamchatka into the northern Kurile Islands. By the 1740s there were trading posts and churches on the northern island of Shumshu, and local Ainu were rapidly being Russified: adopting Western dress, Russian names, and Orthodox Christianity. Japan's response to this challenge was predictable. To protect the northern border from Russian encroachment, it was clearly necessary that the Ainu should be redefined as Japanese. In the words of the famous geographer Honda Toshiaki (1744–1821), who advocated the Japanese colonization of the Kuriles, Sakhalin, and Kamchatka: "we must establish a mutual frontier between Japan and other countries and create a fortress to withstand foreign enemies" (Kaiho 1970, 129). The form which this Japanization of the periphery should take was a source of lively debate in scholarly circles. While some writers focused narrowly on the strategic significance of the region, others (including Honda's student, the explorer Mogami Tokunai), advocated the large-scale agricultural development of Ainu territory and suggested that the Ainu themselves should be taught the Japanese language, encouraged to adopt Japanese styles of dress and diet, and instructed in the arts of farming (Mogami 1972). These projects for assimilation were in part inspired by the experiences of the northern Honshū domains of Tsugaru and Nambu, where the pressures of a hungry population had made it in practice impossible to maintain the separation of Ainu and non-Ainu populations. As more and more *Wajin* families moved into Ainu areas, the domain governments had eventually abandoned their separatist approaches and, by about the middle of the eighteenth century, adopted policies of assimilating Ainu into the general commoner population (Namikawa 1992).

As far as Matsumae was concerned, the ideas of men like Mogami had some impact on the thinking of the central government. As the Russian threat intensified, Ainu territory was placed under direct Shogunal control (the east of modern Hokkaidō, together with the southern Kuriles, was transferred to Shogunal rule in 1799, and the west together with southern Sakhalin in 1807). The initial government instructions drawn up for running the territory spoke of the need to encourage the Ainu to "turn into Japanese" (*wajin ni henka suru*) by gradually encouraging them to live in Japanese houses, to abandon their "uncivilized" habit of eating meat, to cut their hair in Japanese style, to take up farming, and to study the Japanese language (Takakura 1972, 139). Many of these measures, however, proved in practice to be beyond the financial and administrative resources of the Shogunate, and assimilation policies, as they were put into effect, concentrated on outer appearances. Strenuous (though not entirely successful) efforts were made to persuade Ainu men to cut their beards and tie up their hair in a style that would define them as *hyakusho* ("commoners" in the Tokugawa status system) (Amino 1994). Some religious ceremonies were suppressed, and a number of Ainu communities, particularly those near the border with Russia, were induced to adopt the traditional Japanese farmer's dress of cotton jackets and straw sandals. In several areas, Japanese officials organized public ceremonies to "celebrate the improvement of customs" (*kaizoku no gi*), at which cooperative Ainu were paraded in their new costume, treated to Japanese-style banquets, and sometimes presented with "assimilation medals" (*kaizoku hai*) (Takakura 1972; Kikuchi 1991, 11–13).

Two points about these policies are particularly interesting. The first is the acknowledgment that people could be "turned into *Wajin*": that is, that national identity was a matter of following certain customs, rather than an immutable matter of race. The second is the form of "Japaneseness" imposed upon the Ainu. At a time when writers like Motoori Norinaga were developing a particular image of Japan-as-opposed-to-China (an image which emphasized spontaneity and natural appreciation of beauty), the official version of Japan-as-opposed-to-Ainu was still surprisingly Chinese. That is to say, it followed the Chinese *ka-i* formula in stressing outer appearances and etiquette as the main distinctions between civilization and barbarism, and, where it addressed issues of personal ethics, it did so mainly in Confucian terms (Howell 1994, 87). One of the few Japanese works to be translated into the Ainu language (written in Japanese phonetic script) for the purposes of moral instruction was, curiously enough, a handbook of ethics generally attributed to a Japanese Confucian scholar, but which was itself actually a work by the Sinophile Ryūkyūan scholar Tei Junsoku translated into Japanese around the beginning of the eighteenth century (Takakura 1972, 356).

A sense of the encroaching presence of the Western powers influenced eighteenth-century Japanese views of the world to the west and south, as well as to the north. In 1785 the astronomer Hayashi Shihei produced his *Illustrated Outline of the Three Countries* (Sangoku tsūran zusetsu), the first attempt to define Japan's position in relation to its neighbors, Korea, the Ryūkyū Kingdom, and the Ainu. Unlike the screen-painters of the early Tokugawa period, Hayashi colored his map in a way that defined Japan as a single unit, clearly distinguished from its neighbors, and in the process firmly defined the Ryūkyūs and Ainu territory as foreign countries. Hayashi not only advocated the Japanization of the Ainu but also discussed the climate and fertility of the then-uninhabited Ogasawara Islands, and argued that they should be colonized by Japan (Hayashi 1979, 77–79). However, nothing came of this, and Hayashi was soon afterward imprisoned for his temerity in publishing his views on the need for stronger Japanese maritime defenses (Goodman 1986, 213–215). It was only in the north that the threat from Europe seemed close enough to warrant practical action, and even there efforts at assimilation were dropped as the Russian menace receded. In 1821 control of the northern frontier was returned to Matsumae domain, and the doubtless bewildered Ainu were promptly ordered to stop wearing Japanese clothes and abandon their efforts to learn the Japanese language (Takakura 1972, 280–281).

Modernity, Civilization, and Assimilation

A comprehensive effort to "Japanize" the periphery began only after Japan's wholehearted entry into the modern world order in the mid-nineteenth century. In 1855 Japan and Russia completed the first of many attempts to define their mutual border, and in 1869, the year after the Meiji Restoration, the Land of the Ainu was incorporated into the new state under the name "Hokkaidō" (North Sea District). Control of the Ryūkyūs was more contentious and caused serious strains in Japan's relationship with China. In the end, however, neither the

Ryūkyū Kingdom itself nor China had the strength to resist the demands of the self-assertive Meiji government: In 1879, the last king, Shō Tai, was forced to abdicate and the Ryūkyū Kingdom became Okinawa Prefecture. Another area which caused much concern to officialdom were the Ogasawara or Bonin Islands, which had been uninhabited when Hayashi Shihei included them in his *Illustrated Outline of the Three Countries,* but had subsequently been claimed by both Britain and the United States and settled by a motley band of adventurers from various parts of the world. In the 1870s, when Britain and the United States relinquished their claims on the islands to Japan, the Ogasawaras had a population of seventy-one, whose places of origin included England, the United States, Spain, Germany, Hawaii, and Guam and who were hastily naturalized by being enrolled in Japanese family registers (Yamagata 1906, 367).

Once the outlines of the state had been defined, there followed a period of cultural coloring in: an attempt to blend the societies of the periphery into the official image of a united and centralized nation. But the Japanese society to which the people of the periphery were to be assimilated was itself in the midst of rapid and profound change. The idea of civilization which inspired the Meiji government's *mission civilisatrice* was no longer the Chinese notion of *ka,* with its emphasis on order and outward propriety, but rather the Western-inspired version of civilization for which Meiji scholars were obliged to invent a Japanese translation: *bunmei.* Unlike *ka, bunmei* was a dynamic concept, laden with overtones of progress. Its basis was not harmony and hierarchy but production: the ability to create material wealth which would release the human spirit from the bonds imposed on it by nature. In the words of its most famous Japanese theorist, Fukuzawa Yukichi, the attainment of *bunmei* involved successive stages of development. First, the "primitive" stage in which "neither dwellings nor supplies of food are stable" and "man . . . cowers before the forces of nature"; next, the "semideveloped" stage where "daily necessities are not lacking, since agriculture has been started on a large scale," but where people only "know how to cultivate the old," not "how to improve it"; and, finally, the stage of full civilization, where, on the basis of material abundance, "today's wisdom overflows to create the plans of tomorrow" (Fukuzawa 1973, 13–14).

In relation to *bunmei,* Japan found itself again in much the same position as it had in relation to *ka* in the early seventeenth century.

Once more it was relegated to the periphery of civilization, faced with the task of creating anew its own local world order in which it could constitute itself as the center. In the seventeenth century, this had involved turning the societies of the frontier into tributary foreign states; now it involved turning them into parts of the civilized nation-state. For, as Fukuzawa comfortingly pointed out, civilization was a relative thing, and if Japan looked "uncivilized" when compared to the Western great powers, the Japanese (*waga Nihon jōkoku no jinmin*—literally, "people of our Japanese imperial nation") "can be called civilized" when compared with the Ainu (Fukuzawa 1973, 14).

This shifting vision of the world order had three crucial consequences for Meiji assimilation policy. First, it meant that assimilation went far beyond the outward forms of clothing, hairstyles, or even language, to transform the texture of daily life and work. Its central element now was a restructuring of the relationship between humans and nature, imposing on the periphery an idealized image of a society of hard-working, small-scale peasant farmers. In "Japan proper," the traditional pattern of *de facto* ownership of land by individual peasant families had been given a new gloss of civilization by the Land Tax Ordinance of 1873, which conferred *de jure* property rights on farmers and imposed on them a uniform duty to pay a monetary land tax. This now became the standard of civilization for the periphery. In Hokkaidō, the government (advised by Horace Capron, a former U.S. secretary of agriculture who had played an important role in suppressing Native American resistance to the conquest of the American West) embarked on a plan for the large-scale colonization and agricultural development of the island. The Ainu—a dwindling minority in their own country—lost their traditional hunting and fishing grounds, which became the property of the Japanese state or were transferred to the private ownership of colonists from Japan proper.

The main instrument in the assimilation of the Ainu was to be the Former Natives Protection Law (Kyūdojin hogo hō) of 1899, which stipulated that Ainu families were to be given two to five hectares of farmland together with grants of seed and tools. The land could not be sold without official permission and was to be confiscated by the government if it was not farmed within fifteen years. At the same time, the financial assets of Ainu communities were placed under government control and disbursed as the state deemed fit to meet the "welfare" needs of the Ainu.

Not surprisingly, the law served none of its stated purposes. As an assimilation measure, it failed because it marked the Ainu as different: people who could not be relied upon to act as proper citizens without government guidance. From the start, it had no prospect of providing a reasonable livelihood for Ainu villagers because it merely handed back (under strict conditions) a tiny fraction of the land previously confiscated by the state. The plots of land provided were often in the most remote and least fertile areas and were generally too small to be viable. Notions of individual small-scale farming were at odds with the traditional structure of the Ainu community, and even when families succeeded in growing crops on their land, these were hardly sufficient to make up for the loss of traditional hunted and gathered food sources. In many cases, plots were rented out to Japanese settlers on long-term leases at low rents, while their Ainu owners went to seek work in the rapidly growing towns or the coastal fisheries. This, ironically enough, turned some Ainu into "absentee landlords" and ensured that they experienced a final round of dispossession in the land reforms introduced after World War II by the democratizing forces of the Allied occupation (Hokkaidō Utari Kyōkai 1990, 861).

To the south, in the newly created prefecture of Okinawa, the course of events was initially very different. The Ryūkyū archipelago had a substantial and fairly prosperous ruling class, many of whom had close emotional ties to China. Having offended the Chinese by destroying the kingdom, the Japanese government was wary of provoking further conflict by too obvious a policy of Japanization. Although Matsuda Michiyuki, the official in charge of the establishment of Okinawa Prefecture, warned Okinawans that they would "experience the same situation as the American Indians and the Ainu" if they did not "change their old attitudes," little was done at first to enforce such change (Okinawa Ken 1977, 237). The officialdom of the old kingdom was replaced with a new superstratum of Japanese administrators, but the existing form of communal land-holding was retained, and Okinawans were initially neither given the right to elect members to the new Japanese parliament (opened in 1890) nor required to serve in the new conscript army.

During the late 1890s, however, this policy of "preserving old customs" (as it was called) underwent a dramatic change. The overwhelming victory of Japan in its war with China (1894–95) removed Japanese inhibitions about offending the Chinese, and the strains of maintaining the traditional tax system in an age of rapid economic change provoked protests from local taxpayers. The establishment of a new order was marked by the introduction of the Okinawa Prefecture Land Reorganization Law (Okinawa ken tochi seiri hō), passed in the same year as Hokkaidō Former Natives Protection Law and serving the same basic purpose of replacing communal with private land ownership. The tradition by which the village controlled farmland, and had the power to redistribute it from time to time among inhabitants, was replaced by a system of individual property rights vested in the heads of households, while the numerous Okinawan taxes in kind were replaced by a single monetary land tax (Okinawa Ken, 1977, 80–83). This removed some of the arbitrary and oppressive aspects of the old regime, but (like the Japanese Land Tax Ordinance itself) opened the way to the rapid consolidation of farm holding in the hands of landlords, many of whom, in the Okinawan context, were Japanese merchants.

Because it reached so deeply into everyday life—imposing national uniformity on a wide range of economic, social, and cultural institutions—the Meiji assimilation process forced the state to confront complex problems of defining standards. A second major consequence of the vision of *bunmei,* indeed, was the emergence of a much more ambitious and totaling vision of "Japaneseness" than had existed in the Tokugawa period. Tokugawa efforts to assimilate the Ainu, for example, had been accompanied by some attempts to teach them Japanese, but these had been sporadic and largely left to the initiative of local officials. In the Meiji period, by contrast, the institutionalized enforcement of Japanese as the national language was a central element of assimilation. As the Okinawan education authorities observed in 1901:

> The educational level of this prefecture has become equal to that of other prefectures. There has been progress in the development of a sense of national citizenship and in exterior appearances such as the clothing of boys and girls. However, there are still some areas in which there is a sense of foreignness and underdevelopment compared with other prefectures. Not only many uneducated people, but also some schoolchildren and people who have completed general education speak the local dialect, and even when they speak normal language [*futsūgo*], their intonation and pronunciation sounds odd.
>
> (Okinawa Ken 1977, 99)

But the enforcement of "normality" required a definition of what was normal. The idea that a single, recognizable norm of Japanese behavior should exist in all areas of human life was widespread, not just among officials but also among sections of the population in the periphery itself. The *Ryūkyū shimpō* (Ryūkyū News), a journal established by young Okinawan intellectuals in the 1890s, advised its readers that their aim should be "to become like the people of other prefectures in tangible and intangible ways, for better and for worse, from A to Z. In graphic terms, we might say that when they sneeze, they should sneeze like people from other prefectures" (Ōta 1969, 23). The Meiji state did not go so far as to propose a uniform Japanese way of sneezing, but it did succeed in imposing order on many aspects of the existing regional diversity of Japanese culture, including the multiplicity of regional dialects which existed throughout the country. Efforts to enforce the use of "normal language" in Okinawa and among the Ainu were accompanied by heated debates about the relative merits of the Kyoto or Tokyo dialects or of various forms of artificial *lingua franca,* as the official form of "standard Japanese"—debates which were ultimately won by those who favored the Japanese of the Tokyo middle classes (Twine 1991, chap. 8).

Social standardization was imposed, on both the people of the frontier and the people of the various Japanese regions, through the education system and through military training. A highly centralized system of compulsory education, officially introduced in 1873 and gradually extended to the people of more remote rural and frontier regions, proved a particularly powerful instrument of nation-building (Marshall 1994, 25–89). Conscription, which was introduced to Okinawa in 1898 (thirteen years ahead of parliamentary representation), not only fostered a uniform ideology of loyalty to the emperor, but also brought together people from all over the country, helping to create a sense of the nation as community and to accelerate the spread of standard Japanese as the common means of communication.

Time, Space, and Difference

But the most interesting implication of the notion of *bunmei* was the way in which it allowed difference to be transposed from the realm of space to the realm of time, so that "foreignness" increasingly came to be reinterpreted as "underdevelopment." Fukuzawa's vision of a series of stages of development allowed the unfamiliar features of Ainu or

Okinawan society to be perceived as remnants from a more primitive stage of human history. As a result, the frontier areas, which had once been seen as having their own distinctive sets of foreign customs, now began to be homogenized in the popular mind into a uniformly backward periphery. As one governor of Okinawa remarked in the early twentieth century, it was the prefecture's misfortune to be regarded "in the same light as the recently developed area of Hokkaidō," with the result that "any attempt to reform an institution or improve a regulation is always rejected by citing the example of Hokkaidō" (quoted in Ōta 1969, 27–28). Even the cosmopolitan Ogasawarans, who were at first allowed to have a bilingual education in English and Japanese, came to be regarded as an obstacle to development as the islands were opened up to colonization from other parts of Japan and were in some cases sent off to the mainland to have their "lifestyle elevated and their customs improved" (Tokyo Fu 1929, 190). So the vision of a world made up of concentric circles, where foreignness increased the farther one moved from the center, came to be replaced by a vision of a single nation where "development" and "modernity" diminished the farther one moved from the capital toward the geographic extremities. Although this view was initially applied mainly to those frontier areas which had been included within Japan's borders, it could also be used to reinterpret the relationship with more distant societies. As we shall see in Chapter 5, therefore, this new version of "civilization" became a useful tool in redefining Japan's relationship with its Asian neighbors, particularly with its most significant neighbor, China.

The transfer of difference from geography ("foreignness") to history ("backwardness") was encouraged by early twentieth-century academic research on the societies of the periphery. Inspired by the evolutionary sciences of the West, scholars like the archaeologist and ethnographer Torii Ryūzō (1860–1953) demonstrated links in material culture between the Ainu, Okinawans, and the earliest Jōmon inhabitants of the main Japanese islands. The pioneering anthropologist Koganei Yoshikiyo (1858–1944) took this hypothesis one step further, using the study of skeletal remains to develop the argument that the Ainu were direct descendants of the earliest inhabitants of Japan. Although this genetic link remained a topic of controversy, the idea that Ainu culture reflected the material culture of an earlier stage of Japanese history was widely accepted. Hayashi Yoshishige's research into Ainu farming methods, for example, led him to the conclusion that the

Ainu, "being a static hunter-gatherer people," had preserved the Japanese agricultural techniques of fifteen hundred years ago "almost unchanged to the present day" (Hayashi 1969, 3).

However, perhaps the most striking example of the incorporation of the Ainu into the Japanese past was the academic tendency to ignore Ainu agriculture altogether, redefining the Ainu simply as "hunter-gatherers." A large volume of archaeological and documentary evidence shows that Ainu communities in the sixteenth and seventeenth centuries lived mainly on hunted and gathered foods, but also grew small crops of millet and vegetables, while Sakhalin Ainu farmed dogs, which they used for food and fur and as hunting and draft animals. There are also clear records indicating that trade with the Japanese in the eighteenth and early nineteenth centuries discouraged Ainu crop growing, partly because of comparative advantage and partly because Japanese traders deliberately tried to prevent the Ainu from farming, thus forcing them to spend more time on the fishing and hunting activities which provided the basis of the northern border trade (Hanazaki 1993, 79 and 132; see also Morris-Suzuki 1994). In much the same way, indigenous metal working disappeared from many areas as access to imported Japanese and Chinese metalware increased. Mamiya Rinzō, who described the techniques of Ainu and Nivkh blacksmiths on Sakhalin, also states that blacksmiths had once practiced their craft widely throughout Hokkaidō (Ezo), but had gradually vanished as Japanese metalware made growing inroads into the island's economy (Mamiya 1972, 336; see also Fukusawa 1995).

Yet most standard texts on the Ainu are strangely silent about this evidence, preferring instead to follow an approach typified by the 1992 edition of the *Encyclopedia Britannica,* which states that Ainu were "hunters, fishers and trappers, until the Japanese moved into Hokkaidō and attempted to settle them in farming." One of the best-known contemporary Japanese examples of this approach is the work of the philosopher Umehara Takeshi, who argues that the hunter-gatherer culture of Japan's pre–metal-working Jōmon period (which existed before the gradual spread of the rice-growing Yayoi culture from about 300 B.C.) continues to exist in Ainu society "in its purest form" (Umehara and Fujimura 1990, 13).

To the south, in a somewhat similar way, the famous ethnographer Yanagita Kunio (1875–1962) eagerly pursued links between the folk practices of Okinawa and those of various parts of Japan. As we shall see in Chapter 4, Yanagita began by emphasizing the diversity of social forms within the Japanese archipelago, seeing different areas and different social structures as having their own particular histories. From the late 1920s onward, however, his approach shifted to one that defined difference increasingly as a product of time rather than space. The central areas of Japan now came to be seen as representing the most modern forms of Japanese society, and the periphery as containing remnants of more ancient linguistic and social structures (Fukuta 1992, 135–156; Yanagita 1963b; Yanagita 1964d; Christy 1993, 623). So Okinawan culture could be represented as an anthropological treasure house whose contents revealed "the shape of things as they were in the beginning" and as they had once been throughout the entire Japanese archipelago (Okinawa Ken 1977, 692–699). All of this gave substance to idea, not simply that the Ainu and the people of the Ryūkyū Islands were Japanese now, but that they had *always been* Japanese, but had been marooned in some earlier phase of national history.

This attachment to the image of "timeless" frontier cultures, which preserve prehistory unaltered, is curious because so much twentieth-century research points in a different direction: to a history in which the many social patterns that we now label "Ainu" culture or "Okinawan" culture, just like those now referred to as "Japanese" culture, are historical products of a continuous process of cultural interaction with neighboring societies. So-called Jōmon society itself was almost certainly highly diverse network of small autonomous communities involved in complex cultural interactions (Kaner 1996). And, from the period around the beginning of the common era, it was transformed in turn by influences from various directions. In southwestern Honshū and northern Kyushu in particular, waves of immigration from China led to the rapid development of wet rice cultivation and to the emergence of larger centralized polities. Farther south, extending into the Ryūkyū Archipelago, southern Chinese and Southeast Asian influences seem to have been especially significant. Meanwhile, from about the fifth century onward, the societies of the north developed strong interactions with the eastern fringes of Siberia and with the maritime communities of the Aleutian Islands, leading to the incorporation of northeastern Hokkaidō into the complex known as "Okhotsk culture" (from approximately the sixth to the twelfth centuries).

Amino Yoshihiko argues that the concept of Japan—"Nihon" (Sun

Origin, a name presumably derived from the fact that Japan lay to the east of China)—was one which only gradually extended from its origins in southwestern Honshū, where it seems to have been used at least from the eighth century, to encompass other parts of the archipelago. As late as the fifteenth or sixteenth centuries, the far north of Honshū and the some of the maritime areas of Kyūshū and the outerlying islands were at best marginally linked to "Nihon" (Amino 1990, 7–17). Meanwhile, the patterns of production and consumption commonly associated with "Ainu" society are now generally seen as having taken shape from approximately the end of the fourteenth century onward, and the various distinctive societies of the Ryūkyū Archipelago were unified into a single kingdom at the beginning of the fifteenth century (Pearson 1996). These ongoing and interrelated historical processes, however, are obliterated by a perspective which defines the societies of the frontier as remnants of "Japan's prehistory."

The modern transfer of difference from the dimension of space to the dimension of time was closely linked to the emerging sense of ethnicity as the chief criterion of nationhood. In Tokugawa Japan, as we have seen, constructions of identity were built primarily around notions of manners and customs, rather than of blood. European racial theories, however, were enthusiastically studied and adopted by Japanese scholars in the Meiji era, and by the beginning of the twentieth century Japanese national identity was increasingly being linked to the idea of an organically united Japanese "Volk" (*minzoku*). The concept of *minzoku* (discussed in more detail in Chapter 5) allowed a convenient blurring between the cultural and genetic aspects of ethnicity, while emphasizing the organic unity of the Japanese people. In this process, the word "Japan" (*Nihon*) itself played a central and problematic role. On the one hand, the Japanese state was defined as the bearer of progress in the archipelago's history; on the other, the name of the state itself was transformed into an ethnonym, so that "Japanese" (*Nihonjin*) was seen as a racial designation. This meant that Okinawans and Ainu were left in the curious position of being commonly defined as ethnically distinct from *Nihonjin* at the very same moment as they were being claimed as Japanese citizens. This ambivalent relationship of the word *Nihonjin* to the various categories of political citizenship, race, and ethnicity was to haunt debates on national identity throughout the twentieth century.

As Thongchai Winichakul (writing of the Thai experience) ob-

serves, the definition of the geographic boundaries of the modern nation gave birth to the image of the nation as a "geo-body," possessing a
primordial integrity and life of its own (Thongchai 1994). In the Japanese context, the vision of the peripheral societies as remnants of the
Japanese past provided a convenient means of reconciling visible cultural difference with the ideological construction of the nation as a
united "body" (*kokutai*) made up of a single *minzoku*.

A somewhat similar process seems to have accompanied the development of modern nationalism in some European countries. Late-medieval
English descriptions of the Welsh, Scots, and Irish, for example, depict
them as alien and bizarre, "as if Nature were amusing herself in private
with greater licence in the most distant regions than in public near the
centre of the world" (Caxton 1988, 162). With the emergence of the
British as an imperial nation, however, the view from "the centre of the
world" shifted: By the mid-nineteenth century Whig history had redefined the Celtic fringe (and the Scottish highlands in particular) as a
region trapped in a primitive stage of evolution likened to that of
American Indians, its people "kept . . . far behind the Saxon" by insufficient exposure to "the civilising influence of the Protestant religion
and the English language" (Macaulay 1986, 365).

To return to our starting point, the imagining of national communities is an imagining across time as well as across space: a process by
which certain people and events are defined as belonging to "our" past
and others are excluded. The way in which the history of "Japan" is
usually written leaves the people of the frontier with a very attenuated
past: a prehistory, perhaps, as part of the complex ethnic mix which
made up the "Japanese" people, but little sense of a continuing participation in a regional interplay, with constantly shifting boundaries and
identities, between the large societies of Japan, China, and Korea and
the smaller societies of the Ryūkyūs, Taiwan, the Ainu, Uilta, Nivkhs,
and others. More often than not, the societies of the frontier seem to
fall into the cracks between the imagined history of nation-states, ending up in obscure monographs of "special-interest" ethnography.

The problem was interestingly demonstrated in 1993 when the Japanese national broadcaster NHK took the bold step of presenting a
dramatized version of seventeenth-century Ryūkyū history as its main
historical drama of the year. *Ryūkyū no kaze* (entitled in English
"Dragon Spirit") was its first attempt to present the history of the
frontier in the format of Japanese TV drama, but the series in the end

was criticized by Okinawan scholars for focusing too much upon the royal court and its connections to Japan and was relatively unpopular with the general Japanese viewing public because it contained too many unfamiliar names and "foreign" words.

The production of *Ryūkyū no kaze,* is, however, a sign that in the 1990s the changing shape of the regional and world system is yet again forcing redefinitions of "Japaneseness." International links between ethnic minorities and indigenous peoples in various parts of the world are encouraging a revival of regional identity among Ainu and Okinawans. The collapse of Cold War tensions is recreating lost historical links between the Ainu and the "Clans Beyond the Sea" in Sakhalin ("Getting Back Our Islands" 1993, 7–9), and between Okinawans and the Chinese part of their historical heritage (see Chapter 8). At the same time, the growing number of foreign workers in Japan and of marriages between Japanese and foreigners is creating new challenges to the attempt to construct Japan as a racially or linguistically homogeneous nation.

By retracing the historical interplay between shifting definitions of "Japan," "Ainu," and "Okinawan," we can help to open up space for a rethinking of the nature of the nation. Rediscovering history, not as the biography of the nation-state but as a dance of identities between many contiguous social forms, re-emphasizes the importance of spatial difference, as well as temporal change, in the making of the modern world. As we look at the creation of the frontier, we can begin to see some of the multiple histories and traditions which were enfolded into the nation-state and gain some sense of the varying strategies which the state used to manage difference and create uniformity. The chapters which follow consider how, from the mid-nineteenth century onward, notions of tradition, spatial difference, and temporal progress came to be embodied in new concepts of culture, race, and ethnicity and how these concepts in turn were used to deal with diversity within the bounds of the modern Japanese nation-state.

3

Nature

Visions of nature are central to modern constructions of national identity. In defining themselves as citizens, individuals are encouraged to envisage a national landscape which extends far beyond the familiar scenery of daily life. So U.S. citizens who may never have ventured farther than the boundaries of Texas or Kentucky learn to conceive of their land as "America, America . . . from sea to shining sea." And in Australia almost every child knows at least part of Dorothea McKellar's poem, "My Country":

> I love a sunburnt country
> A land of sweeping plains,
> Of ragged mountain ranges,
> Of droughts and flooding rains.
> (Quoted in Bambrick 1994, 15)

This splendid evocation of the vast arid plains of northwestern New South Wales has helped to mold popular perceptions of the meaning of "Australia" for generations, despite the fact that it bears very little relationship to the fertile coastal landscapes in which most of the Australian population actually lives. Images of nature, in other words, are also images of the geographical space which houses "the nation."

In Japan, images of nature have played a particularly central role in molding the imagery of nationhood. The anthropologist Ishida Eiichirō (whose work is discussed further in Chapter 4) once defined the essence of Japanese culture in terms of a unique national feeling for nature, a "broadly based, characteristic 'natural sense' [*shizensei*] stretching back to the pre-agricultural era" (Ishida 1972, 24). This concept has been strongly echoed in many more recent writings. The philosopher Umehara Takeshi and the archaeologist Yasuda Yoshinori, for example, both see sensitivity to the aesthetic and environmental value of mountain forests as a defining feature of Japanese culture (Yasuda 1990; Umehara 1991). Yasuda, indeed, has sparked some sharp debate by contrasting Europe's "civilization of deforestation" with Japan's "forest civilization" (Yasuda 1990, 2–4). To support this distinction, he points not only to the wide range of measures introduced to preserve Japanese forests in the preindustrial age but also to Japan's animist heritage, in which every grove and every tree was believed to be imbued with the spirit of the divine. Indeed, Yasuda goes so far as to present the animist vision embodied in Shintoism as a "grand model" which may "offer an answer to the pressing issue of how to preserve the global environment, and how to let nature and man coexist" (Yasuda 1989, 7–8).

Such ideas are not confined to Japanese scholars. One of the most influential exponents of this theme, in fact, was the U.S. historian of technology Lynn White, who suggested, in a much-quoted article, that Christian theology had endowed Western societies with a culture in which humanity is "superior to nature, contemptuous of it, willing to use it at the slightest whim." By contrast, White saw in Eastern religions like Zen Buddhism a view of the human being as equal to—and part of—the wider natural order (White 1967, 1203–1207). Since White's article was published in the 1960s, others have taken up and developed his message. Edward Olson, for example, emphasizes Japan's legacy of Shinto beliefs, with their concept of "man as an integral part of nature" (Olson 1975, 645) and suggests that this "latent essence of Japanese culture" survived intact, although often submerged beneath overlays of cultural borrowing, until modern times. Against this background, it is not surprising that some writers have interpreted Japan's twentieth-century environmental crises as the product of alien cultural and economic influences: "If Japan is offensive to 'ear, eye and nose,' it is largely because Japanese civilization has been infected by Western technology and industrial methods" (Hargrove 1989, xix).

This conclusion, though, leaves some important questions unanswered. If Japan really lacked the concept of "humans as subject and nature as object," why has Japanese society since the middle of the nineteenth century been so quick to adopt and absorb Western scientific and technological ideas, to which this concept is central? Besides, how could Japan, which acquired so much of its cultural heritage from China, have failed to be influenced by China's long tradition of inter-

vention in and control over nature (a tradition which resulted in drastic
deforestation of large parts of the Chinese countryside) (Elvin 1993)?

One possible answer to these questions has been suggested by the
Norwegian scholar Arne Kalland, who argues that the feeling for nature expressed in the Japanese arts had little to do with a practical
interest in preserving the natural environment and much more to do
with a particular use of nature as a source of metaphors for spiritual
and philosophical values. Natural features such as cherry blossom or
pine trees are appreciated because they represent the fleeting nature of
life or the victory of life over death. In this use of nature as symbol, it
matters little whether the cherry blossom or pine trees flourish abun-
dantly in the wild or are seen in the tame and confined surroundings of
an urban backyard (Kalland 1994, 250–255).

S.N. Eisenstadt also emphasizes the ambiguity of Japanese views of
nature, though from a slightly different point of view. Eisenstadt points
to the deep interconnectedness of "culture" and "nature" in Japanese
thought. Nature was seen not as the creation of a transcendent god, but
as a constantly changing, constantly "becoming" reality in which
human beings were deeply embedded. This reality was often depicted
in binary forms: as divided into realms of "order" and "chaos" or of
"purity" and "pollution." In Japan, however, such dualities were understood not in terms of conflict but, rather, in terms of ebb and flux: they
were "flexible, complementary categories" whose boundaries might
shift as circumstances altered (Eisenstadt 1994, 194).

Kalland's and Eisenstadt's studies highlight some important complexities in Japanese environmental thought. However, I want to look
at the issue somewhat differently, by focusing on the multiplicity of
views of "nature" which existed, and still exist, in Japan and on the
changing ways in which these views have shaped visions of national
identity. This relates to the problem of "culture," which will be discussed more fully later in the book. In Chapter 4, I look critically at
notions of "national culture" as they evolved in twentieth-century
Japan. "Tradition" is often assumed to be roughly synonymous with
"culture," but here I want to start by suggesting that, although ideas of
an organically integrated "national culture" are highly questionable, it
is meaningful to speak of "traditions"—always in the plural. "Traditions" in this sense are bodies of thought or practice which are passed
on from one generation to the next and are constantly given new meanings as they are experienced, retold, and reworked by each generation.

They form part of the store of "symbolic resources"—the heritage of language, ideas, images, and physical attributes—out of which individuals weave their identity through interaction with others (see Chapter 9).

Traditions carry a burden of history—the language in which they are embodied is resonant with memories of past debates and dreams. They are therefore not wholly malleable. Yet within limits they are open to a range of interpretations and acquire new nuances as they come into contact with fresh ideas and changed social circumstances. In nations like modern Japan, the population is not heir to a single "tradition," but to a multiplicity of "traditions," some with their central roots in Japanese history or in the history of more local communities; others whose main origins lie abroad or are too complex to be traced at all. My argument here, in other words, is not that Japanese nationhood was defined by a given "natural environment" or that harmony with nature is central to Japanese national culture. Rather, it is that different ways of understanding the natural environment evolved over time and created a store of vocabulary and imagery which have been central to modern constructions of what it means to "be Japanese."

Visions of Nature in Tokugawa Japan

To understand this process it is useful to begin by looking at evolving concepts of nature in eighteenth- and nineteenth-century Japan. As a starting point, we might draw a distinction between two contrasting traditions which seem to run through the intellectual history of both China and Japan. Olson describes these, in the Chinese context, as "two poles of thought represented by Confucius and Lao Tzu" (Olson 1975, 638). In the Taoist philosophy identified with Laozi (Lao Tzu), human beings are a small part of a single, vast and dimly comprehended natural unity.

> Compared with the universe, the world as we know it is like a small depression in a huge swamp. Compared with the world, China as we know it is like one kernel of grain in a giant granary. There are a multitude of creatures, and man is only one of them. Even in China, which itself is a speck in the universe, man constitutes merely one of the countless things it contains. In short, against the numerous things that exist, man is no more than the tip of a hair underneath the stomach of a horse. (Chuang Chou [Zhuang Zhou], quoted in Li 1975, 48)

From this perspective, the destiny of humanity was thought to be fulfilled not by acts of virtue, but by immersion within the flow of existence, the "One." This Taoist view of nature exerted a powerful influence on many Chinese Buddhist scholars, particularly those of the Chan (Zen) school, and their ideas in turn were eagerly absorbed by Japanese Buddhism, in part perhaps because they harmonized with the respect for nature implicit in age-old Japanese animist traditions (LaFleur 1989, 195–196).

The opposite pole or ideal type, identified with Confucianism, was less concerned with the role of human beings in the natural order and more interested in defining rules of conduct for the interaction between one human being and another. Virtue here was expressed through action, and, for the ruler, one of the most important forms of virtuous action was the dispensing of mercy and compassion to the common people. An important part of this perspective was the view that the sufferings of the people could be relieved by applying the wealth of nature to human purposes. At times, as in the writings of the Confucian philosopher Xunzi (300–237? B.C.) this could produce a highly interventionist attitude to nature:

> You glorify nature and meditate on her:
> Why not domesticate her and regulate her?
> You obey nature and sing her praise:
> Why not control her course and use it? . . .
> You depend on things and marvel at them:
> Why not unfold your own ability and transform them?
> (Quoted in Chan 1968, 37)

The two poles of Taoism and Confucianism, however, represent only the opposite ends of a complex continuum of ideas. In between lay a wide range of syncretic philosophies which borrowed from both extremes. The most important of these, from the perspective of Tokugawa Japan, was the neo-Confucianism of the Song dynasty Chinese philosopher Zhu Xi (1130–1200), whose teachings centered on the twin concepts of *qi* (*ki* in Japanese) and *li* (*ri* in Japanese). Of these, *qi* referred to the matter and spirit of which the universe was formed, and *li* to the pattern or "organizing principle" underlying the workings of *qi*. This "organizing principle," however, often came very close to the Taoist notion of the Way, which unites and inspires the workings of the natural order. "*Li* is the Tao [organizing] all forms from above, and the root from which all things are produced" (quoted in Ronan and Needham 1978, 239). In spite of this, neo-Confucianism continued to place a far greater emphasis than did Taoism on the importance of the social order and opposed the leveling impulses of Taoist thought with its own firm belief in natural inequality of things.

During the Tokugawa period (1603–1867), some Japanese thinkers put forward a vision of the universe very close to the "Taoist" end of the spectrum: a vision in which human beings are inseparably integrated into the web of natural relationships. One of the most powerful examples of this approach is to be found in the writings of the utopian eighteenth-century thinker Andō Shōeki (1703–1761). A little caution is needed here, because in Andō's writings, the word "nature" (*shizen*) means far more than "the physical environment": Rather, it is a metaphysical concept implying the self-existent, the ground of all being. Nevertheless, Andō's works probably come closer than others to illustrating that absolute absence of division between humans and nature which has sometimes been seen as characteristic of Japanese thought:

> In the world of Nature, human beings work in accordance with the operation of Heaven and Earth: there is not the least divergence between man and Nature. Spring comes both in Heaven and Earth giving life to blooming flowers and all other living things; in consonance with it, men begin to sow the seed of the five cereals and various vegetables. Summer comes both in Heaven and Earth and all things flourish; men cut grass and cultivate cereals and vegetables. Autumn comes both in Heaven and Earth bringing all things to maturity, when men harvest the crops. Winter comes both in Heaven and Earth making everything dry; then men bleach the husks of various cereals which they put into granaries. . . . This truly indicates the very concord of man and Nature in which Heaven's way of giving growth to everything conforms to the human way of direct cultivation. (Norman 1949, 221)

The seventeenth-century philosopher Kumazawa Banzan (1619–1691) is also often quoted as an example of the conservationist attitude of premodern Japanese philosophy, and it is true that his writings are full of references to the importance of *chisan chisui* (the management of mountain and water resources). But even in Kumazawa's thought human beings are something more than an undifferentiated part of the natural order. In a charming and revealing simile, Kumazawa likens the universe to the plum tree in his garden:

> The roots which are hidden in the earth are like the origins of the universe, the tree is like heaven and earth, the branches are like countries, the leaves are like the myriad things [i.e., the natural environment], and the flowers and fruits are like human beings. Both leaves and fruits are born of the one tree, but the leaves do not serve to make a tree. They are many, but they merely decay. Flowers and fruits are few, but they contain the whole tree within themselves. Therefore when they are planted in the earth they can become a great tree. (Kumazawa 1971, 13)

Kumazawa's plum tree suggests an image which recurs in much Tokugawa writing: the image of human beings as parts of a wider whole, but as parts with a special role to play in the survival and growth of the whole. The point to notice is the way in which the image allows for subtle shifts of interpretation, from emphasis on the wholeness of the whole to emphasis on the uniquely active role of human beings. In Tokugawa Japan we can trace the evolution of a current of ideas in which the second emphasis gradually became more and more important.

A key concept in this evolution of ideas was the notion of *kaibutsu*—a term which means literally "the opening up of things," but might be interpreted either as "revealing the nature of things" or as "developing" or "making use of" the natural world (Saigusa 1973, 371–374). Like many of the central concepts in Tokugawa thought, the idea itself was derived from classical Chinese writings (in this case from the *Yi Jing*) but was embellished and interpreted in ways which particularly suited the philosophical concerns of early modern Japan. The first Japanese scholar to emphasize the concept of *kaibutsu* was the rural philosopher and botanist Kaibara Ekiken (1630–1714). In Kaibara's writings *kaibutsu,* in the sense of "revealing the nature of things," is the motive behind his search for a universal principle in nature which would provide a basis for human morality. This search takes place at several levels: a deepening awareness of and reverence for nature makes human beings better people, but at the same time a richer understanding of the workings of nature also offers practical ideas for improving agricultural productivity and making people better off (Saigusa 1973, 373; Najita 1987, 45–47).

This somewhat utilitarian approach was enthusiastically developed in the writings of Kaibara Ekiken's contemporary and associate Miyazaki Yasusada (1623–1697), who wrote the most influential Tokugawa treatise on agricultural techniques. Although he does not actually use the term *kaibutsu,* Miyazaki's vision of nature is very close to Kaibara's. In this vision, nature is not a hostile force but is instead abundant and benign. There is no place here for the notion that, as John Stuart Mill put it, "all praise of Civilization, or Art, or Contrivance, is so much dispraise of nature" (Clayre 1977, 307). On the contrary, "art" or "contrivance" ("technology," in short) is the means by which the perfection of nature is revealed; and it is precisely human beings' ability to apply "art" to "nature" which gives them a special place in the natural order. "Of all the myriad creatures of heaven," wrote Miyazaki, "none is more esteemed than human beings. This is because human beings have inherited the spirit of heaven—a spirit which cares for and nurtures all creatures under heaven" (Miyazaki 1972, 84).

By applying agricultural knowledge and techniques to the natural environment—by selecting seeds, grafting trees, fertilizing the soil— human beings fulfill the purposes of nature itself. But the greatest of these purposes, as it turns out, is to provide the basis for moral human conduct. Writers like Kaibara Ekiken and Miyazaki Yasusada were fond of quoting the Confucian maxim that, until they had food and clothing, people could not be expected to behave with righteousness. Agricultural techniques, by increasing the abundance of nature, helped to create the foundations for human morality and therefore agriculture was, in Kaibara's words, "the basis of government" (quoted in Miyazaki 1972, 73).

It is also important, though, to place these varying Tokugawa traditions in their economic and political context. The early Tokugawa period marked the zenith of Confucian influence in Japanese society, but it was the neo-Confucianism of Zhu Xi in particular which was adopted and actively propagated by the first Tokugawa shoguns. Andō Shōeki's writings, with their striking similarities to early Chinese Taoist writings, represented the highly unorthodox views of an eccentric far removed from the centers of power and prestige (Norman 1949, 225). Kaibara and Miyazaki, on the other hand, occupied a somewhat different position in the spectrum of social ideas. Although they belonged to rural rather than urban society, they were neither radicals nor outsiders, and their works reached a wide readership in eighteenth-century Japan. Their aim was not to challenge the Confucianism of the Tokugawa rulers but, rather, to make it more accessible to the common people. In order to do this, they reiterated and re-emphasized the neo-Confucian idea that an active engagement with nature was the source of both morality and physical well-being. The view of humans as the most active and important elements in the natural universe was part of their search for a Confucian code of ethics for farmers—an alternative to the aristocratic ethos, which depicted the warrior class as the chief possessors of virtue.

Hiraga Gennai and the Development of Nature

During the eighteenth and early nineteenth centuries, however, the notion of the opening up of nature—*kaibutsu*—came to be extended still further. As the merchant class prospered and craft production expanded, so *kaibutsu* became incorporated into a still more drastic reinterpretation of Confucian concepts of human morality. Some of the inspiration for the extension may also have come from the introduction into Japan of a remarkable Chinese technological text, the *Tiangong kaiwu* (Development of the Works of Nature; in Japanese, *Tenkō kaibutsu*), which was completed and privately published during the final years of the Ming dynasty by a official named Song Yingxing (Sun and Sun 1966). The *Development of the Works of Nature* is a compendium of the technological achievements of over a thousand years of Chinese history, containing descriptions and illustrations of discoveries such as the chain-pump irrigation system and complex pedal-driven equipment for silk reeling (Song 1969).

One curious point about Song's *Development of the Works of Nature* is that it seems to have been little known in China itself after the end of the Ming dynasty. Although other encyclopedias of techniques (such as the *Nongzheng quanshu,* or Complete Treatise on Agricultural Administration, written in the 1620s) remained in use in Qing China, Song's work disappeared from view until the 1920s, when it was rediscovered by Chinese historians of science and technology (Yabuuchi 1982, 137). In Japan, however, the story was very different. Song's text was probably imported from China around the end of the seventeenth century and was published twice in Japanese editions, once in 1771 and once in 1830 (Kikuchi 1988, 85). Its considerable influence on Japanese writers can be seen from the enthusiasm with which they borrowed, adapted, and embellished its illustrations.

In Song's text the concept of *kaibutsu* is extended far beyond the limits of agriculture, to include the making of textiles, dyestuffs, pottery, metals, and paper, the building of ships, the forging of armaments, and the brewing of wines and beers. This wider vision of the application of human knowledge to nature is repeatedly echoed in the writings of Japanese scholars of the late eighteenth and early nineteenth century; and not only in their writings, but also in the practical use to which they put their ideas.

The most striking example of this is provided by the life of the irascible, eccentric polymath Hiraga Gennai (1729–1780). Hiraga's unusual life began conventionally enough: He was a low-ranking samurai from the domain of Takamatsu, who—like many eighteenth-century scholars—acquired an interest in the study of natural history (*honzōgaku*) and compiled a number of studies of Japanese animals, plants, and minerals. In addition to these orthodox scholarly activities, however, Hiraga also *inter alia* experimented (unsuccessfully) with sheep farming; established a pottery, where he planned to produce ceramics for export; made the first Japanese copies of Dutch thermometers; assisted the Domain of Akita in the development of its copper and silver mines (using techniques probably derived from Song Yingxing's *Development of the Works of Nature*); and built several machines for generating static electricity, which he copied from Dutch models, but then unblushingly claimed as his own invention (Jōfuku 1986). In between times Hiraga also acquired a reputation as a writer of erotic literature and as one of the first people to introduce the techniques of Western painting to Japan (Jōfuku 1986, 89–94).

Hiraga was in many ways a man ahead of his time. His more outlandish enterprises were often greeted with derision by his contemporaries, and his colorful life came to an appropriately dramatic conclusion in 1780, when he killed a colleague in a drunken brawl, attempted to commit suicide, and died in prison of his self-inflicted wounds (Jōfuku 1986 141–151). But Hiraga's ambitious (if often unsuccessful) schemes were part of a wider stream of evolving attitudes to nature and technology in eighteenth-century Japan. The tradition of natural history to which Hiraga was heir had, of course, been imported from China. As far back as the sixth century A.D. Japanese scholars had been aware of the Chinese practice of studying and compiling encyclopedic lists of plants and minerals, particularly those with medicinal properties, but it was not until the late seventeenth century that detailed surveys of Japan's own natural history began to be produced.

Natural history in Japan was thus the first major practical application of the philosophical concept of *kaibutsu*. In the early stages, however, it tended to be much concerned with categorization and classification. It was not until Hiraga's time that the emphasis shifted from the correct naming of plants and animals to exploring the practical uses of natural resources, whether animal, vegetable, or mineral (Maes 1970, 46–48). This approach to natural history was popularized from the 1750s onward by "exhibitions of products" (*bussankai*), which introduced an insatiably curious public to natural rarities and wonders collected from all over the country. Hiraga Gennai and his teacher, Tamura Ransui, were leading organizers of these exhibitions (Maes 1970, 47–48; Jōfuku 1986, 25–28).

For Tamura Ransui, Hiraga Gennai, and their associates, the study of nature was less concerned with elucidating the laws of the universe than with harnessing natural resources for human use. As another disciple of Tamura's put it, human beings are "the image of the universe, the possessors of the five virtues and the supreme spirits among living things [*yūsei no saireibutsu*], who therefore use nature to sustain themselves. Humans in turn sustain nature, and it is through humans that nature becomes potent" (quoted in Bitō 1956, 63).

By this time, however, a significant new element was beginning to enter the notion of opening up of nature, an element which is particularly apparent in the writings of Hiraga Gennai. From the 1630s onward the Tokugawa shoguns had attempted to impose tight restrictions on Japan's foreign trade, but in spite of this there proved to be some essential commodities which could not be produced at home. (These included many of the ingredients of Chinese medicines.) Japan therefore continued to conduct an import trade via the Dutch and particularly via Chinese merchants in Nagasaki, and, since the country had relatively little to export, this trade led to a constant outflow of precious metals to foreign countries. The national dilemma was repeated at the local level in many Japanese domains. The spread of the money economy and the expenses of the alternate residence system (under which domain lords had to spend extended periods of time in attendance at the shogunal capital) resulted in a steady flow of wealth from outlying domains to the metropolises of Edo and Osaka, and during the eighteenth and early nineteenth centuries, one domain after another faced financial crisis. To address the crises, many regions began to introduce policies for "developing industry and promoting enterprise" (*shokusan kōgyō*)—in other words, for exploiting local resources to create commodities which could be sold on the market. These included schemes for the production of cash crops such as raw silk and sugar, for the expansion of mining, and for the creation of handicraft industries such as lacquer production, which made use of naturally occurring rare plants and minerals.

It was this economic problem, rather than the higher issues of human morality, which provided the main motive behind Hiraga's study of nature. By discovering new natural resources and experimenting with their uses, he argued, the state could strengthen the basis of its wealth and power. He applied this idea with enthusiasm both in the advice which he provided to various domain governments and also at a national level in his advice to the Shogunate. In the handbill which he wrote to advertise his "exhibition of products" in 1762, for example, Hiraga suggested that "if we but search the deepest mountains and ravines" most of the materials which were then imported would be found to exist in Japan itself. The study of natural history should be used as a means of opening up these undiscovered resources and so solving the trade imbalance (Jōfuku 1986, 27). To put his own advice into practice, Hiraga undertook several scientific expeditions which resulted, for example, in the discovery of sources of a medicinal chemical, probably magnesium sulfide, used as a purgative in Chinese and Japanese medicine and previously unknown in Japan (Jōfuku 1986, 35).

Hiraga's writings and scientific exploits, therefore, extended the concept of the development of nature in two ways. First, inspired by Song Yingxing, they emphasized the value, not just of agriculture but also of mining and manufacturing technologies as a means of tapping the potential wealth of nature. In this way, they implicitly offered a justification for the activities of the expanding class of merchant manufacturers, with whom Hiraga, despite his samurai origins, had close contacts. Second, by harnessing the concept of *kaibutsu* to the service of nationalism, they helped create a powerful mixture which was to find a wide and receptive audience in the closing phases of the Tokugawa age. Although Hiraga's more ambitious developmental schemes were too radical to be accepted in his own day, they foreshadowed ideas put forward with increasing force in the century following his death.

Nature and National Learning: The "Natural Shinto" of Motoori Norinaga

The growing power of the merchant class and a quickening sense of national consciousness were crucial influences on many eighteenth-century Japanese thinkers, but responses to these influences varied widely. While Hiraga Gennai responded by pursuing the practical development of *kaibutsu* for national purposes, his contemporary, the pioneering scholar of "National Learning" (*kokugaku*) Motoori Norinaga (1730–1801), approached the problem in a different way. The son of a merchant from the Ise region, the site of Japan's most ancient Shinto shrines, Motoori criticized Confucianism as being a moral code which was so deeply concerned with the concept of the just ruler that it had little to say to commoners, who were never likely to be directly involved in the administration of the state: "when one has no country to rule and no people to gratify, what use is the way of the sages?" (quoted in Matsumoto 1970, 36).

In answer to this question, Motoori sought to develop a form of personal ethics and aesthetics appropriate to the ruled as well as the ruler. His underlying approach to the concepts of nature, humanity, and morality was in many ways close to the Taoist approaches discussed earlier. He too saw human beings as existing within a vast and utterly mysterious universe and believed that both human beings and other creatures were sustained by a creative power which he identified with the first figure in the Shinto pantheon, Musubi no kami. This did not mean, though, that humans were equal to other creatures. On the contrary, Motoori wrote:

> All living things in the world, even birds and insects, are, owing to Musubi no kami, aware of and able to do what they should do. Men above all, having been born as especially superior beings, know what they ought to know, and do what they ought to do. Why is it necessary to coerce them into doing something more? (Quoted in Matsumoto 1970, 101)

The implication, in other words, is that humans are endowed with an innately pure heart (*magokoro*), which they must recover by (as it were) wiping away the cobwebs of imposed ideas and conventions. The key to this "pure heart" lies in the spontaneous empathetic reaction which humans feel when they, for example, see a cherry tree in full bloom or recognize the joy or sadness in a friend's face. Motoori's emphasis on the power of nature to evoke this profound sense of "the pathos of things"—*mono no aware*—did not mean that he viewed nature in a purely aesthetic light. He recognized that it had practical uses, too. However, the practical uses of nature should, as far as possible, be carried out with sensitivity to its aesthetic values.

But, despite the visible influence of Taoist traditions in Motoori's thought, Motoori sharply distinguished his own philosophy from the ideas of Taoism and Buddhism as well as Confucianism. Writing at a time when the Japanese state was trying to claim from China a central place in the *ka-i* world order, Motoori bitterly attacked the dependence of Japanese scholars on imported Chinese ideas and sought to ground his own philosophy firmly in the native traditions of what he called "natural Shinto" (*shizen no shintō*—a phrase which may also be read as "the natural Way of the Gods") (Wakabayashi 1986, 35–39; Matsumoto 1970, 63–67). This approach was supported by a lifetime of painstaking work (inspired by the advice of the historian and poet Kamo no Mabuchi) studying and interpreting the Shinto myths set out in the *Kojiki,* or "Record of Ancient Matters," an eighth-century document which had been held in scant regard by most early Tokugawa scholars, but which Motoori regarded as the truest link to Japan's sacred origins.

Radically rejecting rational analysis of human origins, Motoori argued that, since the origins of the universe were utterly unknowable, human beings must accept on trust the convoluted Shinto creation myths set out in the *Kojiki* and other early writings. These taught that, while all creatures owed their being to the creative forces of Musubi no Kami, Japan was unique in that it was the birthplace of the sun goddess Amaterasu Ōmikami—hence (Motoori argued) the origins of the place name *Nihon* (sun origin). This connection endowed both Japanese nature and the spirit of the Japanese people with special qualities: qualities which Motoori sought to define by his readings of ancient Japanese literature. Before his day, the classical Japanese literature of the *Kojiki* and of works like the *Tale of Genji,* with their emphasis on the depiction of human love and other profound emotions, had been criticized by many Japanese scholars as expressing crude and sensual feelings which made them inferior to their Chinese counterparts. To Motoori, on the other hand, this quality reflected precisely that spontaneity and sincerity which demonstrated Japan's affinity with the clear, natural light of the sun goddess (Motoori 1983, 414). In China (*Morokoshi*) or "foreign countries" (*hito no kuni*)—expressions which Motoori often uses almost interchangeably—this original human spontaneity had been gradually overlaid by the constricting scholastic "cleverness" of generations of Confucian and Buddhist philosophers, in the process destroying the purity which only Japanese culture had retained (for example, Motoori 1983, 427–429). Motoori's writings, in other words, established a connection between Shinto mythology, Japanese nationalism, a belief in spontaneous human virtue, and a profound sense of the natural environment as the chief stimulus to that virtue. His criticisms of China and his emphasis on the superiority of "our imperial land" are expressed in strictly cultural and aesthetic terms which distinguish them from the later biological discourse of race, yet it is also easy to see how they provided a framework of ideas onto which notions of racial superiority could easily be grafted.

It is important to emphasize that these were radically new ideas which provoked intense controversy in Motoori's day. At the same time, they were also ideas with considerable public appeal. As an ethical and aesthetic philosophy relevant to "the common people," Motoori's nativism attracted a following, not only among the expanding urban classes but also among rural people, whose local beliefs were incorporated into the framework of nativist thought by Motoori's pupil and reinterpreter, Hirata Atsutane (Harutoonian 1988, 23–33).

Kaibutsu in the Writings of Satō Nobuhiro

Growing interest in Shinto, however, was not necessarily associated with a vision of humans as naturally virtuous and nature as a site for an awareness of the "pathos of things." A much more pragmatic and state-centered interpretation of the same Shinto myths is most eloquently expressed in the writings of the early nineteenth-century agricultural expert and political philosopher Satō Nobuhiro (1769–1850). Satō was a prolific writer whose practical handbooks on everything from silk farming to armaments gave his opinions wide currency beyond the ranks of the scholarly elite. His approach to both science and politics was extremely eclectic, cheerfully combining ideas from the Chinese classics with Shinto mythology (which he derived from Motoori Norinaga and Hirata Atsutane) and Western knowledge derived from the Dutch. His major work on astronomy, for example, uses the Shinto creation stories as an intellectual framework for explaining the astronomical theories of Copernicus and Kepler (Satō 1977a, 361–423).

The basis of Satō's ideas was a belief (similar to Motoori's) in a benign creative life-force which he associated with the gods of the Shinto pantheon. But, far from leading to a sense of peaceful coexistence between humans and nature, this theology led Satō to the conclusion that the most important task for human beings was to improve and make use of the resources provided by a benevolent nature. "The development of products [*bussan no kaihatsu*] is the first task of the ruler" (Satō 1977b, 536). What this means in practice is evident from the fascinating if slightly sinister utopian text in which Satō put forward his image of an ideal society. Here an all-powerful government is divided into six ministries (based on the sixfold divisions of ancient Chinese administration). These include a Ministry of Basic Affairs (or agriculture) (*Honji-fu*), whose duties involve experimentation with new crops and seed types; a Ministry of Development (*Kaibutsu-fu*), which is responsible for both forest management and the surveying and opening up of new mines; and a Ministry of Manufactures (*Seizō-fu*), whose tasks include the building of roads and bridges as well as the supervision and improvement of manufacturing techniques (Satō 1977c, 488–517).

In Satō's writings, *kaibutsu* provided the basis for another crucial concept, again borrowed from the Chinese classics but given a special emphasis by scholars in late Tokugawa Japan. This is the idea of "enriching the nation" (*fukoku*), which was sometimes linked with the phrase "strengthening the army" (*kyōhei*) to create the term which became the key political slogan of the Japanese government in the early phases of industrialization (Satō 1977b; Satō 1925, 867–879). This new interest in military strength was, of course, related to the growing awareness of the expansion of the Western powers and the increasing concern with national boundaries discussed in Chapter 2. Satō's *Economic Digest* (Keizai yōryaku), for example, presents four principles of sound economic policy. Two of these are "development" (*kaibutsu*), defined as "making the nation fertile by developing grains, fruits and all sorts of marine and land products," and "enriching the nation" (*fukoku*), which means "bringing together all the fruits of nature within your borders to create great national wealth" (Satō 1977b, 525). Through *kaibutsu*, Satō argued, the ruler could create the conditions not only for national welfare but also for the military expansion which he eagerly espoused in many of his writings (for example, Satō 1977d, 426–485).

Satō Nobuhiro, then, brings together a number of recurring themes in the Tokugawa vision of nature. Like Motoori Norinaga, he sees nature as a creative force associated with the gods of the Shinto pantheon. Like Kaibara Ekiken and Miyazaki Yasusada, however, he believes that the full potential of this force can be realized only through the application of human knowledge and that the development of nature is the true path to human morality. By reducing poverty, *kaibutsu* is a way of preventing the evils born of desperation, such as the practice of infanticide, which Satō fiercely condemned. Like Hiraga Gennai, however, Satō also links the opening up of nature not just to personal virtue but to national power and, in so doing, provides an apologia for the increasingly active role of the state in promoting the exploitation of natural resources.

Many aspects of Satō's writings echo the teachings of the Chinese classics as far back as Xun Zi and beyond. His concept of a strong state has a lineage stretching back to the *Rites of Zhou* (Zhou li), and his emphasis on "enriching the nation and strengthening the army" is particularly reminiscent of the ideas of the eleventh-century Chinese statesman Wang Anshi (Liu 1959, 560–558). At the same time, however, Satō's position also illustrates the way in which traditions from varied sources could be woven into a coherent whole. By combining Chinese administrative ideas, newly reinterpreted Japanese traditions and a dawning consciousness of European developmentalism Satō was able to produce a hybrid philosophy in which the vision of *kaibutsu* reached its apotheosis.

Nature and Industrialization in Meiji Japan

A journey through pre-Meiji ideas of nature reveals the existence of a rich resource of ideas on which scholars and political leaders could draw as Japan entered into the process of industrialization and modern nation building. At one end of the spectrum, the practical concept of *kaibutsu*—the opening up of nature—offered a philosophy which could readily be related to imported notions of industrial development. At the other, Motoori Norinaga's association of personal morality with a distinctively "Japanese" sensitivity to nature provided inspiration for emerging nationalist imagery. Writers like Satō Nobuhiro had already shown how these two themes could be interrelated and reconciled. Here we shall look more closely at some ways in which these themes were reworked in the changing economic and social circumstances of the later nineteenth and early twentieth centuries.

As Japan deepened its links to the West, the idea of *kaibutsu* proved to be a concept which could offer a bridge between familiar Japanese notions of morality and the new ethos of Western science and technology. This point emerges in the writings of early Meiji scholars like Sakatani Shiroshi, the oldest and most cautious of that group of Westernizers known as the *Meirokusha,* or 1873 Society. Sakatani's essays reveal the huge philosophical challenges posed by Westernization. To what extent, he asks, are Western ways compatible with Confucian ethics? How could Japan import Western social and scientific ideas without sinking into cultural subservience to foreign countries? For Sakatani, the answer to these questions lay in the notion of *kaibutsu,* which he used primarily in the sense of "revealing the true nature of things." If one studied and understood the laws of nature, he concluded, one could create the proper foundations for a combination of Japanese and Western knowledge (Sakatani 1976, 428–435). The basis for this combination was a recognition of the way in which human activity (whether political or technological) fulfills the workings of nature:

> When looking down from an elevated position, affairs of the universe seem to be entirely encompassed by Heaven's Reason and Nature without room for human contributions. On the other hand, when one looks up from the humble position . . . it appears that matters of the universe are wholly human and wholly contrived and that nothing depends on Nature or on Heaven's Reason. Yet the fundamentals of Heaven's Reason and the Human Way are one, and the two function by mutually assisting one another. (Sakatani 1976, 428–429)

In Sakatani's writings, the laws of nature, or of "Heaven's Reason," define the different environmental and cultural conditions in each country. Once we understand those laws, we can use the "Human Way" to develop resources and enterprises appropriate to the conditions of our own country. Nature, in other words, provides the parameters for human action, but, as Sakatani put it, consciously quoting the

Western cliché, "God helps those who help themselves" (Sakatani 1976, 429).

Sakatani's discussion of *kaibutsu* is concerned primarily with philosophy and ethics, but a more practical extension of this approach was being developed simultaneously in the writings of leading architects of Japan's industrialization such as Ōkubo Toshimichi (1830–1878). According to Ōkubo, Britain's rise as an industrial power was a shining example of a wise government building upon the laws of heaven and nature (*tennen no ri*). Nature had endowed Britain with an environment ideal for maritime trade, and Britain's rulers had extended the blessings of nature by actively supporting the country's shipbuilding and commerce until Britain emerged as the world's leading economic power (Ōkubo 1964, 219). Japan's "laws of heaven and nature" (that is, its natural environment) resembled Britain's, and, in Ōkubo's eyes, it was only a weakness in the temperament of the Japanese people which had prevented them from building on their natural resources as Britain had done. The duty of the government, then, was to help the Japanese people overcome this spiritual weakness and acquire the knowledge and technology to exploit their natural environment to the full (Ōkubo 1964, 220).

The idea of *kaibutsu,* whose development we have traced from Tokugawa scholars to Meiji politicians, helps explain some of the paradoxes of Japan's environmental history. One way of understanding that history is to assume that there must have been a sharp cultural fissure between Tokugawa and Meiji society. The former, after all, developed a system of forest protection which would be the envy of many modern environmentalists, while the latter pursued industrialization with hardly a thought to its environmental consequences. But the approach to nature implied by the concept of the "opening up" of nature suggests a rather different way of looking at things. Writers like Satō Nobuhiro, Miyazaki Yasusada, and even Kumazawa Banzan saw human beings as the crowning glory of a rich and benign natural order. Humans had not just a right but a duty to develop the resources of nature for their own purposes. Careless use of these resources—a use not based on "the laws of heaven and nature"—was wrong because it made people (and the state) worse off rather than better off. But because human beings and their environment were not separate but were part of the single tree of life, there was no particular value in an independent nature, untouched by human hands. On the contrary, the notion of *kaibutsu,* as it evolved in late Tokugawa and early Meiji Japan, implied that the most perfect nature was the nature most thoroughly improved by human beings.

It was precisely this emphasis on the integration of humans and nature which provided an intellectual basis for the Meiji government's supreme indifference to the destruction of nature by the process of industrialization; for how could industrial growth be a threat to the ecosystem when, as one Meiji entrepreneur and social thinker put it, "industry itself is an instrument for achieving the moral principles of nature" (quoted in Yoshida 1989, 285)?

Nature and the Critique of Industrialization

While the architects of Japan's rapid modern industrialization extended Satō Nobuhiro's notions of *kaibutsu* and *fukoku kyōhei,* however, twentieth-century critics of government industrialization policies also borrowed and reinterpreted Tokugawa intellectual traditions in different ways. One vivid example of this process comes from the first major environmental protest movement in Japan, a famous series of demonstrations against pollution from the Ashio copper mine, which began in 1890 and were to continue intermittently for twenty years. The mine's origins go back to the seventeenth century, but it was in the 1880s, as industrial growth led to a rapid expansion of output, that its impact on the surrounding countryside became a serious social issue. The Furukawa company, which owned the mine, stripped the mountainsides of trees to fuel the copper smelters, resulting in serious flooding and soil erosion. Fumes from the smelters damaged local crops, and, most seriously of all, toxic waste from the mine was dumped into the nearby Watarase River and then spread over ricefields when the river flooded.

The leading figure in protests against the mine was the local parliamentary representative, Tanaka Shōzō, the son of a prosperous peasant and village head from a community on the banks of the river. Tanaka's outspoken and somewhat eccentric personality was to earn him an almost mythical status in Japanese history (Strong 1977; Shoji and Sugai 1992). Not only did he pursue the cause of the farmers in the Diet (the parliament), but he also succeeded in winning the support of an array of prominent Japanese citizens including the Women's Christian Temperance Movement, Christian reformers such as Uchimura

Kanzō, and conservative politicians including Katsu Kaishū (the founder of the Japanese Navy). This rather unlikely coalition of interests had some success, and the government eventually forced the Furukawa company to introduce a number of pollution control measures. These, however, failed to resolve the problem, and until his death in 1913 Tanaka Shōzō, with a dwindling band of supporters, continued to fight the government and demand compensation for impoverished farmers.

Tanaka's campaign drew inspiration from Kumazawa Banzan, who had indeed been responsible for designing one of the major dikes protecting the Watarase River. Like Kumazawa and other Tokugawa writers, Tanaka was not opposed to agricultural development which was in harmony with the processes of nature and which helped the local population, but he bitterly attacked the Meiji approach to development as being based upon mindless avarice:

> No men love mountains and rivers now. When trees are planted on the hillsides, it is not done from love, but from greed, for what the timber will fetch. Who plants a tree in his garden and thinks of nothing but the fuel it will give him? The gardener loves his trees. Planting in the mountains and in the garden may look the same, but the spirit is different. Forestry is based on greed, not love; even when trees are planted as they should be, where rivers rise, it is not done with love, it is not the Way of forestry. (Quoted in Strong 1977, 224)

At times, his ideas are couched in terms which seem to echo the more radical philosophies of Andō Shōeki. Consciously criticizing the vision (proposed by some Tokugawa scholars) of humans as the "supreme spirits among living things," Tanaka argued:

> Humans should not be the supreme spirits of living things; they should rather be the slaves of living things [banbutsu no dorei], their servants and messengers.... They should dwell in the midst of nature and become its reflection, living at peace rather than in conflict with other creatures, correcting their own faults and nurturing their own energy, never cutting themselves off in solitude.... Thus they may grow close to the Spirit. (Quoted in Amamiya 1954, 329)

On the other hand, Tanaka's supporter the Christian reformer Uchimura Kanzō took a slightly more cautious approach. Rather than calling for an immersion of human beings in nature, he (like some Meiji leaders) borrowed the idea of *kaibutsu*. Uchimura, however, used this concept not to advocate the all-out pursuit of industrialization but, rather, to call for a more balanced and less socially disruptive development of the Japanese countryside. While strongly supporting the "opening up" of nature, he criticized the Ashio mine above all because it was a foolish and badly planned form of "opening up," reflecting a single-minded focus on private profit, and it thus caused more social suffering than it relieved. As Uchimura put it (echoing Tokugawa sources): "the wilderness must be opened by its own resources, and poverty must be made to rescue itself. . . . In this way alone was this our fruitful Nippon opened to cultivation in the days of the gods. All was wilderness then; and without any help, by their own efforts, with the land's own resources, they made fields, gardens, roads and cities as we see them today" (Uchimura 1955, 16).

National Identity and the Environment:
The Concept of *Fūdo*

While ideas about the "opening up" of nature provided the framework for heated debates on the course of industrialization, Motoori Norinaga's fusion of Shinto, spontaneous ethics, and sensitivity to the natural environment was providing a rich source of inspiration for evolving ideas of nationalism. The modern reworkings of these themes are too numerous to be discussed in detail, but some mention needs to be made of the most influential early twentieth-century works to bear the imprint of this influence: the interwar writings of the historian and philosopher Watsuji Tetsurō (1889–1960); these writings in turn provide a key source of inspiration for contemporary ideas of a unique Japanese relationship with nature. Watsuji, like Motoori Norinaga, was intrigued by the *Kojiki* and other Shinto classics, which he studied both with the help of Motoori's commentaries and in the light of more recent archaeological evidence (Furukawa 1961). Although he had little sympathy for Motoori's literal interpretation of Shinto mythology, preferring to treat the myths as symbolic expressions of the emergence of the Japanese state, Watsuji was powerfully influenced by Motoori's philosophies and wrote a famous essay on the concept of "natural empathy" (*mono no aware*).

Watsuji also drew inspiration, however, from different sources,

most notably nineteenth- and early twentieth-century German philosophy, on which he was an eminent expert. Crucial influences on his
thinking were Dilthey's and Heidegger's philosophies of time and
being (*Dasein*). Indeed, in his introduction to his most famous work,
Fūdo, Watsuji explains that the concept behind this study occurred to
him in the summer of 1927, while he was in Berlin reading
Heidegger's *Sein und Zeit* (Being and Time) (Watsuji 1963, 143).
Heidegger's concern with the philosophy of time had, Watsuji felt, led
to a neglect of the equally important dimension of space. For the next
fifteen years, therefore, Watsuji devoted himself to a study of "being
and space" which was published in various stages and in several revised editions, becoming the volume known as *Fūdo.*

The word *fūdo*—made up of the characters for "wind" and
"earth"—is translated variously as "climate," "landscape," or "environment." It expressed, in other words, Watsuji's belief that human
societies are profoundly shaped by their natural setting. In *Fūdo,*
Watsuji defined three major types of environment, each of which he
identified with different aesthetic orientations and different patterns of
human relationships. Monsoon environments, which Watsuji identified
primarily with India, are typified by a relaxed and resigned attitude to
the forces of nature; desert environments, typified by the Middle East,
promote an active and aggressive relationship toward one's natural
surroundings and other people; grassland environments, like those of
the European Mediterranean, are characterized by regular cycles of
seasons and encourage a rationalist approach to the control of nature
(Watsuji 1963, 145–227).

But Japan, according to Watsuji, had a unique *fūdo* which combined
the unpredictability of typhoons and monsoonal floods with the regularity of the seasons, and this, he believed, had created a distinctive and
complex sensitivity to nature, vividly represented in Japanese art, architecture, and literature. Rather than expressing resignation to nature
or imposing an artificial symmetry on nature, Watsuji argued, the Japanese arts involved an empathetic coming together of the human spirit
and nature, which is very close to Motoori's emphasis on spontaneous
human appreciation of the "pathos of things." Classic examples are the
Japanese garden, where the gardener works with the spirit of the natural landscape to produce something almost more natural than nature
itself, or the brush painting which eschews symmetry and regularity,
yet produces perfect balance (Watsuji 1963, 284–285). Watsuji de-

scribes the Japanese environment in vividly evocative prose which condenses the considerable variety of Japan's regions into a powerful image of climatic uniqueness. The core of this uniqueness was its "duality," its combination of the extremes of the heavy winter snowfall typical of northern climates with the heavy summer rains typical of the monsoon belt:

> In these conditions of powerful sunlight and plentiful moisture, tropical plants flourish here in abundance. The summer landscape hardly differs from that of the tropics. Its outstanding representative is rice. On the other hand, the cold weather and lower moisture of winter means that plants of the cold regions flourish in equal abundance. Their chief representative is wheat. So the wide earth is covered in winter with wheat and winter grasses, and in summer with rice and summer grasses. But those plants that do not change with the seasons must embody duality within their own forms. The sight of the tropical bamboo weighed down with snow is often cited as a symbol of the Japanese landscape, but the bamboo, which has learned to bear the weight of snow, is itself different from the tropical bamboo. It has turned into Japanese bamboo, which is flexible and can be drawn with a curved line. (Watsuji 1963, 239)

Later chapters show how Watsuji linked this vision of nature with a vision of Japanese human relationships, which he saw as characterized by a similar duality of passion and calm, flexibility and strength. Here, though, it is important simply to notice how his vivid and attractively schematic concept of nature—of "being and space"—relied on resonances among diverse philosophical traditions. Although Watsuji's understanding of the world differed in many ways from that of eighteenth-century nativism, it drew certain powerful images from that nativism. In particular, it illustrates how the nativist contrast between an emotionally spontaneous "Japan" and a rigidly scholastic "China" could readily be reworked to paint a contrast between an emotionally spontaneous Japan and that new center of power, the rational "West." Watsuji's writings also picked up and made explicit similarities of approach between eighteenth-century Japanese nativist thought and European philosophies of nature and nationhood and wove them together into a new synthesis which had particular appeal to many readers in the intellectual environment of interwar Japan, and which has continued to exert a powerful influence on Japanese perceptions of "Japan" as a spatial entity ever since.

An exploration of some themes in intellectual history from the Tokugawa period onward shows that it is far too simple to identify "traditional" Japanese attitudes toward nature with an animist respect for the spirit of trees. On the other hand, it would be rash to leap to the opposite conclusion, as some recent critics of Japan have done, and suggest that Japan is condemned by its culture to be "the world's number one environmental despoiler and exploiter" (Reader 1990, 16). Rather, the Tokugawa heritage offered a wide spectrum of environmental views, from the strongly "developmentalist" approach of writers like Satō Nobuhiro to the profoundly "quietist" approach of writers like Andō Shōeki, and from the practical ethics of Miyazaki Yasusada to the mystical nativism of Motoori Norinaga. Although all these views drew on and reinterpreted aspects of Sino–Japanese philosophical traditions, they did so in different ways and for different social purposes. They in turn therefore offered alternative versions of "tradition" to be quoted and reinterpreted by nineteenth- and twentieth-century politicians, scholars, and activists from Ōkubo Toshimichi to Tanaka Shōzō and Watsuji Tetsurō. Although all these modern figures can in some sense be described as drawing on historical "traditions," the traditions which they chose to emphasize varied and were used to support radically different political ideologies and values. Japanese philosophies of nature, in short, were not imprisoned like fossils in a cultural bedrock, but changed over time as successive generations gave new meaning to inherited ideas.

The diversity, conflict, and change evident in Japanese ideas about nature, indeed, force us to look more closely at the other side of the equation—"culture." If Japanese images of nature varied from one social stratum to another, or even from individual to individual, and if they evolved and shifted over time, how can we speak of Japanese environmental thought as having been shaped by a distinctive "culture"? What meaning can we give to the word "culture" at all? These questions are the starting point of Chapter 4.

4

Culture

S.N. Eisenstadt was right to observe that, in pre-Meiji Japan, there was no obvious sense of a sharp dividing line between "nature" and "culture" (Eisenstadt 1994). This, however, does not simply reflect the distinctive characteristics of Japanese visions of "nature"; it also reflects the fact that the very idea of "culture" itself is quite modern. Concepts of "culture" emerged from the intellectual ferment of the European enlightenment and began to make tentative inroads into Japanese thought only in the second half of the nineteenth century. A comprehensive analysis of the usage of the term *bunka*—culture—in Japan could fill volumes. Yet some exploration of the idea is important because notions of culture have played such a central role in modern Japanese definitions of nationhood and because these notions have recently acquired increasing visibility in historical debates, both in Japan and elsewhere.

In a keynote address to a conference on Asian history in the early 1990s, for example, Professor Yü Ying-shih of Princeton University argued that the most significant current trend in historical studies is the recognition of "culture as a relatively autonomous force in history" (Yu 1991, 21). For too long, he suggested, historians have looked at the past through a narrow window shaped by the values of the West, particularly by the all-powerful Western notion of history as the pursuit of "scientific truth." To break through this constricting frame we need to recognize "that the history of every society or people deserves to be studied not only as a part of world history but also on account of its intrinsic values" (Yü 1991, 26); we need, in other words, to accept Watanabe Hiroshi's notion that every society or region may be " 'particular' in its own way like an individual" (Quoted in Yü 1991, 23).

The increasing visibility of culture as a topic of debate in history (and other disciplines) can be readily understood. In the past three decades, the grand edifices of eighteenth- and nineteenth-century social thought have come under attack from many directions. The authority of Marxism as an intellectual system has crumbled from within, and the challenges of feminism and ecological thought have eroded the foundations of traditional liberalism. Emphasis on the distinct cultural traditions of differing societies takes this challenge one step further by confronting a central claim of nineteenth-century positivist philosophies: their claim to universal relevance. The new cultural history represents post-enlightenment Western thought as the product of a particular society and era and opens up the possibility that the traditions of other societies may contain the seeds of new theories to fill the gap left by the withering of old certainties.

On the other hand, interest in culture seems also paradoxically to reflect a contrasting trend. The increasing penetration of science and technology (themselves profoundly shaped by eighteenth- and nineteenth-century European thought) is transforming society throughout the world, but particularly in the rapidly industrializing Asian countries. Developments in transport and communications, and the increasingly rapid flow of capital and people, threaten to undermine conventionally accepted images of "national culture" in these countries. The desire to define and mobilize cultural tradition seems to be at least as much a response to these internal uncertainties as it is to the worldwide fluidity of social theory and ideology.

In Japan, the dilemmas of "internationalization" and of the country's growing power in world affairs has made the question of culture particularly salient. In order to make sense of the re-emergence of "culture" as a key issue in historical debate it is, however, important to understand the concept itself in its historical context and to discover the many layers of meaning, implicit as well as explicit, which it has accreted in its long and not always honorable career. The arguments here therefore focus on trying to bring out some of the paradoxes of the concept by examining its evolution in the work of a few Japanese scholars who have reflected particularly deeply on the meaning of "culture" as a framework of analysis.

The Origins of "Culture"

The use of the word *bunka* as in the phrase *Nihon bunka*—Japanese culture—began to be widely used in public debate only around the

1920s. Maybe this should not surprise us, for the appearance of the English word "culture" in the same anthropological sense is also very recent. Other meanings of the word are older. In the fifteenth century, "culture" had already acquired the modest and restricted sense of "cultivation," as in "agri-culture"; by the sixteenth century it was expanding from the physical into the spiritual sphere, so that "culture" might now also mean the refinement of human manners and intellectual attainments. But it was only in the late eighteenth to early nineteenth century that the German *Kultur* came to be applied (in the works of Johan Cristoph Adelung and Gustav Klemm) to the whole complex of beliefs and customs of particular societies, and not until the 1870s that Edward Tylor imported this use into English, in a book significantly entitled *Primitive Culture* (see Kroeber and Kluckhohn 1963, 11, 44–46, 62–63; Gamst and Norbeck 1976, 32–33).

Some of the notions which would, in the nineteenth and twentieth centuries, attach themselves to the word "culture" have, of course, been around for a long time. The idea that different groups of people have different "customs" or "manners" is an old and widespread one. Herodotus spoke of the differences between the customs of the barbarians and the Greeks, but was broad-minded enough to admit that barbarian customs could sometimes be superior (Baldry 1965, 21). From the Hellenistic period we even have a record of an Arab camel driver complaining of employment discrimination because "I am a Barbarian . . . [and] do not know how to behave like a Greek" (Walbank 1981, 115). This sense of "different customs" is not unlike the Tokugawa-period Japanese image of "foreign countries" and "outer barbarians," with their distinguishing peculiarities of dress, diet, hairstyle, and so on.

With the emergence of European nationalism in the seventeenth and eighteenth centuries, ideas of difference were rearranged into the popular notion of "national character," which attributed personality traits such as capriciousness, haughtiness, and diligence to various European peoples (see Yoshino 1992, 54–56). In Meiji Japan, the concept of "national character" was taken up by writers like Haga Yaichi (1867–1927), who described the Japanese as being (among other things) patriotic, practical, realistic, fond of nature, and humorous in temperament (Haga 1977). The rise of nationalism also brought with it a new interest in tracing, defining, and celebrating the intellectual and artistic heritage of particular ethnic groups.

It was the modern evolution of the anthropological term "culture," though, which would weave these various elements together, creating the vision of a coherent and inner-directed whole: a vision which continues to have enormous influence on social thought in the last decade of the twentieth century. This anthropological interpretation of culture as "the civilization of a people (particularly at a certain stage of development)" first appears in the *Oxford English Dictionary* in 1933, but for many decades the English use of "culture" remained unstable, hovering uncomfortably between the older notion of "mental and moral cultivation" and the newer notion of "the practices and beliefs of a particular society."

This adolescent awkwardness is obvious, for example, to anyone who reads T. S. Eliot's *Notes toward the Definition of Culture,* published in 1948. The title is misleading: The book tells us a great deal about Eliot's views on religion, education, politics, the British Council, and many other things. The one thing it does not do is provide a coherent and consistent definition of culture. In some places Eliot stresses that culture is "a way of life" including "all the characteristic activities and interests of a people: Derby Day, Henley Regatta, Cowes, the twelfth of August, a cup final, the dog races, the pin table, the dart board, Wensleydale cheese, boiled cabbage cut into sections, beet root in vinegar, nineteenth-century gothic churches and the music of Elgar" (Eliot 1948, 31 and 41); in others, the definition is much more value-laden: "Culture may be described simply as that which makes life worth living. And it is what justifies other peoples and other generations in saying, when they contemplate the remains and the influence of an extinct civilization, that it was *worth while* for that civilization to have existed" (Eliot 1948, 27; emphasis in the original). It is this interpretive tension which allows Eliot to depict a Britain, assailed by the twin horrors of mass education and religious decline, poised on the brink of a cultural void where Christianity, the Henley Regatta, and the cup final will all alike be churned into formless chaos.

Like the English word "culture," the Japanese *bunka* is burdened by the karma of previous incarnations. Its origins go back to the Chinese classics, where the character combinations *bunka* and *bunmei* (used in modern Japanese to mean "culture" and "civilization" respectively) appear in a particular and restricted context. They are part of a conceptual dichotomy whose other side is represented by the character *bu* (*wu* in Chinese) meaning "military." In this context, *bunka* and *bunmei* imply the ordering and improvement of society by the use of *bun*—the written word, learning or scholarly rule—rather than by the use of *bu,* the sword (Suzuki 1981, 40–43). Both *bunka* and *bunmei* were adopted in Japanese as titles for the reign of emperors, but were not widely used in general discourse until after the Meiji Restoration, when the famous phrase *bunmei kaika* (generally translated as "civilization and enlightenment") was coined by Japan's Westernizers to describe their entire project for the transformation of Japanese society.

This historical context helps to explain a particular flavor which crept into the Japanese use of the word *bunmei* (civilization) when it was introduced by scholars like Fukuzawa Yukichi in the mid-nineteenth century. In Europe, there was a divergence of approaches to the distinction between "culture" and "civilization." Scholars like Wilhelm von Humboldt appear to have defined "culture" as the control of nature by science and technology, and "civilization" as the improvement of human customs and manners; conversely, Mommsen and later Tönnies, Alfred Weber, and others identified "culture" with the intangible world of social values and ideals, and "civilization" with the tangible achievements of human science and technology (Kroeber and Kluckhohn 1963, 25–30; Braudel 1994, 5–6). Their distinction, however, was not only between nonmaterial values and material systems, but also between the spatial and temporal visions of difference sketched here in Chapter 1. Culture, in other words, was the realm of spatial difference—a world divided by the differing social mores of distinct communities—while civilization was the realm of time—a universal trajectory toward which different societies moved at different speeds. It was this second vision of civilization (*bunmei*) as dynamic and universal which (as seen in Chapter 1) was embodied in the writings of Fukuzawa Yukichi.

The word *bunka* grew from the same root as *bunmei,* but its eventual destiny was very different. It was first extensively used by early Meiji Westernizers like Nishi Amane, but its context suggests that it was at this stage a mere abbreviation of *bunmei kaika*—civilization and enlightenment. In other words, it referred to the achievements which flowed from the European scientific and industrial revolutions (Suzuki 1981, 49–56). There were, it is true, a few exceptions to this common usage. The very earliest case I have encountered of *bunka,* used in a context which seems to refer to cultural peculiarities, occurs (interestingly enough) in a discussion of the customs of the Ainu written in 1854 (see Takakura 1972, 325). This was, however, very much the exception to the rule. Until at least the mid-Taishō period, the common usage of the word *bunka* is better illustrated by the local government report, which, discussing the problems of urbanization, observed that "it is a fact common to all countries that with the advance of culture, the part of the population employed in agriculture should decline and that employed in commerce and industry should increase" (Kanagawa Ken 1966, 54).

"Bunkashugi" in Interwar Japan

As Immanuel Wallerstein has pointed out, the notion of "culture" has two distinct aspects, whose compression into a single word is the source of endless confusion. On the one hand, "culture" refers to a horizontal division within particular societies between "that which is 'superstructural' as opposed to that which is the 'base' " (Wallerstein 1990, 32). In this sense "culture" is distinguished from "technology," "economy," and so on. On the other hand, however, culture also refers to a vertical division separating humanity into different "cultural" groups. Here the key distinction is between French culture, German culture, Chinese culture, and so forth.

In Japan, the metamorphosis of *bunka* from an emblem of Westernization to a key concept in theories of Japanese uniqueness was linked to a shift in interpretation from the first meaning of culture to the second. From World War I to the early 1930s, a new interest in culture manifested itself both in popular consciousness and in academic debates. Public recognition of "culture" as an important indicator of social development was symbolized by the establishment in 1930 of the Asahi Cultural Awards (*Asahi Bunka Shō*) and, seven years later, of the state-funded cultural awards (*bunka kunshō*) which honored leading Japanese scholars, writers, and artists. At a more popular level, the identification of "culture" with the "higher strata" of social existence gave rise to the curious phenomenon of the *bunka jūtaku,* or cultural residence, which symbolized a shift from the Meiji equation of civilization with industrial *production* to an equation of social advance with the new *consumption* patterns of the expanding middle classes. The cultural residence was a suburban family house whose exterior was embellished with unfamiliar materials like wood shingles, cement, or stucco. Its guestroom had wallpaper on the walls (probably hung with reproductions of French paintings), carpeting or linoleum on the floor,

Western-style furniture, electric lighting, and, as likely as not, a piano in one corner. It was, in short, the most tangible symbol of the popular equation of "culture" with the novel and the foreign. The same equation was evident in the fashion for tacking the word *bunka* onto the name of any newfangled commercial product which one wished to sell to a gullible public (as in the case of the electrically driven *bunka sempūki,* or "cultural fan") (Ogi 1986, 78–79).

In the world of the intelligentsia, the conception of culture as a "superstructural" phenomenon was expressed through a growing interest in the history of art and architecture, and through heated debates on the social role of literature and the visual arts. This *bunkashugi* (culturalism) can, as Harootunian has suggested, be linked both to the expansion of consumer society in the early interwar years and to a reaction against the Meiji identification with *bunmei*—material civilization, scientific rationality, and industrial progress (Harootunian 1974, 15). But, while *bunkashugi* in its early stages had a cosmopolitan flavor, its emphasis on the private rather than the public and on aesthetics rather than science flowed smoothly into a new and more overtly nationalist stream of thought, which emerged from the late 1920s onward. A key element in this intellectual trend was a questioning of the values of "modernity" as expressed in Western scientific, social, and political thought. Influenced by Japan's isolation from the community of industrialized nations and its growing expansionism in Asia, as well as by the social dislocation which had accompanied Japan's industrialization, a prominent group of thinkers began to look within Japan itself for modes of thought and action which would help resolve the social and spiritual dilemmas of modernity. The key figures in this quest—among them Miki Kiyoshi and Watsuji Tetsurō—belonged to the Kyoto School, which derived its inspiration from the work of eminent philosopher Nishida Kitarō (1870–1945) (see Najita and Harootunian 1988, 734–49). Nishida's famous philosophical system, worked out in his mature works from the late 1920s onward, sought to go beyond the limitations of European neo-Kantian thought by drawing on ideas derived in large part from Japanese Buddhism (see, for example, Nishida 1965a; Nishida 1965b; Suzuki 1977).

From here it was a relatively short step to the view that "Eastern" thought had special power to solve the problems of dualism inherent in "Western" modernity (see, for example, Nishida 1965c, 85–87). In *The Problem of Japanese Culture* (Nihon bunka no mondai), published five years before his death, Nishida attempted to apply his philosophical theories to defining a specifically Japanese mode of consciousness. Through an analysis of history as a creative interplay of subject and surrounding world (*kankyō,* or "environment")—"that which is made" and "that which makes"—Nishida outlined a particular form of Japanese consciousness emerging from the relationship between Japanese people and the territorial space which they occupy: a consciousness which was profoundly "vertical" (or chronological) and in which "subjectivity" tended constantly to be dispersed into "environment." At the core of this consciousness stood the abstract figure of the emperor, the transcendent locus uniting the contradictions of selfhood—"the eternal now which contains past and future" (Nishida 1966, 340).

Although Nishida argued against the transformation of Japan into the unreflective "subject" of a drama of imperialism, his emphasis on the universal destiny of Japanese culture in a new world order reverberates with echoes of less subtle forms of 1940s nationalism. This vision of Japanese culture as possessing the seeds of a new mode of cognition—one which Japan had a duty to communicate to the wider world—also exerted a powerful influence over a wide-ranging group of writers and intellectuals who, after the outbreak of the Pacific War, debated Japan's role as a pioneer in the process of "transcending modernity" (*kindai no chōkoku*) (see Fukuda 1965; Najita and Harootunian 1988, 758–768; Iwasaki 1995).

Yanagita Kunio and the Redefinition of *Bunka*

Nishida was just one of many writers who, in the late 1930s to early 1940s, turned their attention to "the problem of Japanese culture" (see, for example, Nihon Bunka Kyōkai 1939). The analytical struggles which these writers faced, however, is perhaps best illustrated by the example of the famous ethnographer Yanagita Kunio (1875–1962). During the course of his long career, Yanagita's intellectual framework passed through several important stages of development. In his very first forays into folklore (published around the time of the Russo–Japanese War) Yanagita seems to have taken a relative simple approach to the unity of Japanese society and to have seen the peculiarities of outerlying regions of the nation as symptoms of "backwardness." As he embarked on systematic fieldwork, however, his attitude changed. A recent reappraisal of Yanagita's work by Fukuta Ajio points out that the products of this early fieldwork not only emphasized the diversity of social forms in rural Japan—the difference, for example, between the people of the mountains and those of the plains and between various types of village structure; they also tended to present each of these forms as having its own distinct historical lineage (Fukuta 1992, 139–148 and 154–156; see especially Yanagita 1963a). Throughout these early stages, the term "Japanese culture" rarely appears in Yanagita's writings. In the 1930s and early 1940s, however, the focus of his study underwent a further significant shift. The search for integrating frameworks increasingly displaced the emphasis on local peculiarities, and at the same time the expression "Japanese culture"—*Nihon bunka*—made an appearance at center stage.

This metamorphosis in Yanagita's thought needs to be seen in the context both of growing concern about the nature of "Japaneseness" and of changing ideas about the meaning of "culture." From about the 1890s onward, many intellectuals, including Yanagita, had been struggling with the problem of creating a framework for the understanding of Japanese society. As the political scientist Kang Sang Jung has pointed out, these efforts to define Japanese social identity were inescapably shaped by a pre-existing self-definition of "the West" as rational, progressive, scientific, individualistic, and meritocratic (Kang and Murai 1993). In the face of this monumental and daunting vision of "the West," a limited number of reactions were possible. One, typified by the writings of the philosopher Miyake Setsurei, was to define Japan as opposite but complementary to the West: a *ying* whose hollows fitted the curves of the Western *yang*. Thus Japan, although it might lack the material wealth of the West (and although it had its own social deficiencies) possessed spiritual qualities which could "make up for the failings of the white races" (Miyake 1977, 16).

An alternative was to argue that, although surface customs might differ, the underlying qualities of the Japanese "national character" were in fact *equivalent* to those of the West. This approach was perhaps most articulately argued by Yanagita Kunio's close associate, the educationalist and diplomat Nitobe Inazō, best known for his English-language study of *Bushidō*—the Way of the Samurai. In Nitobe's writing, the samurai, with his emphasis on benevolence, courtesy, truthfulness, honor, and loyalty is above all a *gentleman*, and *Bushidō* itself is not so much an esoteric philosophy as a mildly exoticized version of the British public school ethos. Indeed, Nitobe himself likens the Way of the Samurai to the moral code of Tom Brown, whose ambition was to "leave behind him the name of a fellow who never bullied a little boy or turned his back on a big one" (Nitobe 1905, 8). The notion of equivalence comes out still more strongly in a remarkable paper written by Nitobe in the late 1920s. Here, comparing the influence of China and the influence of the West on Japan's history, Nitobe argued in essence that Japan had been superficially "orientalized" by the influence of China and that "the liberating power of Western thought" was serving only to release the real, dynamic, energetic Japan whose true nature had been obscured by the weight of "Celestial didacticism" (Nitobe 1931, 20–21). In this thesis we can hear echoes of an important early twentieth-century historiographical debate, in which the rediscovery of Japan's very early history was used (as Stefan Tanaka has pointed out) to trace non-Chinese roots to Japanese culture and thus to distinguish a more clearly defined "Japan" from a wider *tōyō* (Orient) (Tanaka 1993, 153–187).

The problems of dealing with "Japaneseness" were compounded by problems of terminology. Was the defining characteristic of Japaneseness to be sought in "national character" (*kokuminsei*), in ethical systems like *Bushidō,* or (as Nishida Kitarō had suggested) in distinctive perceptions of reality? The solution devised more or less simultaneously by Yanagita and a number of his contemporaries was to adopt the notion "Japanese culture" as a broad framework which could embrace all that was distinctive in custom, ethos, mythology, and material technology. This solution, however, required some careful redefinition of terms. Thus Yanagita, like T.S. Eliot, was led to compose his own notes toward the definition of *bunka:* a definition which, Yanagita suggested, did not have to coincide with European uses of the word "culture," but should provide sufficient conceptual unity to create a firm basis for debates within Japan (Yanagita 1964a, 194–195).

Yanagita's contribution to the debate was a careful exposition of the idea that "culture" was not just the foreign and novel, nor did it mean just the old and traditional; rather, it referred to a "complex" (*fukugōtai*), "the existing state of harmony of many elements, both old and new," woven together by society like the many-colored threads of silk brocade (Yanagita 1964a, 191 and 199–200; see also Yanagita 1964b, 212). For Yanagita, then, Japanese culture was something dynamic and adaptive. Each age had its own culture—Kamakura culture, Momoyama culture, and by extension Meiji culture and Shōwa culture—which blended old and new, imported and indigenous in its own particular way. But in spite of this conceptual flexibility, Yanagita's definition, like T.S. Eliot's, remained awkwardly suspended between what *is* and what *should be*. This conflict between description and prescription becomes clearly evident where Yanagita turns his attention to a subject particularly close to his heart, the question of regional differences.

Yanagita, of course, was more aware than most of the varied traditions which existed in different parts of Japan and of the fact that regional society could often be exclusive and hostile to outsiders. He was also acutely conscious of the gap between the relatively Westernized society of the big cities and the poorer, more "traditional" society of village Japan. His discussion of these differences concludes with some revealing comments. After a detailed description of the local partisanship and rivalries permeating Japanese society, he goes on to argue that attachment to a sense of "local culture" is a barrier which prevents city dwellers from developing a proper desire to "improve their town for the sake of the nation." This worrying lack of social cohesion has a simple cause. It arises because people are led astray by "the delusion that it is acceptable for a variety of different cultures to exist in the same nation at the same time" (Yanagita 1964a, 199). "Culture," in short, *must* be something national, because defining it in any other way would erode social harmony; so the definition slips quietly from being a description of *actual* social beliefs and practices in all their dynamic complexity, to being a description of *the beliefs and practices which must be created:* a utopian goal symbolized, for Yanagita, by the traditional festival (*matsuri*) in which all social division dissolves in the ecstasy of communal celebration (Yanagita 1964a, 201–202).

The shifting focus of Yanagita's thought can be related to the changing fortunes of both his own career and Japan itself. At one level, Yanagita was responding to the crisis of war and to the upsurge of interest in "Japanese culture" in intellectual circles. At another, he was perhaps influenced by his own particular position within those circles. By the late 1930s, Yanagita had become an eminent scholar whose comments were sought on a wide range of issues, including the ethnography of Japan's expanding empire. His articles began to appear in colonial journals such as *Chōsen minzoku* (The Korean People) and *Taiwan minzoku* (The Taiwanese People), contexts which encouraged reflections on the comparative anthropology of entire nations (Suzuki 1973). The integration of the local into the national, besides, was made easier by the gradual shifts in Yanagita's methodological perspective which had occurred since the end of the 1920s. On the one hand (possibly inspired by the methods of Bronislaw Malinowsky), he had begun to apply a more systematic approach to studying the *internal structure* of local communities (Kawada 1993, 117–125). By 1935 his early, rather eclectic research techniques had been replaced by a well-defined methodology which categorized ethnographic material into three groups: "outer forms of life" (*seikatsu gaikei,* i.e., the visible realm of material culture, festivals, etc.); "explanations of life" (*seikatsu kaisetsu,* i.e., language, oral traditions, etc); and "consciousness of life" (*seikatsu ishiki,* the inner beliefs which give meaning to existence). Of these, it was "consciousness of life" which, he believed, constituted the "essentials" of social existence: The main aim of ethnography was to penetrate through the surface phenomena of material culture and language in order to reach and understand those essentials (Yanagita 1964c, 336–337).

On the other hand, Yanagita's view of the structural *relationship between* the diverse forms of Japanese rural life had also changed. Rather than seeing distinct types of community as having their own particular past, he began increasingly to emphasize their chronological relationship as different stages of a single process of historical development. In other words, his view of culture helped to consolidate the processes which we have already examined: processes by which notions of "progress" and "backwardness" were used to incorporate the periphery into a vision of national community. Thus his early view of local peculiarities as symptoms of "backwardness" was reinstated, but in a more complex and systematic way. In his linguistic theories, developed from the late 1920s onward, Yanagita explored the survival of words from older forms of Japanese in isolated mountainous or island communities (see Yanagita 1963b; Yanagita 1964d, 316–17). This linguistic research led on to a much wider reconstruction of his theories, so that remote regions—and particularly Okinawa, the remotest of all—came to be seen as a storehouse of the vanished social forms. In Okinawa, religious belief and rituals, family structures, and landholding systems were all "entirely different from present conditions, but seem to become much nearer as you think back into the past" so that the region could be seen as an "untapped new source" for studying the history of Japan (Yanagita 1964d, 317; Christy 1993). So local differences, rather than being the products of distinct local histories, were redefined as different evolutionary points along the single line of national history. This interpretation is particularly interesting because Yanagita explicitly rejected the evolutionary perspective which Western anthropologists like Malinowsky applied to the study of foreign "primitive" societies, identifying them as survivals of earlier stages of human history (see Kawada 1993, 128–129). The implication seems to be that separate nations or ethnic groups possessed their own trajectory of historical evolution, within which some regions or subsections might be more "primitive" or "ancient" than others, but that national trajectories were independent of one another and could not be lined up into a single linear system of human development.

Having established the bonds between periphery and center and between material and spiritual life, Yanagita was ready, in the immediate postwar years, to present a picture of Japan in which the nation was seen as united around a distinctive cultural core. In response to the social chaos which followed Japan's surrender, he returned with increasing emphasis to the symbol of the festival as the locus of cultural identity. "In these circumstances," he wrote in 1946, "it is particularly necessary to become aware of what it means to form an ethnically homogeneous nation. . . . Until now we have not considered . . . how many ways of seeing things and ways of feeling we have which, for better or worse, are peculiar to the Japanese. The bond between family and ancestral spirits is among these things, but there are also many inexpressible covenants between the gods and the people of the village which have been handed down unchanged from the past, and which we can think of as existing through the medium of the yearly celebration of festivals" (Yanagita 1963c, 284).

Culture as Organism: The Anthropology of Ishida Eiichirō

It was left to Yanagita's disciples and successors, however, to pursue this analysis of the cultural system to its logical conclusion. For the generation of scholars which succeeded Yanagita, the term *bunka* had lost much of its raw newness. The ethnographers and anthropologists of the immediate postwar period were familiar with European and American debates on the concept of culture. Many of them, indeed, had studied overseas, and some had begun their careers at the height of

Japan's empire building, in that brief period when Japanese anthropologists had unprecedented opportunities for fieldwork throughout East and Southeast Asia (as well as parts of the South Pacific). Culture, to these scholars, was a familiar and accepted tool of analysis. Yanagita's definition of *bunka* as a national level phenomenon and as a mixture of old and new—the definition which had seemed so novel in the early 1940s—was now taken for granted.

Typical of this new generation was Ishida Eiichirō (1903–1968), the pioneering anthropologist whose work was to exert profound influence on images of Japanese culture to the present day. Ishida had studied in Vienna in the late 1930s and conducted ethnographic work in Sakhalin (Karafuto), China, and Mongolia during the Pacific War (see Yamaguchi 1979, 71–80). After an early association with Marxism, he emerged as a fierce critic of dialectical materialism, which he described, in a short but controversial article, as having degenerated from science into sterile dogma (Ishida, "Hihanteki seishin no tame ni," reprinted in Yamaguchi 1979, 119–124). In place of Marxism, cultural anthropology formed the intellectual basis of Ishida's mature writings.

What is particularly fascinating about Ishida's work is the way in which it used ideas deeply rooted in the European nineteenth- to early twentieth-century world view as the foundation on which to build a theory of Japanese uniqueness. Ishida's thoughts on the modern meaning of culture begin with a quotation from Edward Tylor's *Primitive Culture,* where, under the heading "the Science of Culture," the object of study is defined as "that complex whole which includes knowledge, belief, art, morals, law custom, and any other capabilities and habits acquired by man as a member of society" (Tylor 1871, 1; quoted in Ishida 1977a, 234; see also Ishida 1977b, 29). The quotation is an apt reminder of the fact that cultural anthropology was born in an age when science (particularly Newtonian physics) was king, and when the respectability of any new discipline depended largely on its ability to dress itself in the costume of the scientist. The "science of culture" was also a child of the Darwinian age: In pursuing "culture," the early anthropologists were searching for that essence which separated human beings from other animals and which could therefore restore the firm line between apes and humans so rudely removed by *The Origin of Species.*

The world view which Ishida borrowed from Western cultural anthropology was one in which phenomena were divided into three levels. At the most basic level was the inorganic world—the realm of the physicist and the chemist; above this came the organic world—the field of study of the biologist or natural historian; and at the highest and most complex level lay the "superorganic"—the world of human culture which was the special concern of the anthropologist (Ishida 1977b). This vision of things was most directly derived (like most of Ishida's concept of culture) from the writings of the U.S. scholar Alfred Kroeber (1876–1960), whose work, in part through Ishida's influence, has played a key role in shaping popular notions of culture in contemporary Japan (see for example Kroeber 1952a).

Kroeber was an almost exact contemporary of Yanagita Kunio and had moved in a somewhat similar way from detailed ethnographic work (in Kroeber's case on Native American societies) to wider speculations about the nature of culture (Steward 1973). A recurring concern of his work was the relationship between history, science, and anthropology. All human thought, according to Kroeber, required some combination of two forms of analysis: the historical (which dealt with unique and changing phenomena) and the scientific (which dealt with constant regularities and laws). The mixture varied from one discipline to another, with the scientific element being stronger in disciplines concerned with the inorganic world, and the historical element being stronger in disciplines which dealt with the superorganic. He suggested, though, that history and the other social sciences had been rather slow to develop the scientific side of their personalities and that this was a gap which anthropology could help to fill (see Kroeber, "An Anthropologist Looks at History," reprinted in Steward 1973, 94–101; Kroeber 1952b).

It was from genetics and the biological sciences generally that Kroeber drew particular inspiration. Anthropology might not aspire to the elegant simplicity of physics, but it could and should aim to strengthen the element of science in cultural research by following the model of biology (or "natural history"), where the study of the irregular and particular was firmly grounded in orderly laws of behavior. In fact, he argued, cultural studies had "an identity of procedure" with all the "admittedly historical sciences that flourish on sub-cultural levels—palaeontology and phylogenic biology, geology and astronomy" (Kroeber and Kluckhohn 1963, 314). Thus the small cultures of "primitive people" could be "accurately and dispassionately analyzed much as a biologist dissects a worm or a crayfish" (Kroeber 1952b, 76).

What impact did this yearning for scientific method have on the idea of "culture"? First, it meant that the analysis of culture was a search for order and pattern. "The study of culture is the study of regularities," wrote Kroeber and Kluckhohn (Kroeber and Kluckhohn 1963, 330). Ishida Eiichirō illustrates this by using the example of the school bell which rings at the end of a lesson. Each event—each ringing of the bell—has its own particular characteristics, but what is culturally important is the single, instantly identifiable message which is understood every time the bell rings and which evokes the same predictable response from the students (Ishida 1977b, 39). The study of culture, in short, requires the ability to perceive patterns within apparent confusion and to extract these patterns from the messy bits of human behavior which threaten to blur their edges. Here Ishida was partly influenced, too, by Ruth Benedict's notion of "patterns of culture," although he was also to make harsh comments about her famous analysis of Japan, *The Chrysanthemum and the Sword* (Ishida 1974, 125–126).

The search for a science of culture also meant a search for the single unifying force underpinning the regularity of observable patterns. Ishida repeatedly criticized ethnographers like James Frazer—and indeed Yanagita Kunio—who had been content to amass huge quantities of data on myth and ritual and then to organize them as though constructing a giant jigsaw puzzle (see, for example, the "Afterword" in Ishida 1956, 288–289). This eclectic assembling of material was not enough. Alfred Kroeber seems for the most part to have identified this "inner essence" of each culture with its basic system of values (Kroeber and Kluckhohn 1963, 338–340). In some of his last writings, however, he sketched an almost mystical notion of "cultural style," resembling the unique shape which evolution endows on each species of living organism (Kroeber 1957).

This organic imagery particularly attracted Ishida Eiichirō. In a passage which is almost entirely lifted from Kroeber's *Style and Civilization,* Ishida explains the interrelationship between a culture's religious practices, myths, language, and material technology by using the analogy of a bird in flight. In a bird, the parts—wings, head, legs, eyes, tail—are all integrated in such a way as to provide perfect function and balance. So too "human cultures seem to be organically integrated: not random collections of parts but unified structures" (Ishida 1977b, 57; compare Kroeber 1957, 77–78). What gives the bird its particular form is genetics, evolution, and ultimately the force of life itself; what en-

dows each society (or *minzoku,* ethnic group) with an organically integrated culture is less clear, but Ishida goes further than Kroeber in
implying the existence of some kind of life force at the center of the
cultural pattern. Where Kroeber intermittently reflected that culture—
as a product of human beings—was never perfectly integrated, Ishida
consistently emphasized the coordination, totality, and independent existence of culture. And where the core of Kroeber's "cultural style"
remained (in his own words) "misty," Ishida was inspired by the German anthropologist Leo Frobenius's more explicit notion of *paideuma,*
a sort of communal cultural spirit which (Frobenius wrote) "is not
made by people, but only 'lives within people' " or "possesses people"
(Froebenius 1953, 56; see also Kroeber 1957, 80; Ishida 1977b, 58).
Ishida quoted extensively from Frobenius, particularly picking out the
passages where he referred to culture as possessing its own "subjectivity": existing and evolving alongside, but independent from, the inorganic and organic worlds as a separate "third realm" (Ishida 1977b,
66–67).

We have come a long way here from the idea of culture as imported
novelties, or even from the idea of culture as the everyday way of life
of a society. Under the influence of anthropology, "culture" by the late
1950s was becoming something altogether more portentous. Now the
study of culture did not simply mean an examination of all those elements, old and new, which Yanagita had seen as forming the "brocade" of national life; it also meant an effort to grasp the elusive force
which wove the threads together. And the fact that this force was
immeasurable, invisible, and intangible did not mean that it was not
real: According to Ishida, "just as biologists conceptualize the phenomenon of life by using the abstract notion 'life,' so anthropologists
distinguish culture from the inorganic world and the non-human organic world by using the concept 'culture' ... culture itself is not
pattern or type or values or ethos, it is above all that particular *objective reality itself* which is revealed in the consciousness, behavior, and
material life of the people who make up a particular society" (Ishida
1977a, 240; emphasis added).

The vision of ethnic cultures as living things, imbued with an elusive but potent animus, was therefore not a Japanese invention but
something that Japan imported and adapted in much the same way that
it imported and adapted modernization theory and Keynesian economics. The originality of Ishida's work did not lie in his cultural theoriz-

ing, but in his application of existing theory to comparative studies of mythology in the Pacific rim and to analyzing the culture of Japan itself. Ishida's search for the organizing principle which underlay Japanese culture was an unfinished one. In one of his last works, *Nihon bunka ron* (published in English as *Japanese Culture: A Study of Origins and Characteristics*), he called for more thorough examination of Japanese folklore, so that the material collected could be used for "discovering what underlies a people's culture, and how to grasp this in a scholarly way and analyze it structurally" (Ishida 1974, 119). For Ishida, as for Kroeber, that Copernican "decisive organizing step" which would reveal the inner nature of culture remained to be taken. Ishida's comments, though, suggest that he identified the unifying principle of Japanese culture with rice-based agriculture, which (he claimed) had produced a powerful sense of group loyalty, ethical responsibility, and particularly that attachment to nature discussed in Chapter 3. European society, by contrast, was based on pastoralism, which had created a culture where "human life is sustained by ruthless power, intense self-assertion, and the rigidity of customs which support these" (Ishida 1974: 136).

The point at issue here is not the value or otherwise of Ishida's characterization of Japanese (and European) culture, but the widespread acceptance of his underlying concept of an organically integrated "culture" as an appropriate way of analyzing Japanese society. The issue is a crucial one because this concept of culture—often without much discussion or reflection—became the touchstone for a whole genre of 1960s' and 1970s' writings on "theories of the Japanese" (*Nihonjinron*). This turning of the anthropological microscope inward to examine one's own society has struck many Western scholars as odd or even slightly morbid. Until relatively recently, U.S. and European anthropologists notoriously tended to ignore their own societies (one of the few exceptions to the general rule being Alfred Kroeber, who applied his ideas of culture to the study of Western Europe and the United States as well as to the more conventional targets of anthropological research): Only in the past two or three decades has this approach been extensively rethought (see, for example, Fabian 1983). In Japan, on the contrary, it seems almost to be taken for granted that anthropologists will have something significant to say about the Japanese culture. This is partly, no doubt, a reflection of the nature of anthropology itself. As a discipline through which European and

American scientists dissected the rest of the world, it seems to have left the Japanese anthropologist with the uncomfortable sense of being at once researcher and laboratory specimen. But the introspective fascination with "Japanese culture" is also an ironic result of the enormously rapid process of change which has transformed every aspect of the Japanese lifestyle—housing, clothes, transport, working habits, leisure, language—over the past hundred years. In the midst of such endless innovation there is something attractive about the notion of an unchanging cultural essence, a still center, which can reassure you that you are still who you always thought you were.

The organic image of culture is therefore appealing (as Yanagita's writings suggest) because it offers a way of counteracting fears of social disintegration and also because (as the work of Kroeber and Ishida shows) it provides a coherent and respectably "scientific" way of analyzing society. By the same token, it is problematic in terms of both ideology and methodology: Ideologically, it imposes a particular utopian vision of integration and harmony on the protean and fluid forms of social existence; methodologically, it subjects those same forms to a biological model of interpretation whose appropriateness is open to serious question.

The notion of "culture," however, was not the only intellectual framework which could be used to give a scientific gloss to images of national cohesion. In Japan as elsewhere, ideas of culture developed alongside impassioned debates about racial boundaries and racial origins. These in turn helped to refine and popularize a sense of the Japanese as a distinct "ethnic group"—*minzoku*—a concept which fused images of race with images of culture. Like *bunka,* the idea of *minzoku* has a powerful and enduring influence on contemporary Japanese identity debates, and it is therefore important to explore its historical lineage more fully.

Ainu having their customs forcibly "improved" by officials (who are cutting their hair and beards). An illustration from the journals of the mid-nineteenth century traveler Matsuura Takeshirō. (Reprinted in Hanazaki Kōhei, *Shizukana taichi*, Tokyo, Iwanami Shoten, 1993.)

Sakhalin Ainu-bred dogs who pulled their sleds, provided a source of fur and meat, and were trained to catch salmon. (Illustration from Mamiya Rinzō, *Kita Ezo Zusetsu*, Tokyo, Meichō Kankōkai, 1970.)

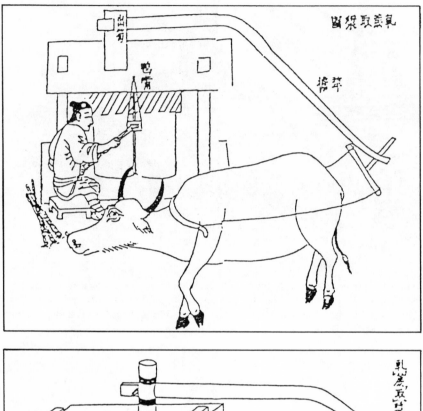

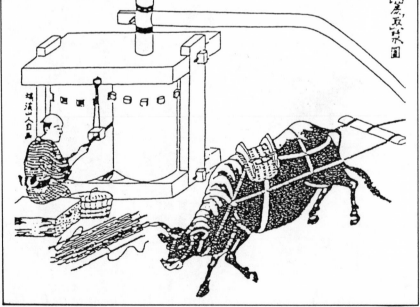

Illustrations of a sugar-crushing mill from Song Yingxing's *Tiangong kaiwu* (top) and Hiraga Gennai's *Butsurui hinshitsu* (bottom).

Illustration from Miyazaki Yasusada's *Nōgyō zensho*. (Reprinted in *Kinsei kagaku shisō*, vol. 1, Tokyo, Iwanami Shoten, 1972.)

"Japan" depicted as an urbanized samurai. From *Chinsetsu kidan ehon bankokushi*. (Reprinted in Torii Ryūzō *Kyokutō minzoku*, vol. 1, Tokyo, Bunka Seikatsu Kenkyūkai, 1926.)

This cartoon from around the time of the First World War—and entitled "ourselves in the past"—suggests a belief in Japan's growing cultural maturity, but also a vision of culture as imported. The "western" adult is feeding the infant "Japan" from a bottle labeled "*bunka*." (Reproduced in Robertson Scott, *The Foundations of Japan*, London, John Murray, 1922.)

A Chinese servant of the Asian race. Illustration from Fukuzawa Yukichi's *Sekai Kunizukushi.*

This photograph of Kaneko Fumiko and Pak Yeor was distributed by right-wing military offices to illustrate the "immoral" nature of political "subversives."

HECHIMA COLOGNE

Wartime pictures of China, like those above (from the newspaper *Fujin Shimbun*) presented repeated images of poverty, backwardness, and misery, which are all the more striking because they are juxtaposed with advertising which creates an image of a prosperous and glamorous Japan (as in this cologne advertisement).

The gendered nation. In this 1910 cartoon celebrating the annexation of Korea, Japan as male (represented by the first colonial governor General Terauchi) rolls back the mythical rock door allowing the eternal light of Japan as female (represented by the sun goddess Amaterasu Omikami) to shine on the suitably diminutive Korean people. (*Tokyo Puck* 1 September 1910). (Reprinted by Ryūkei Shoten, Tokyo, 1996.)

Japan as victim of racism. A depiction of early twentieth century attacks on Japanese immigrants on the West Coast of Canada and the United States. From *Tokyo Puck* 20 September 1907. (Reprinted by Ryūkei Shoten, Tokyo, 1996.)

NHKドラマ・ガイド　朝の連続テレビ小説

おしん

母たちの青春
その光と影を見つめて……

橋田壽賀子＝原作

小木新造＝監修
ＮＨＫドラマ制作班＝協力

Japan as female. The cover illustration of NHK's booklet accompanying the television series "Oshin." (From Fujine Iwao, *NHK dorama gaido Oshin*, Tokyo, Nihon Hōsō Shuppan Kyōkai, 1983.)

Japan as male. This illustration, from Nakane Chie's book of the same name, is entitled "Human relationships in a vertical society." (From Nakane Chie, *Tate shakai no ningen kankei*, Tokyo, Kōdansha, 1967.)

Forbes Japan's vision of the final media battle for the Japanese mainland. (From *Forbes Japan*, December 1996.)

Life on the borderlands. In this cartoon a distinctly "non-Japanese" looking child asks his "Japanese" looking mother (in Japanese) "Mum, what *are* foreigners?" (From Moriki Kazumi, *Kokusai kekkon handobukku*, Tokyo, Akashi Shoten, 1994.)

5

Race

"Upon the whole, every circumstance concurs in proving that mankind are not composed of species entirely different from each other; that, on the contrary, there was originally but one species, who, after multiplying and spreading over the whole surface of the earth, have undergone various changes by the influence of climate, food, mode of living, epidemic diseases, and the mixture of dissimilar individuals." (Buffon 1866, 286). Thus wrote Georges Louis Comte de Buffon, the first scholar to use the word "race" in its modern sense.

As a recent reassessment of his work points out, Buffon's classic *Histoire Naturelle, Générale et Particulière* (published in 1749) embodied a radically new image of the natural world (Sloan 1995, 112–131). It was, indeed, natural *history*. In other words, its vision of nature was animated by a sense of time. Buffon fiercely criticized the Linnean system of classification, where physical characteristics were used to divide and subdivide the living world, creating a flat, synchronic picture of nature. On the contrary, he argued, "it is neither the number nor the collection of similar individuals which forms the species. It is the constant succession and uninterrupted renewal of these individuals which comprises it. . . . The species is thus an abstract and general term, for which the thing exists only in considering Nature in the succession of time, and in the constant destruction and renewal of creatures" (quoted in Sloan 1995, 132). In Buffon's work, race was the product of historical experiences which had gradually created diversity within an originally single human stock. But Buffon was still closer to the world of the Renaissance than the world of Charles Darwin, and he therefore saw the history of race, not as a history of unequal progress from an original "primitive" state, but as a history of unequal degeneration from the original paragon of creation, to which the "white" races most closely approximated (Buffon 1866, 280–281).

The opening quotation also shows how integrally Buffon's concept of race was connected to his recognition of humankind as a single, global species. This connection is crucial. It was no coincidence that the modern idea of "race" emerged simultaneously with the recognition of a global humanity, or that the idea of universal human rights, which was to grow out of this vision of a single human species, developed concurrently with Herder's image of a world divided into radically different "ethnic groups" (*Völker*). The stories brought back by European explorers, and extensively quoted by both Buffon and Herder, confronted scholars with the challenging realization that human beings existed worldwide, possessed a common nature, and had created a previously unimagined diversity of lifestyles. Notions of "race" or "*Volk*" can be seen as efforts to reduce this bewildering variety to manageable order. And, once created, they provided an intellectual framework for practices of racism, which could be used to contain and temper the alarming implications of the emergent ideas of human rights and citizenship. It has often been pointed out that the origins of the idea of Aryan supremacy go back to attempts by elements of the French aristocracy to reassert their place in the post-revolutionary world. Modern racism, in other words, can be seen as behavior, ideas, and structures which seek to exclude individuals or groups, on the grounds of beliefs about their racial origins, from rights to which they would otherwise be entitled. In so doing, it also reinforces the imagined bonds which draw the "included" into the community of the nation-state. If we accept this definition, then the evolution of notions of race and racism has to be understood in conjunction with the evolution of other key modern ideas, including ideas of human rights and of citizenship. Orlando Patterson may be correct to argue that without slavery there can be no idea of freedom, but it is equally true that without a notion of rights there can be no denial of those rights (Patterson 1982).

"Inside" and "Outside" in Early Modern Japan

These remarks obviously suggest that ideas of "race" and "racism," in the present-day senses of these words, cannot really be said to have existed in Japan before the advent of modern Western social and political thought. It is true, though, that many societies, including that of medieval and early modern Japan, had negative, and sometimes monstrous or demonic, images of "outsiders" which fed into the modern imagery of race. (Some of these images were vividly represented the "Charts of All the Nations" discussed in Chapter 1.)

In a recent article on "Human Categorization in Japan," Timon Screech depicts a radical difference between Western and premodern Japanese ideas of race and gender. Europeans have always assumed that there were only two clearly defined sexes, but have accepted the existence of a multiplicity of races. Japan, according to Screech, saw gender as complex and multiple—being "male" or "female" was inherently related to position within the family, and those outside families, such as monks and nuns, as well as people like professional female impersonators, could be seen as occupying a range of intermediate sexes. By contrast, Screech argues, race in Japan was singular and sharply defined: "Japan has always considered itself ethnically pure, and in this it draws a distinction with China and Korea, held to be racially diverse" (Screech 1995, 136).

To support this point, Screech refers to early contacts between Japanese and Europeans. When the first European missionaries and traders arrived in Japan in the late sixteenth and early seventeenth centuries, their presence inevitably resulted in the birth of children of mixed European and Japanese parentage. In the 1630s, all Europeans except the Dutch were expelled from Japan, and at the same time these mixed-race children were also expelled. "Records of mixed-race children appear occasionally thereafter," writes Screech, "stories are told of them, and the mixed-race child full of guile and too clever by half, became a figure of myth. But 'children of Dutch seed' (*Oranda taneko*) ceased to be an acknowledged category." The Japanese government, in short, regarded racial mixture with as much horror as a European government might regard hermaphrodism and had therefore determined that "the blood of foreigners must not be allowed to flow in Japanese veins" (Screech 1995, 132).

I return to the question of gender in Chapter 6, but here I propose a rather different conclusion about race. There are in fact numerous official references to children of Japanese and Dutch parentage during the seventeenth, eighteenth, and early nineteenth centuries. From the late seventeenth century onward, they were treated as Japanese in the sense that, like other Japanese people, they were prohibited from traveling abroad. They were, however, required to register births, deaths, and marriages separately from, and with more formality than, other people

(Koga 1969, 113–125 and 142). It is likely that many faced prejudice and hardship, but we do know that at least one (after strenuous lobbying by his Dutch father) was appointed to an official position in the Nagasaki city bureaucracy and that another, the daughter of the German doctor Franz Philipp von Siebold, became the first woman to practice Western medicine in Japan (Koga 1969; Itazawa 1960, 75–78 and 150–152).

It is difficult, in fact, to find anything in seventeenth- or eighteenth-century Japan which resembles a coherent ideology of race. People might be excluded from or included in the social order, but the grounds for exclusion or inclusion tended to be explained primarily in terms of submission to the power of the state. Perhaps the sharpest line of exclusion throughout the Tokugawa period, indeed, was directed not at "foreigners" as such, but at Christianity, which, after a rebellion by Christians in the Shimabara region of Kyūshū in 1637–38, was regarded as an inherently subversive and destabilizing influence. Although the reasons for the Shimabara Rebellion were social and economic as much as religious, the result was a ruthless suppression of Christianity, one of whose more interesting features was the use of the *fumie.* This was a Christian religious picture on which subjects were required to tread, as a visible sign of their repudiation of Christianity. Throughout the Tokugawa period, villagers and townspeople in domains all over Kyūshū were regularly required to go through the ritual of treading on the *fumie,* and similar rituals were also held in times of social tension in other parts of Japan. The fact that these continued long after the practical threat of Christian subversion had receded suggests that the ritual itself had acquired a deeper symbolic significance as a reassuring public display of social unity and political loyalty.

It is true that submission to the authority of the state could also be symbolized by visible characteristics—the wearing of "correct" dress, hairstyles, etc.—which at times carried overtones of physical difference, but at the same time the dividing line between "inside" and "outside" often cut across what we would now call "ethnic groups." The community of several thousand Chinese living in the port of Nagasaki, for example, was clearly divided down the middle. On the one hand, there was a group of Chinese merchants who were defined as owing allegiance to the Chinese state and were allowed to travel between Japan and China but, while in Nagasaki, were largely confined to a walled ghetto, the *Tōjin yashiki.* On the other hand, there were the "resident Chinese," who were seen as having transferred their allegiance to Japan (Yamamoto 1983; Kimiya 1955). They (like other Japanese) were not allowed to leave the country, but were free to live where they liked in Nagasaki and in practice gradually melted into the general population.

Rather than seeing pre-Meiji Japanese society as bounded by the sharp fault line of racial exclusivity, it probably makes more sense to envisage an inherently unequal social order where everyone theoretically occupied a place in an intricate galaxy of statuses spiraling outward from a center represented by the imperial court and the Shogunal administration. Order, propriety, and virtue were generally assumed to be greatest at the center—in both social and geographical terms—and to diminish as one moved out toward the margins. So semi-incorporated cultural groups at the remotest extremes of the archipelago, like the Ainu and the people of the Ryūkyū Islands, were portrayed by the state (as we have seen) in terms of a set of conventional images of uncouth behavior: They had unkempt hair or unusual headgear, tattooed hands or faces, strange rituals and dietary habits. A similar set of images— untidy hair, tattoos, etc.—was also associated with communities assigned to the lower levels of the social hierarchy. Convicted criminals were commonly tattooed, and tattooing developed into a complex art form in the marginalized communities of prostitutes and entertainers which appeared along the highways and riverbanks of Japan's expanding cities. Other miscellaneous groups of people who occupied the fringes of the social order—including dyers, bamboo workers, river boatmen, stone-masons, leather workers, and undertakers—were required to wear distinctive clothing and to tie their hair with straw cords, in contrast to the neat top-knots prescribed for other social groups. In this world without a distinct sense of political rights, then, there was also no real sense of the exclusion of people from rights on the grounds of race. Rather, there was a concept of an infinite set of social gradations defined in terms of ideas of social function, order, propriety, and political submission.

This helps to explain why some of the most pervasive forms of discrimination in modern Japan have been directed against people who are in no sense "racially" different from the rest of the population: that is, against the communities now known as the Discriminated Villages (*Hisabetsu Buraku*), made up of people whose ancestors belonged to the marginalized occupational groups of the pre-Meiji social order. (In fact, anyone attempting to research questions of discrimination in Japanese society will quickly be struck by the fact that the vast majority of Japanese writings on the subject deal with discrimination against the *Hisabetsu Buraku* community.) The survival of this discrimination into the late twentieth century seems in many ways bizarre and is not easy to explain, though it may be partly understood in terms of the political uses of "minorities"—a subject to which we return in Chapter 9. It is clearly part of a wider phenomenon of "racism without race" which is not confined to Japan but also appears in other twentieth-century societies, one interesting example being the case of the Irish Travelers (or "Tinkers") who are also descendants, not of a separate "ethnic minority" but of marginalized occupational groups. Discrimination, in other words, produces difference just as much as difference produces discrimination.

Race in Modern Japan

The transformation of the Japanese state after the Meiji Restoration redefined patterns of inclusion and exclusion in two fundamental ways. First, Western notions of citizenship were introduced, but only in a very narrow and diluted form. After the Restoration, the status system, along with associated restrictions on dress, lifestyle, and internal migration, as well as the prohibition on Christianity, were abolished. From now on, all people would be encouraged to consider themselves equally "Japanese," in the sense that they were all members of a clearly bounded nation-state to which all owed an equal duty of loyalty. But this equality of allegiance was never intended to confer equality of rights. For one thing, as in most Western countries at that time, the rights and duties of men and women were clearly distinguished; for another, key rights such as the franchise were, until the 1920s, extended only to certain groups of men (those who paid taxes above a specified level). To justify the new social order, with its emphasis on both solidarity and inequality, Japan's leaders made particular use of the imagery of the family (*kazoku* or *ie*). As in the family, all people were part of a single community, but, also as in the family, they had different rights and duties within that community. The imagery of the family was particularly apposite because it created the ideal framework for asserting the paramount place of the emperor in Japanese society. The emperor, previously a shadowy and politically insignificant figure, was now redefined as the father of the nation, the head of the *kazoku kokka* (family-state). The inculcation of this image of the nation was to have profound implications for the ways in which Japanese intellectuals and the wider public digested the imported notions of ethnicity and race.

The second major development of the late nineteenth century was the importation of these notions themselves: first (particularly in the 1860s and 1870s) of the idea of race (*jinshu*) and soon after (from about the late 1880s) of the concepts of the *Volk* or ethnic group (*minzoku*). Significantly, the chief popularizer of the idea of race in Japan was that most eloquent Meiji interpreter of Western civilization, Fukuzawa Yukichi. Western categories of human difference had begun to be introduced to Japan during the seventeenth and eighteenth centuries through the translation of geography texts obtained from the Dutch; the first truly influential representation of the notion of race appeared in 1869, when Fukuzawa published his *Account of the Countries of the World* (Sekai Kunizukushi), intended as a geography text for use in schools. This short and richly illustrated work introduces the reader to a neatly color-coded vision of humanity: Europeans are white, Asians "slightly yellow," Africans black, the people of the Pacific Islands brown, and the inhabitants of "the mountains of America" red (Fukuzawa 1926, 689). Fukuzawa's account of Asia is accompanied by an illustration of "a Chinese servant of the Asian race" which is a perfect replica of nineteenth-century Western Orientalist iconography. This multicolored image of the world was incorporated into generations of Japanese school textbooks, and at least one eminent scholar—the anthropologist Torii Ryūzō—was later to credit it with stimulating his interest in the study of humankind (Torii 1976, 156).

Fukuzawa's role as popularizer of the notions both of race (*jinshu*) and of civilization (*bunmei*) illuminates an important theme of this book. The European intellectual heritage of the eighteenth and nineteenth centuries offered two axes for the definition of difference. The first was the axis of geographical space, represented by the closely related ideas of "race" and "culture/ethnicity." In creating a sense of national solidarity and (sometimes) national superiority, ideologues could draw on the idea of a group linked by the blood bonds of a common origin (race) or on the idea of a group linked by common language or traditions (ethnicity). Both of these notions suggested the existence of deep dividing lines separating distinct human groups from one another. The second axis was that of time, represented by the notions of "progress" or "civilization." These suggested an image of humanity following a single and universal trajectory. Here, national difference was asserted by suggesting that "we" were farther along the path of progress than "they" were (or, sometimes conversely that "we" were more backward than "they" were). In practice, however, the dimensions of space and time—of "race," "ethnicity," and "civilization"—were not necessarily deployed separately, but were combined and interwoven in complex ways. One particularly influential interweaving was represented by the ideas of Social Darwinism (very influential in Japan around the turn of the century), where different races were commonly seen as representing different stages in the march toward "civilization" (Low 1997).

In earlier chapters, we have seen how a shift in emphasis from the dimension of "space" to the dimension of "time" was used to create a sense of national identity in Japan. Outlying regions, most notably Okinawa and Ainu areas, which had originally been seen as "spatially different" or "foreign," came to be reinterpreted as "temporally different" or "backward" parts of a single "Japanese people," and later of a single "Japanese culture." This does not, of course, mean that "internal racism" disappeared from popular discourse. In Hokkaidō, for example, people of Ainu ancestry were often, and sometimes still are, subject to racist stereotypes and insults (for example, Ogawa 1986). Indeed, the whole project of defining Ainu and others as "ancient Japanese" encouraged a complex debate about the racial relationship between Ainu and "modern" Japanese, accompanied by an often demeaning process of anthropological skull-measuring and skeleton collection (Kayano 1994, 98–99; Siddle 1996, 78–88). This process in turn generated crude images of "Ainu" physical characteristics which fed into popular racial prejudice.

In dealing with the world beyond the national boundaries, however, the relationship between "Japan" as political entity and the concepts of "race," "ethnicity," and "civilization" was fraught with even greater tensions. These tensions were intensified by the process of colonization. As Japan expanded its colonial rule into Taiwan (1895), Karafuto and Kwantung (1905), Korea (1910), the Pacific Mandated Territories (1919), and de facto control of Manchuria in 1931 and North China in 1937, issues of the connection between political rule, racial and cultural commonality, and progress along a path of universal human civilization became increasingly complex and intractable. Was Japan's right to rule the colonies based upon the innate racial superiority of the Japanese rulers vis-à-vis their colonial subjects? Or was it based, on the contrary, on racial or cultural *commonalities* between rulers and ruled? Or did it derive from the fact that Japanese society embodied a more advanced form of a single modern "civilization"? Each of these claims had its own implications for colonial policy and for Japan's relationship with the established colonial powers.

It is important to examine interwar and wartime debates on these questions because they have a bearing on continuing dilemmas over ideas of nationhood, ethnicity, and civilization in contemporary Japan. Here I argue that the questions outlined in the previous paragraph were never answered. All three justifications of colonial expansion—the ideas of racial uniqueness, ethnic commonalities, and civilizational advancement—coexisted at different layers within the intellectual world of the 1920s, 1930s, and 1940s, and the use of the ambiguous imagery of "nation" and "ethnos"—*minzoku*—allowed a continuous slippage backward and forward between different levels of justification.

Western notions of race, which were commonly intertwined with ideas about the superiority of the white races, were not necessarily comfortable for Japanese readers. Although the word *jinshu* was accepted as the equivalent of the English word "race" and was widely used by some anthropologists, after about 1890 a growing number of Japanese writers showed a preference for the term *minzoku,* which is perhaps best defined as the Japanese version of the German word *Volk.* *Minzoku,* in other words, can but does not necessarily refer to a group of people who are physically related to one another. It can also refer to a community bound together by ties of language or tradition, and in some cases (as historian Kevin Doak has emphasized) it is used in a sense close to that of the English word "nation" (Doak 1997). It is nearer, therefore, to the concept of "ethnicity" or "people" (as in "the peoples of the world") than to the concept of "race" and contains all the ambiguities tied up in European and North American imagery of "ethnic groups." All efforts at fixing these Japanese terms to stable English translations, indeed, is frustrated not just by the slipperiness of the Japanese words themselves, but also by the fact that the English words "race," "nation," and "ethnic group" are "used with incredible inconsistency" (Wallerstein 1991b, 77).

When the Japanese government was negotiating the abolition of extraterritorial rights and separate residential districts for foreigners in the 1890s, some of the most intensely xenophobic and exclusionist sentiments were expressed by writers who spoke, not of Japan's racial superiority, but of its racial inferiority. The most famous illustrations are provided by the writings of the religious philosopher Inoue Tetsujirō, who opposed "mixed residence" (*zakkyo*) on the grounds that the physically and intellectually inferior Japanese, if forced to live side by side with foreigners, would be unable to survive the competitive struggle for existence with the cleverer and more powerful Westerners (Inoue 1928).

Images of Racial Purity

As Japan's economic and military might increased, however, these fears quickly gave way to expressions of Japanese superiority. In his thorough survey of the subject, Oguma Eiji points out that there were two inherently contradictory approaches to the exaltation of the Japanese race or ethnos (Oguma 1995). The first depicted the Japanese as a racially homogeneous group literally descended from a common blood line whose senior branch was the imperial family. The second, on the contrary, not only admitted but actually emphasized the fact that the Japanese people were of mixed racial origins and frequently identified this hybridity as the source of national strength and of claims to imperial power. The following sections of this chapter outline both these currents of thought and then go on to consider a third, which became particularly influential around the late 1930s: a current which attempted to escape from notions of race altogether and justify imperial expansion in terms of a universal human destiny.

Most writings on Japanese nationalism have emphasized the connection between nationalism and images of racial homogeneity. It is often pointed out that the idea of the *kokutai* (national body or national entity), developed by conservative writers like Hozumi Yatsuka in the last decades of the nineteenth century, combined images borrowed from the Shinto nationalism of the late eighteenth century with more recently imported ideas of racial purity (see Oguma 1995, 53–55; Gluck 1985, 142 and 186–187). The Japanese, it was argued, were linked by blood to a single imperial family, whose origins could be traced back to the age of the gods. In the years following World War I, this idea was taken up, not just by conservative ideologues, but also by some radical critics of the social costs of modernization.

A vivid example of this is evident in the "State Socialism" or "National Socialism" (*kokka shakaishugi*) of Takabatake Motoyuki, the Japanese translator of Marx's *Das Kapital*. Takabatake, whose journal *Kokka Shakaishugi* was first published in 1918, was in many ways deeply influenced by Marxian thought, but differed from Marx on the question of the nation. Takabatake saw the nation as having emerged before the coming of capitalism and believed in a revolution which would restore the nation to that pure integrity which it had embodied in the precapitalist age. All nations, he argued, were similar in the sense that they were structures of social integration and social control, but the Japanese nation fulfilled these functions in a unique way:

> The necessary condition for the ideal state is that its center of control should be established in a firm and unchanging manner. A fluid center of control hampers the development of the ruling authority and is an impediment to the growth of state integration. In this sense we can assert that the Japanese *Kokutai* is truly ideal. Furthermore, our imperial family has maintained a blood kinship between the people of the nation, and thus has preserved its position as the center of control for many thousands of years. For this reason the attitude of the people toward it [the imperial family] embodies a form of mysterious reverence and filial piety which is fundamentally different from the relationship between sovereign and subjects in other countries. (Quoted in Kada 1938, 84)

Images of racial purity and imperial mystique lent themselves to grandiose rhetoric and popular oratory, and it is for this reason that they recur in the popular press and in public statements of nationalism, particularly after the outbreak of conflict in China in 1931. John Dower, in his superb analysis of race in the Pacific War, carefully dissects the wartime rhetoric of race, both in Japan and in the United States. In the Japanese case, visual metaphors, often evoking the symbolism of light and colors, were used to reinforce images of national power and purity (Dower 1986, 210–212). One bizarre but not uncharacteristic example is a book entitled *Basic Research into the Superiority of the Japanese People,* written and published in 1943 by an otherwise wholly unknown retired public servant. The overall tone of the book is conveyed by its opening sentences, which read:

> The Japanese land shines with a golden light, and for that reason the country is the most excellent in the world and its people are the most

excellent people. The Japanese are golden people. What are golden people? They are people who are neither white people nor brown people nor
black people, but are a special race who live only in East Asia. However,
the golden people of East Asia are not all the same. Among them are the
True Golden People (*Hon Ōjin*) and the Quasi-Golden People (*Jun
Ōjin*). The Japanese are True Golden People and the Chinese are Quasi-
Golden People. Why are the Japanese True Golden People? It is because
they are people who live directly under the shining golden light of the
Heavenly (or Imperial) Way (*Tendō*). (Suehiro 1943, 1)

After many more pages in the same vein, the book goes on to
enumerate the many unique advantages of the Japanese physique, beginning with remarkable eyesight.

A similar belief in the racial purity of the Japanese was expressed in
more academic terms by a minority of prewar and wartime archaeolo-
gists and ethnographers. Of these, the most influential was Hasebe
Kotondo, professor of anthropology at Tokyo University from 1938,
who argued that a single race had occupied the Japanese archipelago
continuously since the dawn of humanity (Oguma 1995, 263–267).

Images of Racial Hybridity

This rhetoric of racial purity could be mobilized to challenge the realities of European and North American global power and was commonly
associated with a belief in Japan's divine mission in Asia. In practice,
however, it did not necessarily sit easily with the realities of colonial
rule. As a colonial power, after all, the Japanese state needed ideologies which might appeal to its colonial subjects as well as to the people
of the colonizing homeland (*naichi*). Ideas of the Japanese as a unique
race bound by blood to a quasi-divine imperial family were hardly
calculated to temper the opposition of Koreans or Taiwanese to foreign
rule. As Oguma Eiji observes, this helps to explain why in the interwar
years theories of racial purity were less widely accepted, at least by
Japanese intellectuals, than theories which stressed the diverse racial
origins of the Japanese people. Indeed, despite the views of academics
like Hasebe, at least one anthropologist stated firmly in 1942 that "not
only ethnographers from all countries, but also Japanese experts
equally acknowledge that we Yamato people are an ethnic group with
mixed blood" (Taniguchi 1942, 90).

One of the most eloquent and influential proponents of Japan's racial hybridity was the historian Kita Sadakichi, who spent much of his
career researching the subject. In a study published in 1929, Kita cited
recent anthropological and archaeological evidence. On the basis of
this scientific study, he confidently refuted the mythical vision of the
Japanese as racially pure descendants of divine ancestors:

> From the first, we Japanese people have not been a homogeneous ethnic
> group [*tanjun naru minzoku*]. Rather, many people of different lineages
> have lived together in this archipelago for long periods of time and in
> the process have intermarried, adopted one another's customs, merged
> their languages and eventually forgotten where they came from. Thus
> an entirely united Japanese ethnic group has come to be created. (Kita
> 1978, 214–215)

Japan, Kita argued, had originally been inhabited by a variety of
races, including ancestors of the present-day Ainu. These races had
been subjugated and molded into a single ethnicity by a group of
bronze-age newcomers who included the ancestors of the Japanese
emperors and who were seen—in a somewhat ill-defined way—as
ancient relatives of the Koreans. This, however, was not the end of the
process of ethnic assimilation. Later migrants from Korea and China
had also been absorbed into the racial mix, as had the Ainu inhabitants
of northern Honshū. In other words, the *Yamato minzoku* (the archaic
term by which Kita referred to the inhabitants of Japan) had emerged
from an intermingling of people drawn from most corners of the present-day Japanese empire.

In rejecting ideas of racial purity, however, Kita was by no means
rejecting the central role of the imperial family in Japanese life. On the
contrary, he argued that the "strongest bond" uniting the *Yamato
minzoku* was the presence of "a single imperial line existing from time
immemorial" (Kita 1918, 1). This construction of ethnicity, therefore,
did not abandon the image of the national "family," but merely reinterpreted it in metaphorical rather than biological terms: now the emperor
was depicted, not as a literal blood relative of all Japanese, but as the
descendent of ancestors whose role had been to unite the diverse people of Japan into a single political and cultural community. The
uniqueness of the Japanese was seen as lying, not in their racial purity,
but in their unmatched ability to mold such disparate elements into an

organically united society, for this process of integration had involved a Darwinian struggle between the cultures of many immigrant groups, out of which only the fittest elements had survived: "The customs and languages of the various elements which make up the Japanese ethnic group have not all been preserved in their original ratios. The superior assimilates the inferior, and the inferior is absorbed by the superior" (Kita 1978, 214). This approach, it should be said, created considerable scope for ambiguity in the rhetoric of nationhood. When Japanese writers spoke of the national family, and of the first emperors as the founders of this family, it was often left to the listener to determine whether they were speaking in terms of biology or culture or some combination of the two.

The "melting-pot" image of Japanese origins, of course, meshed beautifully with colonial assimilationist policies. If Japan, in the past, had succeeded in melding together people from a wide range of racial and linguistic backgrounds, surely it could do the same again with its new colonial subjects in Taiwan and Korea. Kita's ideas, in this sense, merely extended the logic which had earlier been used to integrate the frontier regions into the Japanese nation. Japan's colonial subjects— the people whom Kita described as "Japanese in the broad sense of the word"—were seen above all as *incomplete* Japanese: They were still in the process of "merging their languages" and "forgetting where they came from," but their destiny (like that of earlier waves of immigrants) was gradually and irresistibly to be absorbed into the *Yamato minzoku*.

Notions of diverse racial origins also meshed with Japanese nationalism in other ways. A deep source of Japanese resentment against the West was the refusal of the Western powers (led by Australia's William Hughes) to incorporate a clause on racial equality into the Versailles Treaty. This, together with the U.S. exclusion of Asian immigrants in the 1920s, fueled a strong sense of Japanese victimization and formed a recurring theme in the rhetoric of Japan's interwar pan-Asianism. Repeatedly, Japan was presented as a champion of "the colored races," a nation whose destiny was to "stand at the forefront of the global progress toward racial equality" (for example, Takada 1939, 64), and Japan's own history of peaceful racial integration was repeatedly cited as evidence of its fitness to fulfill this mission.

One fascinating version of this logic appears in the writings of the poet and feminist Takamure Itsue. Despite her prolonged commitment to anarchism, Takamure, in the late 1930s and 1940s, became an enthusiastic advocate of Japanese expansion in Asia and argued the cause on the basis of historical research strongly influenced by the historiography of Kita Sadakichi. Takamure's historical starting point was the search for the origins of sexual inequality in Japan. She came to argue that that patriarchy and the subordination of women in Japanese society were the result of importing the alien ideology of Confucianism, and her writings increasingly attempted to reach back beyond the arrival of Confucianism, reconstructing a utopian image of a prehistoric world of pristine sexual equality. At the same time she also developed an interest in the processes by which the various tribes of prehistoric Japan had gradually been forged into a single people. Japan's history of the peaceful assimilation of many peoples through intermarriage, she argued, could be contrasted with the Western history of assimilation through military conquest. This led, in her wartime writings, to an extension of the prehistoric utopia into the present, culminating in the vision of a Japan whose mission was to promote the creation of a single "world family"—a concept summed up in the wartime slogan (itself a quotation from an eighth-century chronicle) "the eight directions of the world under one roof" (*hakkō ichiu*) (Oguma 1995, 186–202; Ryang 1997).

It is worth remarking that this image of a Japanese ethnos whose contemporary strength and unity sprang from historical racial intermingling resonates strongly with nationalist responses to European racial theorizing in other parts of the world. A particularly striking parallel can be found in the stream of Latin American thought which, as Claudio Véliz has pointed out, evolved from the concept of Arielismo (Veliz 1994, 4–8). The idea of Arielismo itself was developed in the first decade of the twentieth century by the Uruguayan thinker José Enrique Rodó (1872–1917), who saw human culture as having two aspects. On the one hand there was the culture of Caliban—the earthbound ethos of material desires and crude utilitarianism, a culture which Rodó saw as being best exemplified by the United States. On the other, there was the ethos of Ariel—"the noble, soaring aspect of the human spirit"—which Rodó identified with Latin Americans. This dichotomy closely mirrors in the division proposed by Japanese thinkers, from Okakura Tenshin in the early twentieth century onward, between a materialist, profit-seeking West and a spiritual East. Rodó's ideas were further developed in the 1920s and 1930s by the eminent Mexican politician and educator José Vasconcelos (1882–1959), whose vision of the world was encapsulated in his most influential book, *La Raza Cósmica* (The Cosmic Race—1925). In this work Vasconcelos presented Latin Americans in general, and Mexicans in particular, as possessing a special historical destiny precisely because of the diversity of their racial origins. Focusing on a rather more recent period of history than the remote past explored by Kita Sadakichi and Takamure Itsue, he argued that the Mexicans had been formed from an intermingling of people from many parts of the world and thus constituted a uniquely complete "cosmic race" whose history was an expression of the divine will (Véliz 1994, 6–8).

In the Japanese case, of course, images of harmonious ethnic integration not only were totally divorced from the repressive realities of Japanese colonial policy but also contained their own inescapable oxymoron. As Takamure Itsue, writing of the prehistoric assimilation of peoples, put it: "In the shift from barbarism to the creation of an ordered world, two approaches are possible. One is to regard the core race with respect and the other races as inferior, and thus create a stratified order, such as we find in the Chinese notion of 'civilization and barbarism.' The other is to treat each racial lineage with equal respect, and furthermore to extend this vision so that one reaches an even more remote, even greater common ancestry, and on this basis to recognize all as being truly compatriots. This is what we find in Japanese Shinto" (quoted in Oguma 1995, 201). Japan's very racial porousness has here paradoxically become the characteristic separating the Japanese from other peoples, and the Japanese lack of a sense of racial hierarchies has become the source of Japan's claim to global racial leadership. The argument, in short, is that we are superior because we do not consider ourselves superior.

In fact, the more one looks at the literature of the 1930s and 1940s, the harder it becomes to sustain simple equations in which belief in racial purity are equated with militarism and imperialism and belief in racial hybridity with tolerance of difference. An intriguing and problematic text, in this context, is the short book *Kokutai no hongi* (Principles of the National Entity), published in 1937 by the Ministry of Education for distribution to schools and colleges. Based on an original manuscript by Tokyo University professor Hisamatsu Senichi, the *Principles* were revised and finalized by a committee of scholars and bureaucrats before publication. In the years immediately after Japan's defeat, the book attracted enormous interest from the occupying Allied administration, whose staff translated and studied its verbose content and seemed to have regarded it as an ideological text equivalent in importance to *Mein Kampf* (Hall 1949, 4–8). This view undoubtedly overestimated the influence of the *Principles*. However, as one of the few attempts by Japanese officialdom to put together a general statement of late-1930s nationalist ideology, the text is of considerable interest.

Laden with references to Shinto mythology and classical poetry, and burdened with archaic vocabulary, the *Principles of the National Entity* offers the quintessential statement of the uniqueness and superiority of the Japanese nation. And yet this "superiority" (which is discussed further in Chapter 6) is always expressed in terms of spirituality, morality, emotion and loyalty, and never in terms of biological race. Indeed, the whole quasi-poetic tone of the work makes it impossible to judge whether the *Yamato minzoku, okuchō shinmin* (one hundred million subjects) or *Yashima minsei* (people of the eight islands), as the Japanese are variously termed, are envisaged as being racially homogeneous or not. What is clear, however, is that one of their main claims to global superiority rests on their "unselfish" ability to assimilate foreign influences. The "importation of culture from the Asiatic continent" is interpreted as a process of "dying to self" which has thereby produced a greater and more purified self: "To have brought forth a culture uniquely our own, in spite of the fact that a culture essentially different was imported, is due entirely to a mighty influence peculiar to our nation. . . . By broadmindedness and assimilation is not meant the robbery of things alien by depriving them of characteristics peculiar to them, thereby bringing about the loss of their individuality, but is meant the casting aside of their defects and making the best use of their merits" (Hall 1949, 134). Thus the Japanese *minzoku* becomes the still center into which cultural difference is continuously absorbed, consumed, and transformed into cultural homogeneity.

The Wartime Critique of Race

Debates about race and ethnicity reached a peak of intensity in Japan shortly before the outbreak of the Pacific War. Despite the presence of an indigenous ideology of "state socialism," German Nazi ideology failed to attract much of a following in Japan. It is true that a few scholars became articulate advocates of nazism: one example being

Fujisawa Chikao of Kyoto University, who toured Germany in the late 1930s and presented a possibly bemused audience at Berlin University with a lecture on his belief that "pure nazism was really a manifestation of the Japanese spirit on German soil" (Fujisawa 1938, 362–363). Nazi theories also had some impact on official thinking, particularly through the efforts of a eugenic lobby group called the Japan Association of Racial Hygiene (Nihon minzoku eisei kyōkai), established in 1930 to improve "the quality of the Nippon Race from the standpoint of racial hygiene [and] thereby to contribute toward the prosperity of the state and the welfare of society" (Kokusai Bunka Shinkōkai 1939, 504). Several prominent members of the association became officials of the newly established Ministry of Health and Welfare (set up in 1938), and their influence is illustrated by a massive report on the global role of the *Yamato minzoku* which was compiled by the ministry in 1943 and which, among other things, issues dire warnings about the perils of intermarriage with races "at a lower stage of cultural development" (Kōseishō Kenkyūjo Jinkō Minzokubu 1981, 303–319; Oguma 1995, 249–258; see also Dower 1986, 262–290).

Nazi racial theories, however, came into direct conflict with the assimilation policies of the colonial governments, particularly in Korea, where an active policy of encouraging marriage between Japanese and Koreans had been in existence since 1937 (Suzuki 1992, 78–87). These theories were also, in the eyes of many Japanese intellectuals, distasteful and embarrassing. Much of the academic debate about race at the beginning of the Pacific War was therefore conducted within the framework of a more sophisticated and therefore more interesting, though nonetheless problematic, view of the world.

Two leading representatives of this wartime rhetoric of race were the sociologist Shinmei Masamichi (1898–1984) and the economic and social historian Kada Tetsuji (1895–1964). Both Shinmei and Kada had studied in Germany during the late 1920s and 1930s and after their return contributed to a sudden boom in Japanese writings about race and racism. Shinmei later became a prominent member of a wartime academic body called the Greater Japan Patriotic Discourse Society (Dai-Nippon genron hōkokukai), and as result was purged from his university position during the postwar Allied occupation (Shinmei 1980a, i–v). In 1951, however, he returned to academia and became well known, particularly for his role in introducing American sociological theories to Japan.

Kada Tetsuji's work was more inextricably connected than Shinmei's with Japan's wartime expansionism, and he is therefore nowadays largely unread, although he was a prolific scholar both before and after the war, and his 1940 study *Race, Ethnos and War* (Jinshu, minzoku, sensō) was a bestseller which had as many as ten printings within a few months of publication. Kada's unrepentant attitude to his past is evident from the preface to one of his last books, published in the 1960s, where he wrote "naturally, I did my best to cooperate in this [i.e., the Pacific] War through scholarship and discourse. The War was lost, but to this day I feel no shame about my cooperation." Just in case any reader should miss the point, he then goes on to describe his postwar resignation from Keiō University as follows: "This occurred, not because I was ashamed about my wartime behavior, but because I could not stand the utterly ridiculous postwar democratic climate, where people who had been valiant militarists during the War suddenly started dancing to the U.S. tune and turned into half-baked democrats" (Kada 1962, 2–3).

Despite their different postwar destinies, Shinmei and Kada shared broadly similar perspectives on issues of race, ethnicity, and nationalism. Both approached the topic from a standpoint defined by their negative reaction to Nazi racial theorizing. Shinmei's 1940 study *Race and Society* (Jinshu to shakai) begins with an account of the emergence in Europe of ideas of race, particularly of Aryan superiority, and proceeds to a detailed critique of these ideas (Shinmei 1980b, 141–162). Shinmei himself accepted that some form of physical distinction existed between different races, but questioned the scientific basis for the concept of an "Aryan race" (Shinmei 1980b, 145–152). Besides, he emphasized that diversity within races was at least as great as the differences between them, and he firmly rejected the view that physical racial difference in any way determined cultural superiority or inferiority. If some races were innately superior to others, he pointed out, one would expect those races consistently to provide the sites of the most powerful and dynamic civilizations, but in fact history showed that the torch of civilization had passed from people to people and from continent to continent (Shinmei 1939, 98–104). Kada Tetsuji took the argument one step further, questioning the scientific nature of the concept of "race" in general. He accepted that "race" existed as a "commonsense" notion. People react at an instinctive level to physical difference, and this instinctual feeling of racial difference has a "use value":

It had frequently been used to promote nationalist sentiments and to justify imperial expansion (Kada 1940a, 50). It was possible, then to speak in a vague and abstract way of a race as "a group of people who share some biological characteristics," but scientific efforts to find a clear dividing line between races based on blood type, skull size, and so on had repeatedly ended in failure (Kada 1940a, 45–50, 88). Here Kada's arguments at times sound similar to Western liberal critiques of racism such as Montagu's classic study *Man's Most Dangerous Myth* (Montagu 1945).

While rejecting the value of race (*jinshu*) as an intellectual construct, however, both Shinmei and Kada made extensive use of the idea of *minzoku*. Their views on this subject are particularly interesting because they in some ways foreshadow more recent debates, involving scholars such as Clifford Geertz, Eric Hobsbawm, Louis Althusser, and Benedict Anderson, about the origins of the nation (see Anthias and Yuval-Davis 1992, 23–27). Shinmei, using the word *minzoku* in the sense of "ethnic group," argues that the *minzoku* predates the appearance of the modern nation-state. The very earliest societies, according to Shinmei, were tribes based on direct family relationships. Later, tribes coalesced into larger societies, and eventually tribal boundaries within these larger societies dissolved, so that all members of the society came to see themselves as belonging to a single "lineage." It is at this point that the ethnos (*minzoku*) appears. Shinmei, however, was quick to emphasize that ethnic groups were not fixed and unchanging, but were dynamic entities which expanded, merged, and evolved, and acquired a new historical significance with the advent of the modern nation-state (Shinmei 1980c, 347–352).

As in the case of race, so too in the case of ethnicity, Kada Tetsuji was more iconoclastic. In his 1940 study *Race, Ethnos and War,* he worked through various common definitions of *minzoku* and rejected them one by one. Many members of a *minzoku* may share a common genetic heritage, but a *minzoku* is not primarily a community based on blood bonds, since virtually every modern society (including Japan) has a mixed biological heritage, and in any case the very concept of race, as his earlier discussion has emphasized, lacks scientific rigor; nor is the *minzoku* based on a shared natural environment, for the Japanese environment differed dramatically in different parts of the archipelago (which Kada defines, interestingly, as extending from the Kurile Islands in the north to Taiwan in the south). *Minzoku* is not primarily a matter of shared language, since peoples like the Swiss have more than one language. Nor does it make sense to define it as a cultural community or as a community with a shared destiny (the German notion of a *Schicksalsgemeinschaft*), since the members of almost all human communities (including, for example, religions) ultimately share some sort of common culture and destiny (Kada 1940a, 86–92). In the end, therefore, Kada comes down to the surprisingly materialist interpretation of the *minzoku* as one form of the phenomenon that he calls the "basic society" (*kihon shakai*), that is "an inclusive human society based upon the acquisition of the materials of existence" (Kada 1940a, 92). "Basic societies," in other words, are the fundamental units of human survival and exist everywhere and in all periods of history, but not all "basic societies" are *minzoku*. Despite his articulate hostility to socialism, Kada uses a dialectical materialist framework to trace the evolution of "basic society" from a primitive communal stage, via tribal, classical, and feudal stages, to the modern stage exemplified in the nation-state. It is only with the collapse of the feudal stage and the emergence of the nation-state, writes Kada, that the *minzoku* becomes a reality (Kada 1940a, 94). The *minzoku* may grow out of a single tribal group, or out of the merging of several tribal groups, but it differs from earlier tribes (*minshu*) both because its identity is invented and conscious, rather than innate, and (more importantly) because, unlike the "static" tribe, it is dynamic and naturally expanding—the bearer of progress.

In Kada's theorizing, then, the nation and the ethnic group collapse into one another. Neither is seen as necessarily based on any primordial tie of blood, culture, language, or destiny: On the contrary, Kada argues that images of common ancestry are promoted by the nation-state to serve its political needs at varying stages of economic development. National or ethnic identity are modern phenomena developed to create a sense of solidarity within the nation-state (Kada 1940a, 111). Moreover, "it must be emphasized that an awareness of sameness goes hand in hand with an awareness of otherness. . . . Contact between one group and another awakens a sense of otherness in relation to the outside, and a sense of sameness toward the inside." These feelings of "otherness" and "sameness" are mobilized by the state to overcome the fragmenting status and regional identities which survive from the feudal age (Kada 1940a, 116–117). In the process, nationalism is able to combat the power of ideologies like religion, whose boundaries do not coincide with the boundaries of the state, but at the same time it increasingly tends to take on the characteristics of a religion itself: It typically adopts the notions of "1. reverence for ancestors; 2. respect for the family system; 3. glorification of national heroes and martyrs; 4. the demand for a spirit of willing sacrifice from its citizens; 5. traditionalism; 6. rejection of a standardized worldwide level of culture. These features are not the scientific product of objective analysis, but are rather assertions or beliefs. They have little in common with rationality, and in this sense are imbued with religious elements" (Kada 1940a, 122).

When I first read the work of Shinmei and Kada, I was frankly surprised to find such hard-headed assessments of race and ethnicity combined with enthusiastic support for Japan's wartime expansion. To explain this combination of ideas we need to turn to the notion of an "East Asian Community" (*Tōa kyōdōtai*), the forerunner of the wartime Greater East Asia Coprosperity Sphere (*Dai-Tōa Kyōeiken*). Both Shinmei and Kada were important ideologues of this community. Shinmei, indeed, was paid by Japan's South Manchuria Railway Company to tour the puppet state of Manchukuo giving lectures on his critique of racism. For Kada, as for other prominent scholars who formed the famous late 1930s think tank known as the Showa Research Association (Shōwa kenkyūkai), the East Asia Community represented a golden opportunity for Japanese intellectuals to play their part in shaping Japan's wartime destiny (On the Showa Research Association, see Johnson 1965, 114–122; Iwasaki 1995). During the 1930s, Kada argued, the rise of crude forms of ethno-nationalism, largely supported by elements in the military, had led to the marginalization of the intelligentsia, who had faced criticism for their excessively Western ideas and lifestyles, and had become timid about expressing their views in public. The new East Asian Community proposed by Prime Minister Konoe in 1938 was their chance to reassert themselves and to lend a new scientific and intellectual credibility to Japan's leadership role in Asia (Kada 1940a, 457–463).

At the core of this vision of the East Asia Community was an unshakable belief in the march of human progress and in Japan's role as the bearer of modernity to the rest of Asia. In Kada's writing, Japan's contribution to the community (by which he largely meant China) would not be derived from any fanciful notions of racial superiority or imperial mythology, but would take the form of a new social and intellectual order based on "the spirit of science" (*kagaku seishin*) (Kada 1939, 491). The community, indeed, represented the highest form of the expansionary impulses of the *minzoku*. Nations, according to Kada, were naturally dynamic and expanding entities. They could, however, expand in a variety of ways: by population growth or colonization, for example. The most advanced and enlightened form of expansion, though, was the creation of economic and political blocs like the East Asia Community, in which waves of economic development emanating from the Japanese center would allow for the gradually and spontaneous merging of weaker and less developed societies into a new supranational identity centered around the core *minzoku*: Japan (for example, Kada 1939, 17–18 and 482–485; Kada 1940b, 141–145). Similarly, Shinmei Masamichi rejected the idea of racial superiority, but had no problem at all with the idea that some countries might be economically, scientifically, and socially more advanced than others. This enabled him to interpret Japan's right to leadership in Asia as being based precisely on its advanced level of development. Drawing on arguments similar to those of Kita Sadakichi and Takamure Itsue, he also claimed that, unlike the European powers, Japan had a long tradition of respect for racial equality and harmony (Shinmei 1939, 108). This tradition meant that Japan was uniquely qualified to lead the East Asian region, and ultimately also the world, in the direction of a truly egalitarian future: Nazism, he wrote, was "creating an excellent new order within European limits, but its racism is incapable of transcending those European limits. . . . We need to advance toward the dream of creating our own ideal, which will go beyond the bounds of the social transformations of Germany and Italy, so that we ourselves, within East Asia, can open a new epoch in world history" (Shinmei 1939, 111). Shinmei too emphasized that nations might expand to absorb other nations and argued in particular that it was the historical destiny of larger and progressive *minzoku* to swallow up their smaller and more conservative counterparts. Discussing the right to national self-determination, he wrote, "in the modern period the notion of the right to national self-determination has acquired historical significance as the fundamental principle for the organization of nation-states. But this does not imply that national self-determination can be applied in an abstract and universal manner. The ethnic groups [*minzoku*] which can form states in accordance with the principles of self-determination are those large ethnic groups which themselves possess a progressive historical character. In other cases, on the contrary, nationalism is in contradiction with the principle of historical progress" (Shinmei 1980d, 426). Although the words "Korea" and "Taiwan" appear nowhere in this text, it is difficult to read the passage without hearing their echoes resounding in the background.

Postwar Reinterpretations

During the 1950s and 1960s, many scholars, both inside and outside Japan, came to accept an image of Japanese prewar and wartime imperialism as essentially a reaction against modernity. Military texts, propaganda documents, and the writings of ultranationalists such as Takabatake were used to illustrate the point that expansionism was inspired by resurrected images of divine origins, racial purity, and obedience to the emperor. Such ideas were seen has having had a particularly powerful influence among sections of the rural population, which had gained little from industrialization and whose members provided a major source of recruits to the armed forces (Smethurst 1974). The inseparable connection between Japanese imperialist ideology and myths of racial superiority is still stressed by many writers on the subject (see Koshiro 1995; Weiner 1995). This interpretation undoubtedly contains a good deal of truth, but it also simplifies the story, overlooking the fact that support for military expansion was a multilayered phenomenon which was rationalized in different ways by different sections of society.

The image of Japan's imperialism as irrational or antimodern was rather comforting. It suggested that, in order to make a break with the past, all that was necessary was to renounce ideas about the racial purity of the Japanese and the divinity of the emperor. Particularly for Japanese intellectuals, this was not very difficult. After all, even among the advocates of Japanese expansionism, there were many who had never taken these ideas seriously in the first place. Besides, identifying militarism with an irrational return to "tradition" helped to isolate the problem as a uniquely "Japanese" one, which had no bearing on wider global dilemmas of modernity and racism. More recently, though, a growing number of scholars have begun to reconsider the role of imperialism in Japanese history. It is coming to be recognized that the colonialism and wartime expansion were often justified in highly "modern" terms and that both provided the basis for the creation of social and economic institutions which continued to serve Japan's growth in the postwar period (Yamanouchi 1996).

A re-examination of the ideas of race and ethnicity expounded by writers like Shinmei Masamichi and Kada Tetsuji forces us to look again at the relationship between prewar and postwar thought in Japan. There are important aspects of their thought which many Western readers at the end of the twentieth century are likely to find sympathetic: the critique of scientific racism, for example, and the vision of nation and ethnicity as modern inventions. The idea that the Japanese were the product of a prehistorical intermingling of diverse peoples is also generally accepted by modern scholars as correct. At the same time, though, there also profound problems in the way in which writers like Kada and Shinmei developed these ideas: problems which have some relevance to contemporary academic theorizing about race and ethnicity in Japan and elsewhere.

In a recent study of notions of nationalism and racism, Sakai Naoki observes that a key characteristic of racism is its power to universalize. In other words (drawing partly on the work of Franz Fanon and others) he envisages racism as an unequal relationship where the dominant group is able to define itself as normal and universal, while the subordinate group is defined (and often comes to define itself) as abnormal or peculiar (Sakai 1996a, 220–224). From this point of view, writers like Shinmei Masamichi and Kada Tetsuji, while they rightly condemned the crude racial theorizing of other prewar nationalists, can be seen in their wartime writings as representing a more subtle but also more profound ideology of inequality, and also a more profound challenge to the power of the West. Their aim, in short, was to claim Japan's place as the "universal center," the vanguard of human progress.

The problems of this approach become evident as soon as we turn from theory to the reality of Japanese colonialism. Like other colonial powers, Japan brought to its empire, not the march of universal civilization inspired by a free-floating "scientific spirit," but a vastly complex, self-contradictory mass of policies and institutions, based on a mixture of human sentiments, including the desire for national power and prestige, the impulses of economic exploitation, the survival instincts of colonial settler populations, bureaucratic fear and ignorance of its own subjects, genuine idealism, and sometimes straightforward violence and greed. Even its most obviously "modernizing" institutions were, from the point of view of the colonized, heavily marked by discriminatory difference. Korean and Taiwanese subjects had only the most limited access to the higher levels of education, where they were required to speak Japanese and follow a Japanese curriculum. Modern media like the radio became sites for a contest between colonially imposed content (including educational programs on "ethics" and the Japanese language) and local projects to promote the culture of the colonized. In Korea, Japanese-language programming was gradually increased beginning in the late 1930s, and Korean-language broadcasting was banned altogether in December 1944 (Robinson 1997). Perhaps the most glaring example of the gap between rhetoric and reality was Manchuria—nominally (after 1931) an independent state, but in practice totally subordinated to Japanese rule. As Gavan McCormack has vividly shown, extensive propaganda campaigns promoting "interracial harmony" in Manchuria (and including events like Shinmei Masamichi's lecture tour) could not obscure the fact that vast tracts of lands were forcibly confiscated from Chinese farmers for distribution to settlers from Japan and that those Chinese who resisted were suppressed with extreme ferocity (McCormack 1991).

It was not even necessary to travel abroad to see such examples of racial inequality. By the time Kada and Shinmei were writing, the importation of forced labor was adding to the numbers of the million Korean immigrants employed in highly discriminatory conditions within Japan itself (Weiner 1994, 190–208). Both migrant laborers and forced labor recruits were generally employed in appalling conditions in mines, manufacturing, and construction. As the war continued, the labor mobilization was also extended to Chinese workers, of whom 42,000 were brought to Japan and some 11,000 were to die from malnutrition, industrial accidents, and so on (Vasishth 1997, 131). The central flaw in Shinmei's and Kada's theorizing was its almost breathtaking ability to overlook these and other awkward realities of the "East Asia Community."

This flaw seems to be related to the role of the idea of *minzoku* in interwar thought and to the fusion of the ideas of nation-state (*kokumin kokka*) and ethnic state (*minzoku kokka*). All of the perspectives on race discussed in this chapter were based on a common belief in the identity of nation-state (*kokumin kokka*) and ethnos, though they interpreted this identity in different ways. For writers like Takabatake Motoyuki, the blood ties of race created the *minzoku,* which in turn created the nation-state. For writers like Kita Sadakichi, the *minzoku* was formed of a common cultural identity based on loyalty to the imperial family, and thus ethnos and state emerged and evolved together. For Kada Tetsuji, it was the nation-state, as Hegelian bearer of historical progress, which had created the *minzoku*—a community whose common identity was based on invented, but necessary, modern myths.

None of these approaches leaves any room for a conceptual separation between the ideas of nation (first) as a political unit whose members have certain privileges and obligations, (second) as a community of people who possess the knowledge necessary to exercise those privileges and obligations, and (third) the nation as a community of people who share a sense of common origins and common history. The result was a pattern of thought and even of *vocabulary* where ethnicity (membership in the *minzoku kokka*), political allegiance (membership in the *kokumin kokka*), and loyalty to a particular political system became inextricably confused. A early example of this process appears in an article published during the Russo–Japanese War of 1904–05, entitled "Half-Japanese" (*han-Nihonjin*). The title does not refer to people of mixed national ancestry, but is a term of abuse directed at Japanese citizens who show insufficient enthusiasm for their nation's war effort (Iketani 1904). In later years, the term *han-Nihonjin* generally came to be replaced by the expression *hikokumin*, literally meaning "nonnationals" and similarly applied to those Japanese citizens who were regarded as lacking the necessary patriotic and imperial fervor.

While suspect political loyalty was labeled with terms suggesting foreignness, particular alien cultural attributes were conversely often construed as signs of treachery—hence the ubiquitous interwar phrase *futei Senjin* (Korean malcontents). Although the term was initially applied to Korean students and workers in Japan who participated in anticolonial activities, it was readily extended to anyone who bore certain recognizable cultural markers of difference, such as the inability to "correctly" pronounce particular Japanese words. The most tragic manifestation of this association of ideas occurred in the aftermath of the Great Kantō Earthquake of 1923, when more than 2,000 Korean and 400 Chinese residents in Japan were massacred in response to rumors that they were plotting rebellion (Weiner 1994, 71–72 and 80–85; Vasishth 1997, 128–129). As Michael Weiner points out, those singled out for slaughter as "malcontents" were commonly selected on the basis of "their ability or inability to speak Japanese" (Weiner 1994, 80). This enduring inability to separate the different conceptual levels of nationhood meant that dreams of a multiethnic empire, though genuinely believed by some idealists, were doomed from the start.

In a sense, interwar debates on race and ethnicity contained their own refutation. If the Japanese nation had truly consisted of people who were united by a sense of common origins into a single *minzoku,* one would have expected there to be at least some consensus about the meaning of the word *minzoku,* as well as about the nature of the ties which bound the Japanese *minzoku* together. Instead, as we have seen, there was a wide range of views, which represented different ways of deploying notions of space and time in the creation of national identity. For writers like Takabatake, Japan was, as it were, removed from time—united by eternal blood ties which somehow transcended the universal evolution of society. For Kada Tetsuji and Shinmei Masamichi, on the other hand, Japan represented the most advanced point in a universal progress whose actors were not individuals or ideas or social systems but ethnic nations. It would, of course, be possible to apply ideas of universal progress to these theories of race and ethnicity themselves: to suggest that concepts of racial purity were in some sense less "modern" than the ideas of race and ethnicity proposed by writers like Kada. But, after all, Takabatake drew on the ideas of Marx and Engels just as much as Kada Tetsuji did. All the ideas discussed in this chapter can, in that sense, be seen as attempts to combine elements of that global body of ideas known as "modern thought" with elements of local intellectual traditions, and each represented attempts to weave these elements into a synthesis which would address particular political concerns and appeal to particular audiences.

These issues are important both because they relate to the intellectual background to Japan's disastrous wartime ventures and because they have continued to haunt debates about nation and identity in postwar Japan. The postwar era and the democratic constitution of 1947 produced significant shifts in perceptions of citizenship. On the one hand, a much wider range of political positions were now seen by the state as compatible with membership in the national community, and the word *hikokumin* fell into disrepute. But the broadening of the *political* meaning of nationality was in part achieved at the cost of a narrowing of possible *ethnic* meanings. Of some two million Korean, Taiwanese, and other colonial subjects who were in Japan at the end of the war, more than half chose to return to their places of origin. But those who remained in Japan lost both their Japanese citizenship and the right to vote in Japanese elections (a right which had been possessed by adult male colonial subjects living in Japan since the 1920s). Recent research has revealed that the government was at first prepared to allow ex-colonial subjects to retain their voting rights, but was dissuaded by advisers who were afraid that Koreans and Taiwanese would use their votes to support the abolition of the monarchy. (The image of *futei Senjin* had put down tenacious roots.) Prominent political thinkers like Nambara Shigeru emphasized the need for Japan to find new unifying forces to replace the lost imperial dream and stressed the new opportunities for national cohesion now that the "outsiders from overseas territories" had returned home and a "pure Japan" had been re-established (Kang 1996, 28–29). In the postwar era, while it was generally accepted that the prehistoric ancestors of the Japanese came from diverse origins, this ceased to be interpreted as having much significance for Japan's contemporary global role. Rather, prehistory receded over the horizon, and for all intents and purposes the historical Japanese were widely seen as a "homogeneous people" (*tan'itsu minzoku*). Once again, however, that slippery word *minzoku* has allowed a convenient blurring of meaning. On the one hand, the concept of a *tan'itsu minzoku* can mean that the Japanese are "ethnically" or "culturally" homogeneous; on the other, it can mean that Japan contains few obvious visible minorities. It has thus helped to erase from public consciousness the presence of peoples with different histories (Ainu, Okinawans, Koreans) within the Japanese archipelago and to encourage a common perception that Japan (unlike other parts of the world) does not have a "race problem." It has also created an environment where those who are neither invisible nor fit into well-established categories of difference—categories such as "Western" = "white"—are easy targets for grotesquely insensitive stereotyping by the media. Some of the most obvious examples of this have been popular portrayals of Africans and Afro-Americans, powerfully analyzed in the work of John Russell (see Russell 1995).

Between the 1940s and the 1960s, therefore, remarkably little was written in Japanese about problems of racism, and issues of human inequality were treated almost entirely within the intellectual frameworks of class or of modernization (Fukuoka 1996, 223–224). During the late 1960s and early 1970s, the influence of the U.S. civil rights movement helped to revive interest in this topic (for example,

Wagatsuma and Yoneyama 1967). But it is only since the beginning of the 1980s that a large number of Japanese scholars have again begun to focus attention on issues of racism. Interestingly, one of the first of this new wave was Iesaka Kazushi's *Japanese Ideas of Race* (Nihonjin no jinshukan), published in 1980, and opening with a chapter which was originally written as an afterword to a volume of the collected writings of Shinmei Masamichi. Iesaka begins this chapter with the words "for some reason, it is difficult for race relations to become a topic of discussion in Japan. It is not that there are no problems within the country involving issues of race relations. There are, for example, the problems of Koreans in Japan and of the *Hisabetsu Burakumin*. All the same, most people try as far as possible to avoid bringing these issues into the open, almost as though such problems did not exist" (Iesaka 1980, 1).

In the past decade, the reluctance to confront questions of racism has gradually diminished: many of the problems raised by Kada Tetsuji, Shinmei Masamichi, and others in the 1930s and 1940s are been energetically debated, and some of the terminology of the debate echoes the language of those mid-century scholars. The re-examination of wartime writings on race and ethnicity can help point out some important directions for the future of this debate. It suggests in particular that the exploration of diverse prehistoric origins and the deconstruction of scientific racism, however valuable in themselves, do not take us all that far down the road to understanding the complexities of inclusion and exclusion, prejudice, and discrimination in modern society. This is important because there has been a recent tendency in some U.S. and European writing to assume that the waning popularity of belief in genetically inherited racial superiority marks "the end of racism" (D'Souza 1995). But modern Japanese history suggests that practices of racial exclusion or subordination can be supported by a wide and complex range of beliefs, including beliefs about "cultural" rather than "racial" superiority and about the relative positions of social groups on a universalized scale of cultural progress. Ironically, even a complacent belief in one's own nation's powers of tolerance or assimilation can become a source of prejudice toward others.

In the end what matters is perhaps not so much whether the logic of belonging and exclusion, superiority, and inferiority is based on notions of biology, culture, or progress. It is, rather, the way in which vocabularies are developed to carve up the world into "them" and "us" and the way that those vocabularies become the bearers of unexamined images where genetic, historical, political, and cultural symbolism can be almost inextricably superimposed upon one another. Contemporary studies need to be sensitive to the multiple meanings of words like *minzoku* (or the English "ethnic") and the ways in which this multiplicity can be deployed for purposes of political self-justification. They need, in particular, to address the continuing tendency to fuse the ideas of nation-state (*kokumin kokka*) and ethnic state (*minzoku kokka*) and to see *minzoku* as the actors in a drama of progress which allows each nation to be seen as a homogeneous "time zone" and ranked in a hierarchy of advance toward civilization.

—— 6 ——

Gender

The key words which form the core of earlier chapters resonate through Japanese debates on national identity—*Nihon, shizen, bunka, jinshu, minzoku.* . . . But gender is largely a silence. This is not to say that the issue was not discussed: questions of the relationship between men and women (*danjo kankei*) and the social position of women in Japanese society were addressed by a wide range of social reformers, academics, and popular writers, from Fukuzawa Yukichi in the early Meiji period to interwar feminists like Hiratsuka Raichō and Yamakawa Itsue, to mid-century activists like Ichikawa Fusae and more recent feminist theorists such as Saitō Chiyo and Ueno Chizuko. Public formulations of national identity, however, rather rarely addressed the images of gender implicit in ideas of nationhood. And yet echoes of gender were almost always present, if only because of the central place of the family in national symbolism.

"In a complex play," writes Jan Jindy Pettman, "the state is often gendered male, and the nation female—the mother country" (Pettman 1996, 49). States, in other words, are part of the public realm, centers of power which are also traditionally the domain of the male political actor. Nations, on the other hand, tend to be envisaged as natural, nurturing bodies vulnerable to outside aggression: qualities which are often incarnated in feminine form, in Britannia, La France, Mother Russia. Julia Kristeva argues that "women . . . are particularly vulnerable to a possible support of *Volksgeist* [national or ethnic spirit]. The biological fate that causes us to be the *site* of the species chains us to *space*, home, native soil, motherland [*matrie*] (as I wish to say instead of fatherland [*patrie*])" (Kristeva 1993, 33–34; italics in original).

This distinction between male state and female nation is partly applicable to Japan, but not entirely. Certainly, for much of the twentieth century, the state was envisaged as a male arena. For all intents and purposes, women were excluded from citizenship until after the end of the Pacific War, not simply because they were unable to vote but also because between 1890 and 1922 they were prohibited from attending political meetings or taking part in political activity of any kind. For many feminists of the interwar period, therefore, one explicit goal was to "turn women into citizens" (*josei o kokuminka suru*) by encouraging their participation in the public realm. Even after the war, when formal barriers to women's involvement in politics were removed, the world of parliament and bureaucracy continued to be—both in reality and in the public imagination—a profoundly male world, so that when in 1989 a total of twenty-two women were elected to parliament, this was seen as being a phenomenon worthy of considerable debate.

But the femininity of the nation is a more complex question. It is true that Japanese culture is often seen as being epitomized in the simplicity and refinement of traditional arts associated with women— flower arrangement and the tea ceremony, for example. Some eighteenth-century nativist writers, most notably Motoori Norinaga, also identified Japan's national spirit with a spontaneous sensitivity to nature which they explicitly defined as "feminine." This equation of woman and nature, however, is a debatable issue which we consider more closely later in this chapter. On the other hand, throughout the first half of the century one of the most ubiquitous symbols of nationhood was the notion of *bushidō*—the Way of the warrior—seen not only by Nitobe Inazō but also by countless other writers as constituting "the soul of Japan." Nitobe's *bushidō* was not in fact exclusively male. Samurai women, too, could participate in the warrior spirit, but their participation always seems marginal and paradoxical and does nothing to alter the vision of *bushidō* as a quintessentially masculine virtue (Nitobe 1905, 138–157).

During the late nineteenth and early twentieth centuries (as Jean-Pierre Lehmann has pointed out), European and American observers often depicted two quite distinct "Japans." Female Japan—submissive, delicate and exotic—was presented in overwhelmingly positive terms: "How sweet . . . Japanese woman is!" wrote a nameless author to Basil Hall Chamberlain, "All the possibilities of the race for goodness seem concentrated in her" (quoted in Lehmann 1978, 87). While Japanese debates about the role the women almost always focused on the image of motherhood, the Japanese women of European orientalist literature tended to be young and unmarried (a tradition which is continued in more recent orientalist novels like *Shogun* and *Rising Sun*). Japan's feminine persona was therefore captured in repeated imagery of littleness and fragility, but at the same time it was also seen as having a timeless quality: In the words of Lafcadio Hearn, the charm of Japanese women "is the charm of a vanished world—a charm strange, alluring, indescribable as the perfume of some flower of which the species became extinct in our Occident before the modern languages were born" (quoted in Lehmann 1978, 89). By contrast, male Japan was modernizing, militaristic, and menacing. The Japan of the Yellow Peril was unmistakably male, for, as one prominent ideologue of the peril wrote: "the Japanese consider themselves to be a thoroughly masculine people, whereas most Western nations, especially those above all, on whom, in any conflict with the Mongoloid races, everything will depend have, without exception, become 'feminine.' . . . The Japanese are manly and strong in matters which affect the fatherland and national feeling—where decisions are made, Mars is in the ascendancy, Venus and her erotic companions must be silent" (Baron von Falkenegg, quoted in Lehmann 1978, 175).

This association of modernity and national power with masculinity was reflected in, and reinforced by, the policies of the Meiji government. During the early years of the Meiji era, the implications of modernization and Westernization for the role of women were enthusiastically debated, and some efforts were made to ensure that women were included in social reform. Compulsory education, for example, was extended equally to boys and girls. But while the desirability of "modernity" and "civilization" for men continued to be emphasized by the state, the impact of social change on women was viewed with growing unease. Sharon Sievers points out the symbolic significance of the government decree of 1872 banning short hair for women. One of the Meiji government's first acts had been to encourage Japanese men to adopt the "practical" Western custom of cutting their hair short, but when some Japanese women sought to follow suit, the response was hostile and swift: The practice was first discouraged and soon after made illegal (Sievers 1983, 14).

The same attitude permeated Meiji policies of technological modernization. Silk production, for example, had been an overwhelmingly female activity throughout the Tokugawa period, and (although there are hardly any written records to support or refute this) it seems likely that many of the incremental technological innovations in the industry during the eighteenth and early nineteenth centuries had been the work of women. But the rapid introduction of foreign technology and the application of science to the industry in the early Meiji period were accompanied by a conscious attempt to move production into male hands. As one official report put it: "Heretofore silk-culture has been considered to be an employment suitable for women, and to be an art which impressed itself upon the mind by means of manual practice; but now that it has taken on such a development, it ought to become the main occupation of whole families" (Adams 1870, 37). So, in spite of the long association of women with the industry, the new institutions set up to teach "scientific" silk production, like the Ueda Sericultural College in the silk district of Nagano, recruited male students who were to be taught not only the skills of silk farming but also the manly arts of judo, fencing, and archery (Robertson Scott 1922, 159).

Here we can see the emerging outlines of a world view in which femininity was associated with the home, and the home with stability and continuity, while modernization was associated with the masculine public domain. This division, of course, was an imagined one and bore only scant resemblance to reality. Women's lives, like men's, were transformed by the social and economic changes of the Meiji and Taishō eras. Women formed the larger part of the factory workforce until World War I and also played a crucial and often neglected role in managing and keeping the accounts of the tens of thousands of small family firms which dominated Japanese manufacturing and commerce throughout the early decades of the century. But the *concept* of woman as source of continuity, and man as agent of change, became a particularly enduring leitmotiv in evolving notions of nationhood.

This chapter examines some aspects of gender in debates on national identity, focusing on the period from the 1930s onward. Japan's growing military involvement in Asia after 1931 created particular tensions in the relationship between images of gender and images of nation. Nationalist ideologies became more strident, and militarism re-emphasized the connection between patriotic attitudes and the warrior ethos (Low 1996). But at the same time the drift toward total war brought changes to the social role of Japanese women. After the outbreak of the Pacific War in particular, women were needed as factory and farm labor and were increasingly exhorted to "go out into society" (*shakai ni shinshutsu suru*). The emergence of mass production from the 1930s onward also led to more rapid changes in domestic technology and patterns of consumption, eroding the conceptual boundary between the household as a place of tradition and the public sphere as a place of technological change (Narita 1995).

After Japan's defeat in 1945, the reforms introduced by the Occupation forces transformed the legal position of women, and of the family itself, in Japanese society. Women obtained equal legal rights to participate fully in political life, and the power of the household head over family members was sharply reduced. Yet the survival of existing attitudes and economic structures prevented these reforms from creating anything approaching equal participation by men and women in the workplace or in the central political institutions of Japanese life. Differences of gender role therefore continue to haunt constructions of "Japaneseness" in the postwar era.

Consuming the Female: The Household and National Identity

Timon Screech (as seen in Chapter 5) argues that the notions "male" and "female" in eighteenth-century Japanese thought were firmly tied to status within the family. This is certainly a fair description of the Japanese state's approach to gender in the late nineteenth and early twentieth centuries. When the relationship between men and women was discussed, it was almost inevitably placed within the overarching structure of the stem family, or *ie*: a family where the emphasis was on vertical relationships between parents and children; where the power of the male household head was paramount; and where the maintenance of the household name was more important than biological blood ties (so that the adoption of heirs, who would take on the family surname, was a common practice).

As many scholars have pointed out, the *ie* was at least in part an "invented tradition" (Ueno 1996, 213). It was a pattern of family relationships which had been common among the samurai class during the Tokugawa period, but bore relatively little resemblance to the realities of family life for commoners in most parts of Japan. It was also a regionally specific institution: Vertical *ie* relationships had been more strongly emphasized in the eastern and northern parts of Honshū than in Western Japan, where horizontal links between people of the same generation within the village community had long been a key element in the social structure.

Repeated official emphasis on the sanctity and inviolability of the *ie* ignored the fact that Japan in the 1880s and 1890s had a relatively high divorce rate (higher than the U.S., Britain, or Sweden) and that sexual relationships in the rural community were sometimes fairly casual (Kondo 1990, 170). Ella Lurie Wiswell, studying a Kyushu village in the 1930s, discovered one woman (admittedly regarded as a bit of an eccentric) who was said to have married "at least ten different men" (Smith and Wiswell 1982, 79; Kondo 1990, 170–171). The anarcho-feminist Kaneko Fumiko (whose ideas are discussed later in this chapter) grew up in just such a social setting: Her parents were unmarried, and both mother and father moved repeatedly from one short-term relationship to another (Hane 1988, 75–78). Nevertheless, it was the *ie* whose authoritative structure was to be imposed upon everyday life by the all-important family registration system (introduced in 1871) and the Meiji Civil Code of 1898, and which was transformed into the central image of Japanese nationalist ideology from the late nineteenth century onward.

Although government edicts like the 1890 Imperial Rescript on Education repeatedly imprinted the image of the *ie* on the minds of the people—"Ye, our subjects, be filial to your parents; affectionate to your brothers and sisters; as husbands and wives be harmonious"—the philosophical underpinnings of family ideology remained fairly unsophisticated until the 1930s, when they were analyzed and debated in the writings of scholars like Watsuji Tetsurō. As seen in Chapter 3, Watsuji was deeply influenced by the hermeneutics of Dilthey and Heidegger, and used this as a basis for reinterpreting the relationship between the nation and its natural environment, the *fūdo*. Watsuji believed that the environment shaped human beings' deepest emotions, but that these emotions were channeled and given social meaning by historically constructed institutions. So the nature of national society was woven out of an interrelationship between the spatial forces of *fūdo* and the temporal forces of national history.

At the core of Watsuji's philosophy of identity is the notion of *aidagara*—intersubjectivity—the fundamental relationship from which both self and society are simultaneously formed; and the most basic of "intersubjectivities" is the relationship between men and women (Watsuji 1963, 242). Human beings' experience of their natural environment—their exposure to heat or cold, drought or monsoon rain, the cycle of seasons or the sudden onset of storms—influences the character of their intersubjective emotions, so that people of fertile, tropical monsoon regions are prone to gentle and mild temperaments and those of harsh desert regions to violence and sudden passion. But Japan, with its climatic completeness—its mixture of warmth and cold, typhoons and clearly marked seasons—produces a personality which Watsuji describes in terms rather different from the language of Meiji patriarchy or of conventional European images of Japan.

The key to the "intersubjectivity" between men and women in Japan, writes Watsuji, is a distinctive form of love (*renai*) characterized by its "calm contained within passion" and its "militancy combined with disinterested self-resignation" (Watsuji 1963, 242). This love allows for a profound self-sacrifice, where individuals merge themselves into a "unity completely devoid of separating interval" (*zenzen hedatenaki ketsugō*) and in doing so, paradoxically, find their true self (Watsuji 1963, 243). For Watsuji, this relationship between man and woman cannot exist on its own, but is always incorporated into the complex of relationships, between parent and child as well as husband and wife, which make up the Japanese *ie*. The family is therefore the site of a boundless, self-sacrificing love which is represented even in the very architecture of the Japanese house: Unlike "Western" houses, which are divided into separate rooms by unyielding stone walls, the Japanese house is divided only by removable screens whose presence never obscures the potential of the whole space to merge into one (Watsuji 1963, 247).

But the household, like the individual, does not exist for itself. It too finds its true self only by the willing sacrifice of its subjectivity to the larger whole: the state. Playing on the construction of the Japanese word for state—*kokka*—which is made up of the ideograms for "nation" and "house" or "family," Watsuji observes that the state is merely a set of intersubjectivities between families. So the forces of militant yet self-sacrificing love ultimately flow into the all-embracing nation-state revolving around the nurturing parent-figure of the emperor (Watsuji 1963, 249–250). This profound unity of individual and household with nation has its roots in an ancient history in which religious belief was inseparable from politics and in which imperial ritual (*matsurigoto*) became the foundation of government (Watsuji 1963, 250–251).

This image of the national community proved a profoundly influential one and is strongly echoed in some official writings, most notably the *Principles of the National Entity* (Kokutai no hongi), whose outlines are discussed in Chapter 5. These echoes are not surprising, since Watsuji was a member of the official committee responsible for preparing the revised version of the *Principles* (Hall 1949, 5). This text, drawing heavily on the concepts of eighteenth-century nativism, traces the origin of Japan back to the original union between male and female ancestral deities, Izanagi no Mikoto and Izanami no Mikoto, out of whose love emerges the Japanese people's love for their homeland: "herein lie the strong ties that inseparably bind *koji* (the ancient myths of ancestry) and *fūdo* (natural environment)" (Hall 1949, 124). The national spirit is thus founded upon the self-sacrificing love which merges the self into a larger whole, although the "spirit of self-effacement is not mere denial of oneself, but the means of living to the true, great self by denying one's small self" (Hall 1949, 134). It is, in other words, a means of realizing one's "true spirit" (*magokoro*)—a term inherited from eighteenth-century nativism (Hall 1949. 100). This "mutual respectful love and obedience, endearment and fostering" which holds the nation together begins with the family, but the family in turn extends the same spirit of self-sacrifice to the nation, so "uniting with the Emperor's great heart of benevolence" (Hall 1949, 91 and 93).

In all of this there is, of course, no hint of the fact that, in practical terms, the nature of the self-sacrifices demanded of men and women was very different or that men and women merged their subjectivities into the household on very different terms. So, among the multitude of quotations from classical mythology, the *Principles* significantly failed to quote the formative point in the narrative of the classical *Nihon shoki* at which the ancestral deities, having made their first circulation around the newly created earth, come together, and the female Izanami cries, "How delightful! I have met with a lovely youth!"; to which the male Izanagi replies, " 'I am a man and by right should have spoken first. How is it that on the contrary thou, a woman, shouldst have been the first to speak? This was unlucky. Let us go round again.' Upon this the two deities went back and met anew, and this time the male deity spoke first and said 'How delightful! I have met a lovely maiden!' " (quoted in Tsunoda, de Bary, and Keene 1958, 27–28).

The disappearance of gender difference into the rhetoric of the loving self-sacrifice of subjectivity is interestingly symbolized by the person of the emperor, who stands at the heart of national imagery in Watsuji's *Fūdo* and even more obviously in *The Principles of the National Entity*. Despite the influences both of *bushidō* and of Western images of the masculine imperial presence, the sexuality of imperial imagery in these works is surprisingly ambivalent. The emperor is, of course, the father of the nation, the head of the national household. But he is also the descendant and contemporary incarnation of the sun goddess Amaterasu Ōmikami (the child of Izanagi and Izanami) and, as such, shares in her maternal qualities. So the *Principles,* for example, describes the emperor as protecting and nurturing his subjects "as one would sucklings" (Hall 1949, 75–76). The opening sections of the book emphasize in particular the central role of the ceremonial rites performed by the emperor, through which he unites the nation by re-enacting the deeds of the Shinto pantheon. Central among these is the "great harvest festival," the *daijōsai,* performed at the beginning of each emperor's reign, which represents the descent of the sun goddess Amaterasu Ōmikami to give the first grains of rice to the earth. Through such rituals, the *Principles* tells its readers, the emperor becomes "one in essence" or "of one august body" with the imperial ancestors and implicitly also with the sun goddess herself.

In a fascinating discussion of gender and the emperor, Fujitani Takashi relates this ambivalence to the notion of the emperor's "two bodies." Medieval tradition in Britain and France perceived the king as having two bodies: a material body which died and turned to dust, and a spiritual or political body which survived eternally, to be inherited by each new monarch on his predecessor's demise. At least one prominent Meiji student of Western monarchies discussed this philosophy and pointed out its practical relevance to Japan (Fujitani 1996, 155–157). This sense of duality, Fujitani argues, can also be seen as underpinning nineteenth- and early twentieth-century constructions of the imperial body. On the one hand, as we have seen in the text of the *Principles* and as Japanese writers like Kanō Mikiyo have emphasized, the unifying role of the emperor was often expressed in female and maternal terms (Kanō 1979). But, on the other, the need to assert the emperor's role as active ruler of the nation, and as equal (or indeed superior) to other modern monarchs, made it also necessary to "masculinize" the emperor's body with trappings such as a beard or mustache, military uniform and sword. By the end of the Meiji era, Fujitani argues, government elites had

> constructed an emperor who could be imagined to have not one but at least two bodies . . . the one imperial body was a human and

masculinised body that represented the mundane and changing prosperity of the national community in history, while the other body, often invisible or described as wrapped in ancient courtly robes, represented the emperor's godliness or transcendence and the immutability of the nation. (Fujitani 1996, 192)

Placed in the context of philosophies of the family state, this image of the emperor's two bodies—one male, the other often implicitly female—is very illuminating. It not only symbolizes a constantly repeated identification of masculinity with visibility, action, and change and femininity with invisibility, equilibrium, and continuity; it also enables the family state, and its symbol—the body of the emperor—to become the place where the harsh realities of gender difference were obliterated. This construction of national identity, in other words, is one where the all-embracing love of the family state is seen as absorbing and consuming gender difference in rather the same way as it was also seen as absorbing and consuming cultural and racial difference. Just as the Japanese state was understood, in many versions of nationalist ideology, to be the still center which endlessly assimilated ethnic minorities without losing its essential "Japaneseness," so too in the person of the emperor, it has become the still center which invisibly embodies and therefore subsumes the female without losing its visible male essence.

Critiques of the Family State

Not all Japanese thinkers of the prewar and war period, of course, saw things from this point of view. Indeed, precisely because of the central position of the *ie* both in the definition of women's social roles and in the formation of national identity, some of the most comprehensive criticisms of prewar nationalist ideology came from feminists. Japanese feminism in the early twentieth century spanned a wide range of political positions. Some prominent feminists focused on the practical goals of campaigning for women's suffrage, while others stressed the need to improve the social status of married women and the quality of social welfare for mothers and children (Tachi 1995). With the rising tide of militarism in the 1930s, a number of activists also sought to win greater recognition for women's social role by emphasizing their own loyalty to the nation and highlighting the crucial contribution of

women to the war effort (Suzuki 1989). As seen in Chapter 5, Takamure Itsue, who had earlier been a sharp critic of Japanese imperialism,
developed a distinctive philosophy linking the history of Japanese
women to a utopian image of empire. At one level, a linking of women
and nationalism could be used to push for improvements in the position of women in the workforce. The activist Oku Mumeo, for example, sought to use the new opportunities created by the war economy to
encourage women's participation in a wider range of employment
(Narita 1995). But nationalist ideology could also combine an exaltation of feminine virtues with reiterations of the stereotypical image of
women as preservers of national tradition within the household. In the
words of a document produced by the Greater Japan Women's Association for National Defence (Dai-Nihon kokubō fujinkai) in 1943: "It is
the mother, not the father, who is the true spiritual center of the household. The mother is the one who experiences the pains of childbirth
and of raising children. It is therefore no exaggeration to say that in
fact the Japanese spirit is maintained and passed on by these splendid
mothers" (quoted in Suzuki 1989, 24).

For a few prewar feminists, however, opposition to the patriarchal
power of the family led inexorably to a critique of the state and its
constructions of nationhood (Mackie 1995). This approach is perhaps
most vividly illustrated by the political views of Kaneko Fumiko
(1903–1926), whose anarchist ideology suggests the possibility—even
in prewar Japan—of a radical rejection of nationalism, but whose suicide in prison at the age of twenty-three emphasizes the extreme dangers of such a political stance. Kaneko's life stands in sharp
contradiction to nationalist images of the family as the site of boundless love. Brought up in great poverty and abandoned by both her
parents, she spent much of her childhood in the care of a grandmother
who treated her essentially as a domestic servant. After spending her
early years partly in Tokyo, partly in rural Yamanashi Prefecture, and
partly in colonial Korea, she returned in her late teens to Tokyo, where
she worked at a variety of casual and poorly paid jobs, among other
things being employed as a door-to-door salesperson of soap powder.
Despite these unpromising circumstances she managed to educate herself, read widely, and develop a profound interest in political and social issues. In the process, she met and fell in love with the Korean
anarchist Pak Yeol, with whom she formed an anarchist group defi-
antly called the "Society of Malcontents" (Futeisha—a title deliber-

ately echoing the catchphrase "Korean malcontents"). Kaneko and Pak were both arrested in the aftermath of the 1923 earthquake and were sentenced to death on a charge of treason. Their sentence was later commuted to life imprisonment, but soon afterward Kaneko hanged herself in Utsunomiya Women's Prison (Hane 1988, 75–79; Kaneko 1991).

Kaneko's writings, as well as the record of her interrogation (which was not published until after the Pacific War) reveal a radical egalitarianism in which rejection of the ideology of family is inseparable from rejection of the ideology of nation. Her bleak perspective on parental feelings, so unlike Watsuji's idealized image of the family, are vividly expressed in her memoirs: "I want to cry out to the fathers and mothers of the world. 'Do you really love your children?' Your love really lasts only as long as your primitive parental instincts. After that you pretend to love your children so long as they can serve your interest" (quoted in Hane 1988, 77). This critical perspective on the family led almost inevitably to a skeptical view of the family state and its parental figure, the emperor:

> We have been taught that the Japanese national polity consists of an unbroken lineage of the imperial family throughout the ages. But the imperial genealogy is really very fuzzy. And even if the genealogy is unbroken through the ages, it signifies nothing. It is nothing to be proud of. Rather, it is shameful that the Japanese people have been so ignorant as to acquiesce in having babies foisted on them as emperors. . . .
>
> The people have been led to believe that the emperor and the crown prince represent authorities that are sacred and inviolate. But they are simply vacuous puppets. The concepts of loyalty to the emperor and love of nation are simply rhetorical notions that are being manipulated by the tiny group of the privileged classes to fulfil their own purposes. (Hane 1988, 124; see also Suzuki 1989, 13–15)

Modernizing the Female: Women and Time

Even among much more mainstream thinkers, the appeal of ideologies based on Shinto mythology was quite limited, and many mid-century intellectuals envisaged the role of the family in terms very different from those embodied in *The Principles of the National Entity*. One particularly interesting alternative approach appears in the work of the historian of science Saigusa Hiroto, whose book *The Philosophy of*

Technology (Gijutsu no shisō), published in 1941, devotes a chapter to the subject of "women and technology." It was an issue to which Saigusa returned, publishing (among other things) a short essay immediately after Japan's defeat on "Women and Their 'Liberation' " (*Josei to sono "kaihō"*). Read from a 1990s' perspective, Saigusa's comments about women often seem somewhat patronizing, but the very fact that he regarded the relationship of women to technology as an important philosophical issue is remarkable. Besides, his comments on the subject go far beyond issues of technological innovation and offer interesting reflections on the role of women in national society as a whole.

While Watsuji Tetsurō saw the family (*ie*) as the place where male and female merged into each other, Saigusa saw it above all as the dividing line between the social roles of women and men, which therefore formed the starting point of women's subjugation. Saigusa agreed with Watsuji in regarding a certain form of restrained passion as characteristic of Japanese culture, but he identified this passion particularly with Japanese women and saw it not as a spontaneous reaction to the natural environment but as the product of women's socialization. Women as child-bearers, according to Saigusa, were naturally destined to a social role different from that of men. And yet, many of the characteristics commonly thought of as naturally "feminine"—love, gentleness, excitable emotions—were a consequence less of biology than of the social institutions which had come to surround the care of children.

The key institution was the family, where labor had become divided such that the man went out to work and the woman remained in the household (Saigusa 1978a, 175). In his postwar essay "Women and Their 'Liberation,' " Saigusa developed this point in a particularly interesting way. While writers like Motoori Norinaga and, in the twentieth century, Takamure Itsue (whose ideas are discussed in Chapter 5) equated woman with nature and rural life, and man with urban artificiality, Saigusa reversed this equation. In the course of Japanese history, women, confined to the household, had become divorced from nature, while men had maintained their connection with the natural world through daily work in the fields and forests. Saigusa illustrated this equation by referring to the famous Japanese folk tale of the old man who cares for wild swallows, while his wicked wife cuts off their tongues because they peck at her washing. The old man is rewarded with a gift of treasure by the birds, but the old woman is punished with a treasure casket which proves to contain a monster. Here it is man who is assumed to be in harmony with nature, and woman who protects the culture of the household at the cost of destroying nature (Saigusa 1978c, 285–286).

These reflections form the background to Saigusa's thoughts about the relationship between women and technology. Women, he accepts, are often nimble fingered and manually skilled. But this does not mean that they have a natural gift for technology. On the contrary, "technology" for Saigusa means an ability to immerse oneself in nature, understand its inner principles, and so constantly develop better ways to interact with nature and use its resources. In this sense, women are doubly handicapped. Their enclosure within the household cuts them off from nature; at the same time the traditional arts which have been developed to purify and temper the emotional female character have provided an inadequate training for participation in modern technology. Traditional arts like the tea ceremony or the composing of *haiku* poetry are, in Saigusa's eyes, a sort of "technology," but a technology which works on the human personality, creating inner calm, poise, and emotional balance. Women have continually refined these arts over the centuries. Yet this process of refinement has been an inward-looking one, which has failed to develop links to other forms of knowledge or to provide the intellectual stimulation necessary for contemporary technological creativity (Saigusa 1978a, 178–180).

Saigusa, in other words, echoes some existing views of gender difference. Women are associated with the household, men with the wider world; women are seen as the bearers of cultural tradition, men as the creators of technological change. To this extent, his work reinforces a divided view of the flow of time, where masculinity is linked to the future—to the dynamism of modernization—and femininity to the past—to the passing on of tradition. But Saigusa's social approach was also a critical one. Writing at a time when women's labor was increasing demand in a "nontraditional" area of industry, Saigusa looked forward to a time when women would overcome the limitations of their existing social training and begin to develop a more creative interaction with technology and the social progress of the nation.

Variations on a Theme: "What Sort of People Should There Be?"

During the postwar decades many aspects of gender relations in Japan were transformed. Women acquired full civil rights, and in the first postwar election thirty-nine women were elected to parliament (although the number was to decline in later years) (Hastings 1996). Coeducation became the normal practice in state junior high schools and high schools, and most gender differences in the school curriculum were removed. Higher education for women also expanded rapidly, although there was a tendency for women to be overrepresented in two-year junior colleges and underrepresented in the most prestigious state universities such as Tokyo and Kyoto Universities. All the same, improved education extended women's choices of career. Meanwhile, the high growth era of the late 1950s and 1960s was rapidly exhausting Japan's supply of labor. One result was that, from the late 1960s onward, an increasing number of women who had left the workforce after marriage returned as temporary or "part-time" workers once their children were in school (though, as many studies have pointed out, this "part-time" work is characterized less by short working hours than by limited benefits and career opportunities).

In spite of these profound social changes, existing images of gender died hard. Here I hope to show how some of the themes of gender in national identity which had emerged in the first half of the twentieth century survived and were revived and reinterpreted in postwar debates about the nature of the Japanese nation-state. A good starting point for this exploration is a short but fascinating document published by the Ministry of Education at the height of the high-growth era, entitled *Kitai sareru ningenzō*—literally, "An Image of the Human Beings That Are to Be Hoped For," though a less clumsy English translation might be "What Sort of People Should There Be?"

Three-and-a-quarter years in the making, *Kitai sareru ningenzō* was clearly regarded by the ministry as an important statement of its vision for the education of the next generation of Japanese citizens. The document was compiled by a committee under the chairmanship of the Kyoto School philosopher Kōsaka Masaaki, and an interim report was published in 1965. This was strongly criticized by sections of the media and the teaching profession as old-fashioned and authoritarian and placing too much emphasis on the role of the emperor. In the final document, released the following year, some of the sections which had provoked the greatest controversy were modified, but the content nevertheless invites comparison with the 1937 *Principles of the National Entity,* which had, after all, fulfilled a similar role in presenting the ministry's grand vision of national identity.

At first glance, the 1966 report seems utterly different in tone from its 1930s precursor. Where the prose of the *Principles* was shrouded in the mists of Shinto mythology, *Kitai sareru ningenzō* begins with a crisp universalism: "One of the characteristics of modern civilization has been the sudden rise of the natural sciences" (Kōsaka 1966, 263). The text then goes on to enumerate recent developments in medical, nuclear, and space science, before discussing the implications of these developments for human society. This sets the tone for the entire document, which repeatedly speaks of the values of democracy, individual responsibility, and international "openness." Both style and content, therefore, bear testimony to the considerable shifts in official thinking which had occurred since 1937. Despite these obvious contrasts with wartime ideologies, however, some interesting continuities also emerge from the text.

In an age of modernization, democratization, and consumerism, the document emphasizes, it is important not to "ignore the special characteristics which the Japanese *minzoku* continue to possess" (Kōsaka 1966, 238). It is therefore necessary to describe not just the sort of human beings, but more specifically the sort of Japanese people who "are to be hoped for." This passive voice of this much-repeated phrase raises the obvious question: Who is doing the hoping? To which the report's chief author gives the remarkably homogenizing and circular reply that the topic of discussion is "the sort of Japanese people hoped for by the Japanese people."

In describing these ideal citizens, the report begins with some philosophical speculation about the nature of the "self" (*jiga*). The role of education, it suggests, is to promote the development of the self with all its unique individuality. At the same time, "the full development of human nature cannot be achieved by oneself alone, but involves relying on others and mutually making up for each others' deficiencies" (Kōsaka 1966, 244). So self-development can occur only through intermediating social institutions: the family (*ie*), society, and the state. The atoms of which the nation consists are therefore families, which are "communities of love." The love which they express is not a selfish or demanding love but, rather, a love purified by adherence to the moral Way (Kōsaka 1966, 248). Thus the family also becomes a child's first place of education, fostering the development of "healthy" individuals who, when they go out into the wider world, will be able to "love their work, develop it and sacrifice themselves to it" (Kōsaka

1966, 252). This in turn will flow into a wider devotion to the nation, which will express itself ultimately in devotion to the emperor, for "it is logically natural that those who love Japan must love its representative symbol" (Kōsaka 1966, 255).

Like the *Principles of the National Entity,* this postwar report makes no distinction between the roles of men and women in the family-community of the nation. Gender differences, however, always lurk in the resonances of its prose and are in fact made explicit in a book-length introduction to the report composed by Kōsaka himself. In a chapter on the individual, the family, and the state which draws heavily on the philosophies of Kierkegaarde and Buber, Kōsaka emphasizes the differences between the roles of man and woman in the household. He is quick to stress that, in contemporary Japan, women can no longer be "enclosed within the household" but must be able to "go out into society." Nevertheless, their roles as wives and mothers clearly distinguish their position from that of men. In particular, it is the destiny of the mother to be her child's "first teacher," passing on knowledge in an instinctive and spontaneous manner quite different from the more formal education of the classroom (Kōsaka 1966, 135–136). On the other hand, the father's guiding role is that of an intermediary who stands between the family and the wider world and acts as "the representative of society to the family" (Kōsaka 1966, 136).

Kitai sareru ningenzō indicates the ways in which the postwar rhetoric of democratization, modernization, and scientific progress could readily be integrated with reworked prewar ideas about the centrality of the *ie* in the national order. Here again, the notion of the *ie* as a community of love whose emotions flow into the emperor-centered polity obscures questions of the differing roles of men and women in both household and public sphere. Yet here again the implicit image is of women as maintainers of tradition within the household, and men as actors in the wider society.

These separate social roles are reflected in enduring postwar conceptions of the distinctive life courses of men and women. Men's lives are commonly depicted in the media, advertising, and fiction as being ideally straight-line, upward trajectories which last throughout the individual's career and are symbolized by the system of *nenkō joretsu,* or age-related pay rises, often described as one of the three hallmarks of the Japanese system of company management (the other two being lifetime employment and company unionism). By contrast, women's lives are more often presented in cyclical terms or in terms of a series of changes which have no obvious trajectory. The middle-aged women interviewed in Margaret Lock's study of menopause, for example, or the part-time workers described in Dorinne Kondo's account of a downtown Tokyo community, describe their own lives less in terms of sequential stages on a ladder of progress than in terms of repeatedly shifting human responsibilities without a definable final goal: from marriage, to childrearing, to juggling the demands of paid work and home, to taking care of elderly parents or in-laws (Lock 1993; 46–77; Kondo 1990, 260–263).

Modern Japan as Male: *Nihonjinron*

This concept of differing relationships between gender and social time is reflected in many of the most influential representations of Japan in the postwar written and visual media and helps to explain the strong overtones of "Japan as male" evident in that important postwar genre of writings which came to be known as *Nihonjinron,* or "theories of the Japanese." Influenced by the holistic images of national culture which emerged from prewar ethnography and which were being further developed by postwar anthropologists (among them Ishida Eiichirō), *Nihonjinron* sought to identify unique characteristics which explained the workings of contemporary Japanese society. Many discussions of *Nihonjinron* trace its roots to Ruth Benedict's classic study *The Chrysanthemum and the Sword,* whose analysis of Japanese culture was based largely on interviews conducted with mostly young and male Japanese prisoners of war in the United States (Benedict 1946). Later works in the *Nihonjinron* tradition drew on and sought to refine Benedict's description of Japan, but these more recent studies (unlike Benedict's) were written in the shadow of Japan's phenomenal postwar economic growth and were therefore often driven by a desire to uncover some of the sources of this unpredicted dynamism.

The major texts of *Nihonjinron* have been widely criticized for their reliance on anecdotal evidence and their insensitivity to regional and class diversity within Japan (Befu 1987; Dale 1986; Sugimoto and Mouer 1986). But it is also interesting that, in seeking out the sources of Japan's economic success, they often managed to produce a projection of "Japaneseness" which was profoundly gender biased. The most striking example, perhaps, is Nakane Chie's study *Tate shake no ningen kankei* (Human Relationships in a Vertical Society), also published in a somewhat different English-language version as *Japanese Society* (Nakane 1967; Nakane 1973). Nakane's argument is that the structure of Japanese organizations such as the corporation or the university is modeled after the structure of the Japanese family (*ie*). As a consequence, members of the organization do not develop strong horizontal relationships with coworkers or age-group peers (as "Western" workers do); rather, their most important relationships are vertical links with superiors and inferiors, which mirror the relationships between parent and child in the family. The "family-like" structure of Japanese organizations also accounts for the strong sense of group loyalty which binds the individual to the firm for life and promotes strong competition between rival organizations. The final section of *Japanese Society,* advisedly entitled "Characteristics and Value Orientation of Japanese Man," examines the life course of "the individual who copes with the system" by tracing the career of a Japanese businessman from university through various stages of company life (Nakane 1973, 108).

In the entire book, no more than a few passing references are made to the social relationships of Japanese women, and this is surprising, first, because Nakane herself is one of the most successful examples of the postwar generation of career women and, second, because the brief comments which *are* made suggest that the experiences of many women may not actually conform to the model of vertical relationships so vividly portrayed throughout the study. For example, discussing the inability of Japanese men to maintain horizontal friendships in their local communities, Nakane writes, "wives may make friends with neighbors, but because husbands are reluctant to join in these associations, they remain partial and shallow" (Nakane 1973, 131). Again, emphasizing the lack of contact between adult siblings, she comments "actual relationships with relatives tend to be closer on the wife's side, although the husband's relatives are accorded precedence on formal occasions" (Nakane 1973, 133). In fact, subsequent studies have suggested that many women, even without their husband's participation, do maintain significant horizontal relationships with neighbors, workmates, ex-schoolmates, and relatives (Imamura 1987; Kondo 1990). Indeed, Nakane's depiction of Japanese society seems to have declining relevance the more one moves away from the male white-collar world of the large enterprise, university, or government department and toward the world of the manual laborer, the part-time worker, the family firm, or the fishing village. Yet the boldness and clarity of her picture of "vertical society" ensured that it had a profound influence on images of Japan both at home and abroad and was widely accepted as a comprehensive picture of Japanese society in all its aspects.

A similarly gendered depiction of Japanese society appears in another classic of *Nihonjinron,* Doi Takeo's *Amae no kōzō* (The Anatomy of Dependence). Based on his experiences both as an exchange student in the United States and as a practicing psychiatrist in Japan, Doi concludes that a key to understanding Japanese society lies in the concept of *amae,* a virtually untranslatable term which generally implies a "tendency to behave self-indulgently, presuming on some special relationship which exists" between oneself and others (Doi 1973, 29). The Japanese penchant for *amae,* Doi suggests, not only helps to explain the strength of group relationships in Japanese society and the different ways in which individuals behave within and outside their "own" group, but also makes sense of social "pathologies" (as he sees them) such as the student demonstrations of the late 1960s and early 1970s. In defining *amae* as the core characteristic of Japanese culture Doi is presenting an image of the Japanese nation as fundamentally male gendered. This may seem a curious contention as "dependence" (in the normal English usage of the word) might more normally be considered a "female" than a "male" characteristic. Besides, Doi sees *amae* as the source of that spontaneous sensitivity to nature which Motoori Norinaga had defined both as uniquely Japanese and as essentially feminine (Doi 1973, 78–79). Doi, however, develops this connection in an interesting way. Aesthetic sensitivity and a deep emotional attachment to the group are, he argues, long-standing characteristics of the Japanese; it is only the shock of defeat in the Pacific War which has enabled Japanese people to understand the true source of these characteristics. They arise from a deep desire for acceptance and nurturing (i.e., *amae*) which originates as "an emotion felt by the baby at the breast toward its mother" and which therefore "must necessarily begin before the 'Oedipus complex' of psychoanalytical theory" (Doi 1973, 20). This analysis allows Doi to develop the concept of *amae* in the light of Freudian theory. For example, citing the example of Natsume Soseki's famous novel *Kokoro*—which deals with an intense and implicitly homosexual entanglement between a younger and an older man—he argues that vertical social relationships in Japan (of the sort described by Nakane Chie) often develop quasi-homosexual overtones. The connection between this latent homosexuality and *amae* is obvious: homosexuality is believed to arise because the individual "identifies with his mother—he becomes his mother, as it were—and thus comes to love objects similar to himself. If homosexuality is in many cases an outcome of closeness to the mother, may it not be possible to see it as an expression of *amae?*" (Doi 1973, 120). Similarly, the "self-indulgent" rebellion of 1960s youth is seen as a phenomenon of a society where fathers have lost their authority, the young are more closely attached to their mothers than their fathers, and Oedipal overtones abound (Doi 1973, 150–157).

Doi's *amae,* to be fair, is not a phenomenon limited to men. He does briefly cite examples of a daughter's dependence on her father and a wife's on her husband. At certain points in his study, he also reflects on the fact that being dependent or indulged (*amaeru*) requires the presence of someone who is depended on or does the indulging (*amayakasu*). Yet his overwhelming emphasis on the receiving rather than the giving of "indulgence" leaves the reader with the lasting impression of a society of Oedipal young men, a society where no child ever grows up to be a mother.

Modern Japan as Female: *Oshin*

The sociological speculations of *Nihonjinron* encouraged an outpouring of works, many of them written by scholars based in the United States or Europe, which analyzed the peculiarities of Japanese management practices, generally by focusing on the experiences of male full-time employees in large firms (for example, Cole 1979; Ouchi 1981; Pascale and Athos 1981). Yet the association of modern Japan with male social relationships was not an inescapable one. Indeed, at the very moment when Japanese economic strength was at its peak and the holistic social images of *Nihonjinron* at their most influential, a shift in the gendering of popular representations of the nation began to be visible. By the 1980s, Japan's economic power was beginning to result both in an increasingly visible worldwide presence of Japanese multinational corporations and in growing pressure for trade concessions from economic competitors, most notably the United States.

In this context, it is interesting to notice the growing influence of popular works in which the nation was unequivocally identified as female. One example is the work of the psychiatrist Kawai Hayao, whose ideas closely mirror Doi Takeo's notion of "dependency," but who approaches the issue, as it were, from the opposite direction. Kawai, in other words, defines Japanese culture as one based on the "maternal principle," which he defines as being characterized above all by "inclusivity," whereas paternal societies are based on "separation." Matriarchal societies, in other words, are based on an indulgent love which nurtures but can also hamper the development of the independent self; patriarchal societies, on the other hand, separate individual from individual, in the process creating strong selves but also often producing social alienation (Kawai 1976, 8–32). In early versions, Kawai used this theory mainly to explain the prevalence in Japan of various psychological problems such as the famous "school avoidance syndrome" (*tōkō kyohi*), where children are reluctant to leave the safety of home for the public world of school (Kawai 1976). By the 1980s, however, Kawai was giving a increasingly positive slant to Japan's "maternal principle," which he saw, among other things, as a reason for misunderstandings of the Japanese system by "foreigners" (= Westerners = Americans) and thus of phenomena like trade friction. Westerners, with their strong male sense of self, for example, demanded quick, clear decisions and written contracts and failed to recognize that this approach conflicted with the relational, feminine Japanese sense of self, which relied on negotiation and consensus (Kawai 1984).

But by far the most influential and memorable vision of Japan as female was surely the NHK television drama series *Oshin,* whose first episodes were shown in Japan in April 1983. *Oshin* was an enormous commercial success, attracting large audiences, not just in Japan itself but also in China, Hong Kong, much of Southeast Asia, the United States, and even Belgium and Iran (Lull 1991, 176). Its appeal lay partly in its spectacular scenery and lovingly recreated period settings, but above all in its script, which embodied the classical elements of the very best of human melodrama (Hashida 1984).

Told as a series of prolonged flashbacks, *Oshin* begins in "the present": that is, in 1983, in a small town in the western Japanese region of Ise. The local Tanokura chain of supermarkets, under the management of its somewhat ruthless director Tanokura Hitoshi, is about to celebrate its commercial success by opening its seventeenth store. But in the midst of the festivities one figure is missing: The matriarch of the family, Hitoshi's mother Oshin, has disappeared, leaving as a clue to her whereabouts just one battered wooden doll. Only her beloved step-grandson Kei knows how to interpret this clue, for Oshin has told him that the doll was a gift from her mother, given to her at a particularly traumatic moment in her impoverished childhood. Kei therefore sets out on a journey to the remote mountainous area of Yamagata Prefecture where Oshin grew up, and there he finds his grandmother, who begins to tell him the story of her life.

She was born, as we discover, in 1901, the sixth child of a poor tenant farmer in the snowy mountains of northern Japan. At the age of seven she was sent out to work as a nursemaid for a local family, who unjustly accused her of theft and threw her out of the house in the middle of winter. She was rescued by a couple of hunters, one of whom proved to be a deserter from the Russo–Japanese War and taught her about the evils of militarism. Later, she went to work for a well-to-do family of rice merchants, from whom she learned some of the secrets of their trade and befriended their elder daughter, Kayo.

Oshin, of course, is Japan itself, and her life therefore takes the viewer on a guided tour of the landmarks of twentieth-century Japanese history. She and Kayo become involved with Kōta, a young activist in the nascent socialist movement. Toward the end of World War I, Oshin moves to Tokyo, in time to be caught up in the postwar wave of consumerism and *bunkashugi* and develops a successful career cutting women's hair in the newly fashionable (and now socially acceptable) Western style. Meanwhile, she struggles to support her ne'er-do-well family, and her diligence and courage attract the attention of a moderately prosperous merchant, whom she marries. Her husband, however, proves unimaginative and unsympathetic; Oshin struggles to modernize his drapery business, only to see her handiwork destroyed in the Great Kantō Earthquake of 1923. Her indomitable spirit keeps the family going through the Great Depression, which bankrupts her friend Kayo's family and drives Kayo herself into prostitution. Oshin's husband, meanwhile, has developed links with the military and, as Japan slides into war, goes into business making army uniforms, but once again fate intervenes, and the family factory is destroyed in wartime bombing raids. By now, Oshin has three children, and her eldest son is old enough to be recruited into the army and die on the battlefield in the Philippines. To compound the disaster, her husband, overcome by shame and despair, commits suicide the day after the announcement of

Japan's surrender. Once again, Oshin takes charge of the family's destiny and sets up business as a fishmonger in a provincial town. As Japan's postwar economy gradually revives, her retail business grows and diversifies, and she becomes one of the first people in the town to start a self-service store. At the same time, she acts as mother not just to her surviving son and daughter but also to two adopted children and copes with the endless personal and emotional complications of her family, including the inevitable conflicts with her daughter-in-law.

But Oshin is Japan in geographical, as well as historical, terms. Her life takes her from the classical site of rural poverty—northeastern Japan—to a fishing village in Kyushu and later to the ancient mercantile heartland of the Ise area, with frequent detours to Tokyo along the way. The historical and geographical authenticity of her journey is emphasized by a superbly illustrated glossy booklet produced by NHK to accompany the series, in which photographs, oral histories, and a detailed chronology are used to anchor the story into the real lives of the various regions of Japan (Fujine 1983).

The drama could, of course, be interpreted as a fictionalized version of *Nihonjinron*—an account of the special virtues which explain Japan's miraculous evolution from rural poverty to commercial triumph (though Oshin, of course, embodies the inverse of *amae*—an enduring, tenacious, forgiving reliability). This, indeed, is how it was understood by at least some of its viewers. James Lull records that in China, where Oshin became something of a national obsession when it was screened in 1986, viewers' comments often echoed the sentiment of a Beijing man who remarked, "No one can compete with [Oshin]. The woman has a certain goal in life that she wants to come true . . . no matter how bad life is, she just keeps going" (Lull 1991, 178). Another commentator praised the program as having the potential "to stimulate people's attitudes and spirit to work for economic development and technological improvement in order to make China strong" (Lull 1991, 179).

But for a large number of Japanese viewers, the drama was not a story about a successful upward march into the present and future, but rather the reverse. Watching *Oshin,* at a point when they knew that Japan had reached the summit of material success, enabled them to indulge in a wondering, bittersweet nostalgia for the hardships of the past (Harvey 1995, 86–88). For the young, who could not remember the events depicted in the series, *Oshin* was a revelation of memories which their own parents and grandparents had never been able to convey to them with such poignant clarity. For the older generation, every thatched roof, every patched-up cotton jacket, every oil lamp or blackened iron kettle brought forth sighs of wistful recognition.

This sense of Oshin as a symbol of continuity with the past is made explicit by the dramatic structure of the story. The viewers learn that Oshin has chosen to set off on her journey of rediscovery at the height of the Tanokura Company's celebrations because she is distressed by her son Hitoshi's hard-nosed devotion to profit-making. Somewhere along the line, she tells her grandson Kei, the family has lost a sense of human decency, which can be recovered only by re-establishing links with the forgotten hardships of the past. The story ends with Hitoshi, whose newly opened store has plunged the company into debt, being rescued from bankruptcy by an elderly neighboring shop-owner. His rescuer proves to be none other than Kōta, the socialist friend of Oshin's youth: Without the human relationships and loyalties of the past, the brash money-makers of the present are doomed to failure.

Oshin is a Japanese *Citizen Kane,* whose battered wooden doll plays precisely the same symbolic role as the sled "Rosebud" in Orson Wells's classic. But *Citizen Kane* is primarily a parable of class, and its viewers are not supposed to sympathize with the grasping and increasingly grotesque capitalist main character, even though they may feel a twinge of regret at the end of the film for Kane's lost innocence. Oshin, on the other hand, is a parable of nation. The main character has her human failings, but she is nevertheless a profoundly admirable character with whom the viewers are supposed to, and do, identify. So her rediscovery of the past is also their rediscovery, the means by which they retie the broken threads of history. Her role as a successful businesswoman is overshadowed by her role as a symbol of the all-important continuity between past and present.

Oshin's gender also enables the series to present an interesting, though slightly problematic, view of that history. It is, in many ways, a liberal and pacifist view. The landmarks of history traversed by Oshin's story are far from a simple litany of national triumphs: They include events such as crop failures and famine, the rice riots of 1918, the emergence of peasants' unions, and the rise of feminism. Oshin is even briefly arrested by the police on suspicion of being a socialist sympathizer. Her friendship with the army deserter and her experiences during the war also give a clearly antimilitarist angle to her story. But, for this very reason, to the extent that Oshin is Japan, the

Japan that is presented to viewers is a peace-loving, suffering Japan, which is in no way responsible for the mid-century disasters which befall it. Seeing the war through Oshin's eyes, the viewer's perspective is confined largely to the home front and to the horrors wreaked on the civilian population by food shortages, bombing, and the death of loved ones. The battlefields of China and Southeast Asia exist for the most part beyond the program's range of vision, and their complex implications do not need to be confronted. This gendered past makes the drama particularly suited to its role as a cultural export to other parts of Asia and as a presentation of a Japan which, with growing economic and cultural ties to its Asian neighbors, hopes to present an attractive and unthreatening face to the other nations of the region.

Gender, Family, and Identity

Constructions of national identity almost always embody explicit or implicit images of gender. The ideas surveyed in this chapter suggest that the nation in Japan has not necessarily been construed as female. Instead, via differing depictions of the ideal family, notions of femininity and masculinity have been deployed and combined in various ways to create visions of the nation which suited particular historical and political contexts. At certain times, the concept of *ie* was used to absorb and obscure gender difference; at others, the family was seen as marking out the space which separates the sexes—women, whatever their other roles, remain centered in the family, while men roam more freely through the "public sphere." Whether the nation was depicted in terms of male or female imagery also depended on circumstance and on the often unspoken awareness of other powerful nations from whom Japan was being differentiated. Japan as modernizing economic dynamo was often depicted in male terms, while Japan as a flexible, unthreatening, nonhegemonic nation (often implicitly contrasted with the male hegemon—China, and later the United States) was seen as female. In all this imagery, the concept of the family commonly embodied gender differences in relation to time: Men were seen as the dynamic face of the nation—the creative, though sometimes disruptive, agents of progress; while women were the face of cultural continuity, a source of stability in a changing world.

These images, of course, capture only a small share of the immensely diverse experiences of men and women in a complex society like Japan's. They are significant, though, because of their implications for the way in which individuals define their own personal identities. The final chapter of this book examines more closely the multiple and inter-secting dimensions of individual identity. For many people in twentieth-century societies, gender and nationality have provided two key dimensions of that identity. In the heritage of (often implicit) imagery explored here, however, Japanese nationality and gender are generally seen as intersecting in a narrow and limiting way: within the household, and in terms of defined roles within the household. So certain sorts of "femininity" and "masculinity" are endorsed as being properly "national," while others are denied; conversely, certain sorts of nationality are recon-firmed as being properly "feminine" or "masculine."

This rhetoric of nationhood poses major challenges to feminists who try to create space for alternative social understandings and practices. During the 1950s and 1960s Japanese feminism was, by and large, closely linked to images of universal social progress. The oppressive structures of the patriarchal family were seen as remnants of a "feudal" or "traditional" Japan, and the pursuit of equal opportunity for women could therefore be aligned with a wider trajectory of national and global social development. The main goal at this stage, in other words, was to enable women to move freely into that sphere of public action which had previously been seen as the preserve of men. The new currents of feminist thought which entered Japan in the 1980s, how-ever, opened the way to very different interpretations (Ehara 1990, 32–34). Ecofeminists like Aoki Yayoi, for example, rejected both the "Western" model of economic development and the goal of equal op-portunity for women within existing social structures. Modernization, they argued, was the chief cause of, rather than the solution to, the oppression of women. The modern emphasis on the "masculine" value of rationality had suppressed the instinctive unity of human beings with nature and had resulted both in sexual inequality and in the mas-sive destruction of the natural environment. What was needed, there-fore, was a rediscovery of the feminine principle—of "the nature within us"—and this in turn implied a rediscovery of traditional com-munal structures, which, in Japan as elsewhere, had been obliterated by the creation of the modern state and the post-Meiji patriarchal family (Aoki 1986).

Such views were fiercely challenged by other Japanese commenta-tors, including the prominent feminist Ueno Chizuko. Ueno argued that images of an inherently maternal and nurturing feminine principle threatened to sanctify those very social structures and stereotypes which are the sources of women's oppression (Ueno 1986; see also Buckley 1997, 2). Some critics have also detected in ecofeminism echoes of the wartime nationalist search for a "transcendence of modernity" (see Aoki 1986, 89). Once again, women are liable to be defined as sources of nurturing love and as the bearers of tradition (in this case defined as a traditional respect for nature), while men are perceived as agents of change in the public sphere (even though their actions are now portrayed in negative terms as the source of environmental destruction).

More recent feminist writings have tried to go beyond the limitations of early versions of ecofeminism, developing an ecological approach which rejects simplistic notions of an essentialized feminine nature. They have argued for a more thorough critique of the socially imposed division between "nature" and "culture," and between "male" and "female." The main target of criticism, in this sense, is no longer a Western-style modernity in contrast to indigenous tradition, but "a modern capitalist system in which the exploitation of nature is integrally related to discrimination and exploitation based on sex, race, ethnicity, culture, region and age" (Ōgoshi 1994, 169). The theoretical underpinnings of this approach are not yet well developed. However, it clearly reflects a growing concern among Japanese feminists about the relationship between gender, ethnic, and national identities. With the expansion of Japanese companies into other parts of Asia during the 1970s, Japanese women's movements began to establish links with their counterparts in other Asian countries, focusing particularly on the exploitation of female workers in Japanese-owned factories overseas. During the 1980s new groups were also established to support the rapidly growing number of Asian women migrants employed in Japan itself—particularly in prostitution and the entertainment industry. These activities helped to broaden the range of perspectives embraced by Japanese feminism. A sense of the crosscutting issues confronted by the contemporary women's movement is vividly conveyed by Sandra Buckley's description of a Women's Resource Center in the early 1990s in suburban Tokyo:

> At one table a group of Japanese and Filipino prostitutes were meeting with two academic feminists to develop a position paper for the prosti-

> tutes to present to a government inquiry into the status of illegal women workers in Japan. At the same time a group of Ainu women were consulting with the center's librarian, who was helping them locate comparative materials in the center archives for use in their campaigns for the recognition of the particular problems faced by women of indigenous populations. Such alliances are frequent and belie any clear-cut distinction between academic and non-academic feminism in Japan. (Buckley 1994, 180)

A particularly central issue for Japanese feminists in the last few years has been the question of the so-called comfort women—women, many of them from Japan's colonies, who were coerced into prostitution by the Japanese military during the Pacific War. The issue is a practical one involving campaigns for the compensation of victims, but it also raises profound questions of the relationship between nationalism, militarism, and concepts of gender and ethnicity. As writers like Suzuki Yūko point out, military prostitution represents in the most stark form the dark, neglected inverse of ideologies of the family state. The image of the good woman as the faithful core of the family, and of man as the venturer who pushes forward the frontiers of national power, implied the covert existence of another group of women: women whose disposable sex served male freedom and power in the public realm without imperiling the survival of the family unit. The identification of family with nation, and of nation with ethnos meant that, to fill these roles, it was convenient to use women from the margins of the empire, or from the most remote and impoverished corners of Japan itself—women whose identification as "Japanese" could be seen as incomplete. In this way, the shadow world of purchased sex could be more easily kept separate from the idealized image of nation as family and of women/mothers as the bearers of national tradition. The result was the creation of a group of women whose gender, ethnicity, and class allowed multiple levels of exploitation and exclusion and whose wartime sufferings in many cases left them permanently unable to bear children. Since their story fitted uneasily, not just into gendered images of the Japanese nation, but also into the nationalist imagery of the newly independent Japanese ex-colonies, their plight was largely ignored for decades.

The nation's past is made up of millions of threads of individual lives, coming together, drifting apart, crossing boundaries. In *Oshin,* a single invented human life is used to weave the story of the past together in a way that emphasizes the central role of women without disturbing the conventional imagery of nationhood. But as the stories of the "comfort women" have become more widely debated in Japan and have begun to be included in the curriculum of history education, they have highlighted some of the many threads which fit less easily with established patterns; which cut across accepted images of the convergence of gender and national identity. The force of the challenge which these stories present to accepted visions of national identity is evident from the strength of the reactions which they have evoked. The inclusion of references to the "comfort women" in school textbooks has become one of the main targets of attack of a revisionist group of historians led by Fujioka Nobukatsu of Tokyo University (Fujioka 1996). Fujioka's impassioned criticism of what he calls the "history of disgrace" suggests that the stories of the "comfort women," in destabilizing comforting myths about ethnic, sexual, and power relationships, are indeed an important starting point for rethinking the connection between gender and nation in the twentieth century world.

7

Civilization

The world of entertainment has, in recent years, provided plenty of examples of unexpected comebacks by aging stars. But in the world of academia the most surprising comeback of the decade is surely civilization theory. Civilization was the great organizing concept of nineteenth-century European thought. The rise and fall of civilizations provided a framework for understanding and justifying the triumph of the European empires, and comparisons between civilizations provided the testing ground for newly emerging theories about culture and social change. Henry Thomas Buckle, for example, studied geography and climate to explain the origins of the worldwide dominance of European civilization, while François Guizot (who, like Buckle, exerted great influence on Meiji Japanese thought) examined the history of European civilization from the perspective of French culture because (as he wrote) "I believe that we can say without flattery that France is the center, the engine of European civilization" (Guizot 1851, 5–6). In the second part of the century, with the upsurge of ethnic nationalism on the fringes of Europe, these ideas began to be put to new uses by men like Nikolai Danilevsky, who saw the world as divided among ten great civilizations and whose belief in the divine destiny of a Slavic civilization, emerging from an alliance between Russians and Serbs, raises disturbingly familiar echoes in the 1990s (see MacMaster 1967).

By the middle of the twentieth century, perhaps in reaction to ideas like Danilevsky's, civilization theory was falling out of favor. Its last great efflorescence seemed to be Arnold J. Toynbee's *Study of History,* a massive and magisterial analysis of the dynamics of world civilizations, which since its publication has sat on the shelves of university libraries, largely unread. In the past few years, however, nineteenth-century notions of civilization have had a facelift, put on some bright new clothes, and reappeared in the spotlight as the latest thing in social theory.

The best-known example is probably the work of Samuel Huntington, whose recent writings present a vision of a world divided among seven or eight major civilizations as the best framework for understanding the post–Cold War order (Huntington 1993; Huntington 1996). It is the conflict between these civilizations, rather than between more conventional political and economic units, which Huntington foresees as the dominant force in the world affairs of the near future.

Huntington's image of the future, however, is not simply the product of a paranoia induced by declining U.S. influence in world affairs. Wider and deeper forces are clearly at work here, for Huntington's map of the world is remarkably similar to that proposed by some of the more controversial recent writings on "civilization theory" in Japan. A major panel at the 1991 conference of the Social and Economic History Society (Shakai Keizaishi Gakkai)—one of Japan's foremost academic associations—addressed the topic "The Advocacy of Japanese Civilization" (*Nihon bunmei no teishō*) and in doing so ranged over panoramas of human progress from the stone age onward. Civilization theory is seriously discussed by some influential members of the younger generation of Japanese historians and has also given rise to recent popular publications like Ueyama Shumpei's multivolume *History of Japanese Civilization* (Nihon bunmei shi) (Ueyama 1990a).

As many writers have pointed out, "the word 'civilization' has a double meaning. We contrast Western civilization with non-Western ones, but we also talk about the emergence, progress and possible collapse of civilization in general" (Arnason 1988, 87). When Fukuzawa Yukichi wrote of "civilization" (*bunmei*) in the mid-nineteenth century, he (like Buckle and Guizot) was using the word in its singular sense. His concern was to define Japan's place in a universal flow of progress from past to future. During the second half of the nineteenth century, however, a growing number of European scholars developed theories concerning the rise, fall, and coexistence of multiple "civilizations." It is this usage which has been taken up by postwar civilization theorists in Japan.

One of the earliest Japanese studies to examine the comparative history of "civilizations" in the plural was Umesao Tadao's essay *Civilization from the Perspective of Ecological History* (Bunmei no seitai shikan), first published in 1957 (Umesao 1989). This work embodied a view of geography radically different from that of most prewar scholars. Where prewar writers had struggled with the problems of Japan's racial, cultural, and political relationship with Asia, Umesao reimagined the geographic space of Eurasia in a way which aligned Japan much more closely with Western Europe than with its Asian neighbors. Eurasian history, he argued, was the product of a continual interaction between, on the one hand, the maritime fringes at the far east and west of the continent and, on the other, the desert regions in the center. The desert was the home of nomads, who, in times of population expansion or drought, burst out of the confines of their homelands to ravage surrounding state societies. The states which bordered the deserts (such as China and Russia) were therefore prone to repeated periods of turmoil and to the repeated rise and fall of political systems. States on the outermost fringe of the landmass (such as Britain and Japan) were insulated from these disruptions and therefore had greater continuity in their social and economic history. This helped to explain their ultimate progress to the stage of industrial civilization (Umesao 1989).

Umesao's theories had an obvious appeal in the high-growth era, when Japan's rapid industrial development seemed indeed to make the nation "closer" to Britain than to its Asian neighbors. But they have also exerted a powerful influence on a new wave of civilization theory which has come to prominence in the very different economic and social environment of the 1990s.

Transcending the Eurocentric Paradigm

The contemporary prophets of civilization theory do not speak with one voice. They come from a variety of different backgrounds and define civilization itself in a number of different ways. Two fundamental shared concerns, however, shine through their writings. The first is a desire to escape from the Eurocentric world view which has dominated the study of history since the eighteenth century. Eurocentrism, they argue, has constricted the focus of historical study and, more importantly, produced theories of history which make sense only of the European (or North Atlantic) past (Kawakatsu 1991, 136–151; Itō 1990, 147–148).

The second concern is to develop an alternative to the Marxian stage theory of history, which has exerted a strong sway over the historical imagination in modern Japan. This second issue is, of course, intimately connected to the first. Marxian stages, and in particular the

Marxian analysis of the emergence of capitalism from feudalism, are seen as classic cases of a Eurocentric view of history (Kawakatsu 1991, 138–149; Itō 1990, 241–242). As the intellectual authority of Marxism has declined, it has left a vacuum into which the new civilization theorists hope to fit a different and (supposedly) more universal theory of the unfolding of human destiny.

To go beyond the limits of Eurocentrism, to go beyond the materialism of Marx—these are aims which inspire much contemporary history writing. In their stated purposes the civilization theorists are not so far removed from the postcolonial historians of Asia and Latin America or the poststructural historians of Europe. But the tools which they use to build their theories are remarkably different. Here there is no talk of elusive concepts like subalterneity or imagined communities. Instead the categories of analysis are bold chronological or geographic blocks: hunter-gatherer society, agricultural society, Egyptian civilization, Chinese civilization. Why have these categories regained such popularity in Japan, and how do they influence the directions of the emerging civilization theory? To answer these questions, I look in some detail at three popular contributions to the recent civilization debate: Ueyama Shumpei's *Nihon bunmeishi no kōsō* (A Plan of the History of Japanese Civilization), Kawakatsu Heita's *Nihon bunmei to kindai Seiyō: "Sakoku" saikō* (Japanese Civilization and the Modern West: Second Thoughts on the "Closed Country"), and Itō Shuntarō's *Hikaku bunmei to Nihon* (Comparative Civilization and Japan).

Civilization and Culture

Ueyama Shumpei, a leading member of the group commonly known as the "neo-Kyoto School," bases his speculations on the nature of civilization firmly on the notion of "culture" explored in Chapter 4, with all its striving after organic models of society. Ueyama begins his examination of Japanese history with a lengthy discussion of the terms "culture" and "civilization," in the course of which he adopts a definition of "culture" inspired by American social anthropology, particularly by the work of Alfred Kroeber's collaborator, Clyde Kluckhohn. Culture consists not merely of the visible "patterns of behavior particular to a [social] group," and not merely of the material products created by that behavior, but also of the invisible "ways of thinking and feeling" which constitute the "inner workings" of social existence (Ueyama

1990b: 42–43). Ueyama then goes on to define "civilization" (borrowing from Philip Bagby and others) as culture which has exceeded a certain level of development. He therefore classifies social difference across two dimensions: a spatial dimension, which (for example) separates "Chinese civilization" from "Western civilization"; and a temporal dimension which (for example) separates "primary (agricultural) civilization" from "secondary (industrial) civilization."

Ueyama argues that modern industrial civilization, based on the principles of "science" and "freedom," has produced great benefits for humanity, but has also produced negative social and spiritual consequences: "poisons" to which it is necessary to seek an antidote. The origins of both the positive and the negative aspects of industrial civilization lie in the cultural heritage of the West. It is therefore necessary to look for an antidote to the poisons of modern society elsewhere, in a society which participates in modern industrial civilization but whose cultural origins lie elsewhere: "Japan was born from the womb of Chinese civilization, which was very different from the old civilizations in which Western civilization has its roots. So from the point of view of creating an antidote for the new civilization, Japan perhaps has the advantage of being in a promising situation" (Ueyama 1990b: 23–24).

The nature, both of the "poisons" and of the "antidote," are implied rather than explicitly delineated in Ueyama's writings. A central issue in his work, for example, is the loss of spirituality. He draws inspiration from the ideas of Dostoevsky and of Nishida Kitarō, both of whom sought "antidotes" in the religious traditions of their own countries, though he is at pains to stress that the solution to the dilemmas of modernity must be forward looking, rather than a simple retreat into the religious systems of the past (Ueyama 1990b, 250–264). Some hints of Ueyama's solutions to the problems of modernity are also contained in his reconstruction of Japanese history. While European societies, he argues, are characterized by a "convex culture" which constantly seeks to impose itself upon others, Japan has been characterized by a "concave culture" which readily absorbs elements from abroad. Japan has passed through two major phases of foreign borrowing. The first was a wave of borrowing from China, which began when Japan entered the era of "primary civilization" (i.e., agricultural society) and when the Japanese imperial system was established; the second was a wave of borrowing from the West, which began as Japan entered "secondary civilization" (i.e., industrial society) and when the

Japanese state was transformed into a constitutionally based imperial system.

In the first phase, borrowing was initially quite indiscriminate, and it was only through a long period of absorption, culminating in the Edo period (1603–1867), that the "individuality" (*kosei*) of Japan began to shine through the veneer of imported Chinese culture. In the modern era of "secondary civilization," though, Japan has yet to transcend the stage of indiscriminate borrowing from the West and "establish its individuality" (Ueyama 1990b, 238). The implication seems to be that the establishment of that individuality and the development of an antidote for the poisons of modernity go hand in hand. And where does the source of that individuality lie? According to Ueyama: "It is intimately related to the fact that Japanese civilization was born together with the emperor system [*tennōsei*] and has developed to this day together with the emperor system. It seems to me that the individuality of Japan and the individuality of the emperor system are inseparably connected" (Ueyama 1990b, 233).

Civilization and *Minzoku*

Kawakatsu Heita borrows his definition of culture from Ueyama Shumpei, but is critical of Ueyama's emphasis on the emperor and the state in the shaping of Japanese civilization (Kawakatsu 1992a, 37–39). Rather than identifying the turning points in the history of civilization with political moments in state formation, Kawakatsu identifies them with shifts in the material culture of societies. His aim, in short, is to develop a post-Marxian, post-Eurocentric version of history, based not on the ideas of Toynbee and company, but on home-grown Japanese philosophies (although various European writers from John Ruskin to Fernand Braudel exert a marked influence on his approach). Three Japanese writers have had a particularly powerful influence on his ideas. First is the philosopher Watsuji Tetsurō, whose famous prewar study of the impact of natural environment on culture, *Fūdo,* is enjoying something of a vogue in Japan at present (Watsuji 1963). The second is Umesao Tadao (though Kawakatsu is critical of Umesao on some points). Third, and most important, is the naturalist Imanishi Kinji. Imanishi's well-known studies of social behavior among monkeys (and other animal species) have produced several concepts which are central to Kawakatsu's history. These include the notion of a natural order of coexistence (*sumiwake*) which species create within their habitat, the idea that culture is fundamental to animal as well as human societies, and the concept of group (as opposed to individual) evolution (Kawakatsu 1991, 155–182). Kawakatsu points out that all these writers have a spatial as well as temporal emphasis in their work. They see not only the linear flow of time but also the vastness of geographical horizons. They are conscious of the decisive force of place, as well as generation, in shaping human identity (Kawakatsu 1991, 154).

The central current of Kawakatsu's thought, however, is explained not only by the influence of these intellectual antecedents but also by his own career as a historian. Kawakatsu, a professor of economic history at Waseda University, began his academic career by specializing mainly in that great staple of economic history research, the role of the cotton industry in the industrial revolution. One of his chief contributions has been the suggestion, accepted by many historians, that the Japanese cotton industry survived the opening of trade to the West because European cotton thread and textiles were unsuited to Japanese tastes. Consumers in Japan were used to thick, chunky cotton cloth which was made into winter clothes. Their reluctance to buy thinner imported cloth gave the domestic industry breathing space, which allowed it to embark on its own path to mechanization (for example, Kawakatsu 1977).

From this small island in human history, Kawakatsu moves out to claim much wider realms, arguing that economics and economic history in general have neglected the role of culture in the human economy. Demand for goods, he insists, is not driven simply by physical need but equally by cultural tradition (Kawakatsu 1991, 208). Up to this point Kawakatsu's arguments, which explicitly echo Braudelian notions of the structures of everyday life, are very persuasive. It is easy to agree that conventional economics has indeed been too reliant on images of human beings as "greedy machines" and has given too little thought to the psychological, social, political, and symbolic aspects of economic life. From this point on, however, the story becomes increasingly contentious.

Putting culture back into the economy, according to Kawakatsu, involves shifting from the Marxist emphasis on production to a new emphasis on consumption. Each ethnic group (*minzoku*) has its own distinctive "product mix" (*bussan fukugō,* consisting of staple foods, clothing, etc.) which defines its identity. Or, to be more precise, it has a product mix which gives rise to a nonmaterial "mix" of meanings, values, and so on (the cultural complex or *bunka fukugō*). In a rather confusing scheme, Kawakatsu then depicts these as supporting a production system (the old Marxian base), which in turn supports a system of laws and political systems (the old Marxian superstructure) (Kawakatsu 1991, 199; see also Kawakatsu 1995, 57–58).

The key point, however, is that it is the interaction, conflict, and accommodation between different ethnic groups and their product mixes which are the driving forces of history. In contrast to Marx's pronouncement that "the entire history of society is the history of class struggle," Kawakatsu proclaims that history has been, on the one hand, a history of environmental destruction and, on the other, "as far as relations among humans are concerned, a history of the interaction and conflict between ethnic groups [*minzoku*]. The interaction and conflict between *minzoku* is what brings about change in cultural and material mixes [*bunka bussan fukugō*]. Ethnic groups are as old as human history and are the basic human groups. These, above all, are groups which create the same cultures" (Kawakatsu 1991, 199–200).

This attempt to define the material culture of *minzoku* as the decisive force in history raises several important problems. In a world where (as Kawakatsu himself so ably demonstrates) material goods and ideas are constantly on the move, being incorporated in different ways by different groups within different societies, how exactly do we recognize the bundle of products and cultural traits which defines the identity of the ethnic group? Are the people of northern China, whose staple crops have long been wheat and millet, a different *minzoku* from the people of southern China, whose staple crop is rice? Are Japanese people born in the 1960s a different *minzoku* from their grandparents, born in the 1910s, for certainly the "product mix" with which they have grown up is almost totally different? On these key questions Kawakatsu is remarkably vague. In some places he seems to equate culture (and therefore presumably group identity) with sets of material products, but elsewhere he insists that despite the massive "Westernization" of Japan's material way of life, the nation retains an irreducible and "self-evident" (*jimei*) core of unique identity, and immutable "Japaneseness" (*wa*) (Kawakatsu 1991, 246–247; Kawakatsu 1992b, 112; Kawakatsu 1993, 295). This desire to see an enduring ethnic identity within rapidly changing patterns of consumption forces Kawakatsu to search for inner characteristics which maintain the cohesion and distinctiveness of the material "product mix." In places, he adopts a vocabulary reminiscent of Nishida Kitarō's metaphysics and speaks of the human subject taking on the identity of the objects which it consumes (Kawakatsu 1991, 205).

Kawakatsu applies his vision of history as a process of interaction between *minzoku* in a number of ways. In his reassessment of the development of Japan in the Tokugawa period, he points out that during this period Japan absorbed and domesticated the same bundle of foreign products—cotton, sugar, porcelain, etc.—which Western Europe absorbed during the industrial revolution. He therefore suggests a sort of parallel or balance between the "revolution in lifestyle" (*seikatsu kakumei*) in Tokugawa Japan and the industrial revolution in Europe (Kawakatsu 1991, 111–117).

Elsewhere in his study, Kawakatsu identifies military power as an essential element in the "product mix" which characterized modern Western culture from the Portuguese and Spanish empires to twentieth-century Pax Americana (Kawakatsu 1991, 228). This is contrasted with the culture of Tokugawa Japan, which chose to abandon the use of firearms, and which saw international affairs not in terms of "war and peace" but in terms of "civilization and barbarism" (where civilization meant, above all, education) (Kawakatsu 1991, 231–240). Although Kawakatsu observes that Japan was only too quick to absorb the Western military-economic complex from the Meiji period onward, he suggests that there may be a modern lesson in the Tokugawa cultural combination of arms reduction and civilization (= education) (Kawakatsu 1991, 240). This is just one of a series of lessons which Kawakatsu seeks to derive from Tokugawa-period Japan. Indeed, he sees the period as a sort of historical treasure house from which Japanese people should draw in order to recreate an identity in an increasingly international age (Kawakatsu 1991, 241; Kawakatsu 1992a, 45). While lamenting the corporate greed, political amorality, and declining aesthetic sensibility of contemporary Japan, Kawakatsu argues that "the limits of the civilization created by modern Western civilization [*sic*] have now been exposed, and we have entered an era which calls for a new perspective on the theory of civilization. This is none other, I believe, than the wisdom hidden in the forms of Japanese civilization which the Japanese people themselves created during the closed country period [i.e., from the mid-seventeenth to mid-nineteenth centuries], and which can be brought to life in the present age" (Kawakatsu 1992a, 45; see also Kawakatsu 1991, 252–255).

One of the key characteristics of the Tokugawa system, according to Kawakatsu, was the development of labor and skill-intensive manufacturing techniques which nurtured an enduring diligence in the Japanese workforce (Kawakatsu 1995, 45–49). Another example of Tokugawa-period wisdom was the practice of restricting the migration of people. The moral which Kawakatsu derives from this is that, in the interests of social harmony, Japan should limit the entry of foreign workers and instead promote overseas investment, assisting people to live and develop in their own natural habitats, and so promoting a harmonious order of "ethnic coexistence" (*minzoku no sumiwake*) (Kawakatsu 1991, 250). At the same time, however, Japan is held up as a model case of willingness to absorb the best elements of other cultures (Kawakatsu 1991, 244–261). In developing this point, Kawakatsu borrows Ueyama Shumpei's notion of "convex" and "concave" cultures. Using an interesting piece of sentence construction, Kawakatsu goes on to observe: "if the height of civilization is measured by the extent to which we absorb the heritage of the human civilizations of the past, we may say that Japan, as a concave culture, stands both on the Eastern and on the Western systems of civilization" (Kawakatsu 1992a, 45).

Civilization and Progress

"Japan," writes the philosopher of science Itō Shuntarō, "needs to develop [the] comparative theory of civilization. This is necessary because the intellectual role of comparative civilization is to conduct a balanced, fair observation and evaluation of various civilizations, free from self-centered righteousness. For this purpose it is necessary to avoid both the [egocentrism of] the Great Powers and Chinese empire and the nationalism into which developing countries so often fall" (Itō 1990, 236–237). In a wide-ranging historical survey, Itō traces the decline of objectivity in European history writing during the eighteenth and nineteenth centuries, but then goes on to outline the emergence of a new comparative perspective in the work of a number of anthropologists and historians since the late nineteenth century. These early theorists of comparative civilization, to whom Itō acknowledges a debt, range from Nikolai Danilevsky, through Oswald Spengler to Arnold Toynbee, Alfred Weber, and Alfred Kroeber in the mid-twentieth century (Itō 1990, 160–232). Another clear though unspoken influence is the work of the Australian-born archaeologist Vere Gordon Childe, who (inspired by the elder Arnold Toynbee's notion of an "industrial revolution") first suggested the division of human history into a series of revolutions—agricultural (or neolithic), urban, and industrial—each producing a higher level of human civilization (Childe 1936).

Like other Japanese civilization theorists, Itō uses his own version of the Childe scheme of history. Itō, however, adds to the list to produce five revolutions: the human revolution (*ningen kakumei*), which separated humans from other species; the agricultural revolution (*nōgyō kakumei*); the urban revolution (*toshi kakumei*); the spiritual revolution (*seishin kakumei*), which produced the great world religions; and the scientific revolution (*kagaku kakumei*). In this series of stages, human *culture* exists from the very beginning, but *civilization* (as the origin of the English word implies) exists only from the urban revolution, which brings with it "the establishment of the state, the separation of social classes and the invention of writing" (Itō 1990, 240). Rather surprisingly, having defined the agricultural revolution as a distinct step in human evolution, Itō relegates the industrial revolution to a subsidiary status under the heading of the scientific revolution. The truly original point in Itō's scheme of things, however, is that he sees humanity as being on the brink of a new epoch-making revolution. The decline of the mechanistic world view, the decreasing power of the old industrialized economies and the challenges of environmental crisis all point to a transformation, which he terms a new "human revolution," or elsewhere a "bio-world revolution" (*sei sekai kakumei*) (Itō 1990, 25 and 324). This revolution, Itō tells us, will involve a synthesis between the spiritual and the material, the individual and the group, the developed and the underdeveloped, and the human and natural worlds.

Another characteristic of Itō's work (which he shares with his fellow civilization theorists) is an emphasis on space as well as time. European historians, he argues, have tended to present history as moving along a single path from Babylon to the Mediterranean to Northern Europe, paying scant regard to the parallel rise and fall of other civilizations. By contrast, he draws a two-dimensional map of history, in which different parts of the world, placed side by side, can be seen moving at their own pace through the various historical revolutions. This allows Itō to point out a very interesting phenomenon: No two revolutions have begun in the same part of the world. His argument here appears to be that, in the core region of each revolution, society becomes so firmly anchored in the systems necessary to sustain that revolution that further innovation is stifled. Subsequent epoch-making developments therefore emerge from a "peripheral" area which has played the role of follower in the previous wave of revolutionary change. The human revolution began in Africa, the agricultural revolution in Southeast Asia (though Africa threatens to spoil things by putting in a claim for an early agricultural revolution), the urban revolution in Mesopotamia and Egypt, the spiritual revolution in Greece, China, India, and Israel, and the scientific revolution in western Europe (Itō 1990, 21). As each stage of progress unfolds, it moves from the original core areas (what Itō calls the "elemental civilizations") into surrounding peripheral areas, and it is from these peripheral areas that the next leap forward always arises.

Once set in train, the logic of Itō's argument marches bravely forward into the present and future. The current bio-world revolution, clearly, cannot begin in the area which gave birth to the previous scientific revolution. Instead, it must occur in a region which is "situated on the periphery of Western culture, and which has absorbed its scientific and technological civilization to a high degree, while at the same time receiving to the full the negative aspects of civilization such as pollution, environmental damage, and exhaustion of resources. From within these sufferings, it must be willing to take on the task of creating the principles for a new civilization which will overcome them. Where, I wonder, could this be?" (Itō 1990, 23).

I would not spoil the mystery too much if I reveal (as Itō does a few pages later) that the answer is . . . Japan. The characteristics of the next stage of civilization imply that "it is we Japanese who must assume the responsibility of pioneering this sixth revolution in civilization. In other words it can be concluded that Japan must play the role of 'core area' in the sixth 'human revolution' " (Itō 1990, 28). It is hard to avoid the impression that, as in most good mysteries (and much history writing), the plot has been constructed with a predetermined dénouement in mind.

The Limits of "Civilization"

But the heart of the problem with Itō's interpretation of history lies not so much in his selection of historical "revolutions," or even in his identification of the birthplace of the next civilization, but rather in his choice of "civilization" as the topic of study in the first place. By basing their analysis on the notion of "civilizations," all the theorists we have just looked at import into their work a particular notion of space and time. The term "civilizations" in the plural may not suggest a simple unilinear vision of history, but it does suggest a world divided into very large territorial blocks, each united by an enduring cultural essence. It builds, in other words, on the notion of an organically integrated culture (of the sort discussed in Chapter 4), but it takes this notion one step further, suggesting a sense of both historical dynamism and extensive geographical reach. Often, indeed, the term "civilization" suggests something with global influence. Thus Kawakatsu Heita speaks of a distinction between a "Japanese culture" which is strictly for domestic consumption and a "Japanese civilization" which has a special role to play in shaping the contemporary world.

Viewing the world in terms of large civilizational blocks obscures the claims of smaller national or regional units to distinctiveness: There is clearly no room in this schema for an "Okinawan civilization" or an "Ainu civilization." Indeed, since it incorporates a vision of human progress borrowed from theories of "civilization" in the singular, its vision of time leaves hunter-gatherer and small-scale agrarian societies suspended somewhere in the remote past, while others press forward toward the future. This view of time makes it difficult for civilization theories—even comparative civilization theories—to escape a tendency toward hierarchical rankings, a tendency to define particular civilizations as more "progressive" than others. As long as civilization theory rests on an image of the march of humanity through a series of "revolutions," its logic inevitably points to the existence in any given epoch of one particularly dynamic civilization which bears the embryo of the next global revolution. This logic is particularly explicit in Itō Shuntarō's writing, but it is surely also implicit in the approaches of Ueyama and Kawakatsu.

Kawakatsu Heita objects to criticism of his work as ethnocentric, but it is nevertheless evident that Japan occupies a special position in his view of the future of global civilizations (see particularly Kawakatsu 1995, 76–82). He writes, "Japan, of all non-Western countries, is the one which has most dramatically accepted Western culture." Now the time has come not for an outright rejection of Western influences but, rather, for Japan "to shift from worship of the West to understanding of the West, and through this process to seek out their own national identity" (Kawakatsu 1995, 81). This identity will be quite different from the sort of reactive nationalism which Kawakatsu sees as typified by Islamic fundamentalism. On the contrary, it will lie in a distinctive universalism: "as many different living civilizations exist within Japanese society, its characteristic is to activate these various elements. Thus if the Japanese can establish Japan's identity as a space in which many civilizations coexist, that is, as a living museum of the world, I believe that Japan's cultural characteristics can turn into a mediating force activating the diverse cultures of the world in all their diversity" (Kawakatsu 1995, 81–82).

Japan's unique ability to serve as a sort of cultural "adaptor," transforming imported know-how to suit the tastes of both local consumers and other Asian markets, is already evident in Japan's twentieth-century industrial success. Universalism and adaptiveness, together with the diligence developed in the Tokugawa period, help to explain the contrasting modern destinies of Japan and other Asian countries. "I believe that an ethos which zealously seeks to create cheap products by one's own efforts and to supply things of use to human beings . . . fits more closely with the national character of the Japanese than the character of Chinese and Indians" (Kawakatsu 1995, 233). This raises not only questions of fact (Has Japan actually been more receptive to "Western culture" than Singapore or Thailand, Brazil or Liberia? Are Japanese workers really more diligent than Chinese and Indians?) but also certain echoes of prewar visions in which Japan's very hybridity justified its claim to international influence. Now, however, it is not racial hybridity but Japan's "concave culture"—its status as a "museum of the world"—which gives it a special destiny in shaping the next wave of civilizational change.

Of course Japanese society (like many other societies) is heir to a wealth of artistic, intellectual, and other traditions which deserve to be better known outside its own boundaries. But in casting these traditions into the frame of a unique "Japanese civilization" (even a "uniquely universal Japanese civilization") contemporary civilization theorists have chosen a questionable basis for launching the search for a truly universal view of history. To explore some of the problems of this approach more fully, it may be helpful to turn first to another, and very different, current in contemporary Japanese thought which has emerged alongside the rise of civilization theory: a current which may be described as the "critique of culture."

Japanese Critiques of Culture and Civilization

During the 1960s and 1970s, as seen in Chapter 6, many writers, extending the arguments of scholars like Ishida Eiichirō, elaborated on the concept of an integrated and unique "Japanese culture." Japan's cultural core was commonly defined in terms of such features as group consciousness, "dependency," and vertical social relationships (for example, Nakane 1970; Doi 1973; Aida 1972). This genre of *Nihonjinron,* embodies a distinctive common view of the world. Sakai Naoki has pointed out that *Nihonjinron* counterposes Japan, not against the wide range of societies with which the nation might meaningfully be compared—Korea, Thailand, France, Britain, Nigeria, Mexico, etc.— but against a monolithic entity called "the West." The West is thus seen as representing the mainstream form of "modernity," while Japan represents the particular: an island of culture which stubbornly resisted absorption into the generality of Western modernity (Sakai 1996b, 19–21). In reacting against the Eurocentric image of "the West" as the source of the universal standards of civilization, *Nihonjinron* has in this sense incorporated the very world view against which it protests.

Nihonjinron quickly attracted criticism from scholars both inside and outside Japan, who strongly disputed its depictions of Japanese society. *Nihonjinron* theorists were criticized for their lack of scientific rigor, their implicit ideological agenda, their reliance on anecdotal data, their willingness to overlook abundant evidence of diversity and conflict in Japanese society (for example, Mouer and Sugimoto 1986; Dale 1986; Befu 1987; Yoshino 1992). The emergence of civilization theory has also coincided with a new upsurge of critical Japanese writings on the subject of culture, but now the critiques go one step further. Since the late 1980s, there has been a growing tendency for critics to question not just the veracity of particular depictions of Japanese culture but the very concept of "Japanese culture" itself. The question now, in other words, is not so much "how should we understand 'Japan'?" but, rather, "how should we understand 'culture'?"

The challenge to established notions of national culture comes in many forms. One approach is represented by the anthropologist Aoki Tamotsu, who does not discard organic visions of culture as such but, rather, questions their usefulness to contemporary society. Japanese culture has had, according to Aoki, a certain coherence and consistency, so that (for example) the process of cultural borrowing in Japanese history can be likened to the way in which a soft-bodied mollusk creeps into borrowed shells: The outer covering changes, but the inner being stays the same (Aoki 1988, 136). But Aoki goes on to suggest that the preservation of this cultural essence has become a millstone around the neck of Japanese society, hampering Japan's efforts to adapt to a more international age. He therefore proposes an "escape from culture," for which Australia's policy of multiculturalism is suggested as a possible model (Aoki 1988, 53–62).

A somewhat more radical approach to the problem is taken by Nishikawa Nagao's study *Kokkyō no koekata* (literally, "How to Cross Frontiers"), whose point of departure is a discussion of Edward Said's critique of orientalist thought (Said 1978). Nishikawa has much praise for Said's work, but observes that a basic weakness of the book is the author's failure to address the conceptual difficulties of the word "culture." Said only begins to question the use of "culture" as an organizing framework in his concluding paragraphs. By implicitly accepting this concept, Nishikawa argues, Said has left himself no escape route from orientalism, no means of proposing a coherent alternative to the world view which he criticizes (Nishikawa 1992, 83–92). Nishikawa therefore embarks on his own critical analysis of the concepts "culture" and "civilization."

An important element in this analysis is a comparison between images of "civilization," which Nishikawa sees as central to the process of nation-building in France, and images of "culture," which he sees as having played a central role in German definitions of national identity. His most important conclusion, however, is that the notion of "national culture" is an ideological construct which, in both Europe and Japan, emerged with the rise of the modern nation-state and helped to serve the demands of the state for social integration. In fact, Nishikawa argues, the culture which exists within any country is both dynamic and diverse, it changes over time and is shaped and reshaped by contact with other societies: "therefore, what is called Japanese culture, or so-and-so culture, divided by some frontier, does not exist" (Nishikawa 1992, 226; Nishikawa 1996, 263). Culture, therefore, may be analyzed at many different levels, but the most meaningful level of analysis is not the group but the individual: "culture is ultimately a matter of values. In the end, it is the individual who decides on values. It is 'I myself' who not only decides my own place in a single culture, but can also choose to abandon one culture and select another" (Nishikawa 1992, 233).

Nishikawa's approach is in many ways a persuasive one. Looking at problems of history, though, I cannot help feeling that the biggest difficulty is in understanding the constraints, the paradoxes, and the conflicts which influence the individual's choice of values. From this point of view, one of the more interesting critiques of culture is that proposed by Sakai Naoki of Cornell University. Sakai's arguments are complex, and here I simply outline some of their key features by focusing on the question of "assimilation."

When we speak of cultural "assimilation," we envisage a situation where immigrants, colonial subjects, or other "foreigners" are incorporated into the society of a nation by adopting national culture and so "becoming the same as everyone else." The problem with this image is that it assumes that "everyone else" is indeed "the same": in other words that all citizens possess a common national culture. But, like Nishikawa, Sakai sees this as an illusion. If "culture" means the possession of the same knowledge, values, and experiences, then any national society clearly contains many cultures. Not only do the cultures of (for example) men and women, or teenagers and pensioners, differ, so too do the cultures of (for example) those who can drive cars and those who cannot (Sakai 1996b, 21–22 and 42–43). "Assimilation" is therefore not actually about the removal of "cultural difference": A more complicated process is at work here.

Central to this process, Sakai argues, is the way in which the state constantly transforms the immeasurable, protean, and infinitely complex substance of "cultural difference" into a taxonomy of clearly bounded categories, usually identified with notions of "race," "ethnicity," or "nationality." Once they have been placed in this taxonomy, however much individuals may become "like" other members of society, they still continue to be seen as different. Thus Jews in prewar Germany or people of Korean descent in Japan have been discriminated against, not because they dress, act, or think in an unusual way, but because they have been placed in a particular position in the nation's taxonomy of difference (Sakai 1996b, 42). The function of this taxonomy is not primarily to assimilate the "foreign" but, rather, to create an illusion of community and homogeneity among the majority of the state's citizens—to feed the dream of "sameness" which the state requires to mobilize and motivate its population. Sakai emphasizes that this dream may exist not only in states like postwar Japan, where national identity has been identified with ethnic homogeneity, but also in self-consciously multicultural societies like Australia, Canada, and the United States. Here, although the boundaries of "nation" and "race" no longer coincide, the same taxonomy of difference survives and is often used to replicate historical inequalities between the so-called ethnic groups which make up the nation's social mix (Sakai 1996b, 45–48).

These critiques help point to some of the central problems of civilization theory in contemporary Japan. The first is what we might call the paradox of post-Eurocentrism. Attempts to extract from "Japanese civilization" a solution to the problems created by the modern Western world view seem to rest on a fundamental contradiction. The notion of "the West" as a coherent entity is itself profoundly "Western" (in the sense in which Ueyama, Kawakatsu, and others use the word). The dualism between "West" and "East" emerged from a world view which was integrally related to the structure of nineteenth-century European thought, and the idea of enduring, integrated national "cultures" (discussed in Chapter 4) grew from attempts to apply the models of classical Western science to the study of societies.

My point is not, of course, that Japanese scholars *should* be capable of creating a totally "indigenous" vision of the world. In an age when Maoist slogans have become the lyrics of karaoke performances and Uzbeks dance to the music of Dire Straits, the search for such radical indigeneity is surely illusory. But the very impossibility of a "Japanese world view," untouched by the influence of imported paradigms, ought to encourage reflection about the complex relationship between worldwide and local patterns of behavior and belief.

Ideas of "civilization" and "culture" emerged with the creation of a global system and are inextricably related to struggles for power within that system. In global society, the creation of group identity—a sense of "we" and "them"—does not occur in isolation, but relies on common frameworks for classifying difference: frameworks which are powerful precisely because they are shared with the very groups from which "we" wish to differentiate ourselves. Any attempt to define national identity in the global system therefore inevitably involves an interweaving of internationally accepted taxonomies of difference (concepts like "nation" or "ethnic group") with local traditions which, on the one hand, are often mobilized in opposition to globalization but, on the other, are themselves often recast into global taxonomies.

In the twentieth century, many different taxonomies of difference have existed simultaneously: notions of "nation," "race," "culture," "civilization," "local community," etc. as well as notions such as "social class," "gender," "religion," and "occupational group." Government officials, academics, journalists, and others who argue over questions of identity have some leeway to choose the classificatory framework which best suits their social purposes. At the same time, complex societies like Japan's (as seen in Chapter 3) inherit a wide variety of intellectual traditions, which are constantly reinterpreted in the light of changing knowledge and circumstance. Global taxonomies and local traditions interact. The choice of a particular framework for classifying identity helps to determine which of the enormous range of local traditions will be seen as defining "our" identity. Conversely, the desire to highlight a particular local tradition may help to determine whether "we" are defined as the people of a particular region, the members of a race, the bearers of a civilization, or whatever. The main aim of Chapter 8 will be to trace this interweaving of global and local ideas in shifting twentieth-century images of Japanese identity and to consider the way in which changes in the structure of the world order may have influenced ideas about the boundaries of that identity and about the nature of "Japanese tradition."

Both Nishikawa and Sakai, however, are surely right to argue that, if "culture" implies shared patterns of behavior, experience, and knowledge, then every modern nation contains many "cultural groups." Every individual, moreover, participates in a multiplicity of groups. Even at the level of the individual, therefore, human identity is surely not a simple, single thing constructed only in relation to a single "culture" or "civilization," but something which has many dimensions linking each individual to gender, age, family, occupational groups, and ethnos. Increasingly, the identity groups in which an individual participates also cross national boundaries, as ideas, fashions, and values flow through the intricate worldwide networks of modern information systems. These dimensions of identity, besides, do not stack neatly inside one another like Russian matrioshka dolls, but (even in the most integrated societies) overlap and jostle against one another, so that the sense of self is created and recreated out of a constant struggle to draw the many dimensions of identity together in actions of everyday life. As a result, culture is (to borrow a rather unattractive word from Laclau and Mouffe) "unsutured": Instead of being a neatly sewn-up whole, it is an always incomplete effort to pull together the jagged edges of conflicting definitions of identity (see Laclau and Mouffe 1985; also Barrett 1991, chap. 4).

In Chapter 9 we return to some of these issues in more detail. It is important to emphasize, however, that these questions of identity are also issues of power. Ideas such as "culture," "race," and "civilization" are not simply different ways of defining identity: They also carry different implicit notions of power relationships between social groups. The idea of "civilization" in the singular was a notion by which the European colonizing powers sought to justify their global expansion: As a study of the Eurocentric world view puts it, "if there is one concept which has a privileged place in the ethnocentric images in which Western peoples see themselves in relation to others, it is the concept of civilization" (Preiswerk and Perrot 1978, 61). The idea of civilization, in other words, elevated particular European traditions to the status of universal standards marking the advance of human progress. Recent comparative studies of civilization try to shrug off this ethnocentric legacy by speaking of "civilizations" in the plural. But because it still embodies a vision of time in which all societies pass through the same series of civilizational "revolutions," though at differing speeds and in differing ways, comparative civilization theory still, almost inevitably, incorporates a sense of hierarchies of civilizational advance.

The Japanese civilization theories which we looked at in this chapter also focus almost entirely (as did earlier *Nihonjinron* writings) on the relationship between "Western" and "Japanese" civilization and have remarkably little to say about the ways in which other contemporary "civilizations" (China? India? Latin America?) might fit into the picture. How might Africa be represented in Japan's "living museum of cultures"? Like the *Nihonjinron* of the 1960s and 1970s, in other words, they still seem to be caught up in a world view where less dynamic "civilizations" are destined to orbit around the sun of a central, hegemonic, universalizing "civilization." Now, however, rather than accepting Japan's place in the outer orbit of particularism, they increasingly tend to stake Japan's claim to a place in the universal center. To put it another way, contemporary Japanese civilization theory, which often seeks to draw inspiration from the ideas of the Tokugawa period, also (in many cases) contains certain echoes of the Tokugawa ideas examined in Chapter 2: It, too, is concerned with reconstructing an imported image of the world order so that Japan can take its place at the center of that order.

Much of the language of these civilization theories is highly attractive and not surprisingly strikes a responsive chord with many readers.
They tend to define the essence of Japanese culture with values such as
peace, open-mindedness, and environmental responsibility. But in as-
sessing these theories of national identity it is important to look not just
at the characteristics that they attribute to the nation but also at the
power relationships implicit in their taxonomies of difference. The idea
of "Japanese civilization" creates a questionable image of the power of
the nation to homogenize the identities of its citizens and contains
uncomfortable implications about the power of Japan in relation to the
material and intellectual traditions of other parts of the world, particularly of less economically dominant regions. Confronting these problems involves further development of the critiques of culture proposed
by scholars in Japan and elsewhere. The final chapters of this book
outline some possible approaches to this task.

8

Globalization

One of the international best-sellers of the early 1990s was a book by Japanese management consultant Ohmae Kenichi entitled *The Borderless World.* Concluding with a stirring "Declaration of Interdependence," Ohmae's work argues that the contemporary global economy has created a world where human values and tastes are no longer tied to geography or ethnicity: "The better informed people are," he argues, "the more they will want to make their own choices, and the less those choices will coincide with boundary lines drawn years ago on maps" (Ohmae 1990, 230–231).

But go into almost any Japanese bookstore today, and you will find Ohmae's works sharing shelf space with books whose titles suggest a very different message. On one side you might see the works of the prominent Finance Ministry bureaucrat Sakakibara Eisuke: books like his *Beyond Capitalism,* which proposes that Japan has developed a market economy based on quite different principles from those of the West (Sakakibara 1996; see also Sakakibara 1995). Sakakibara's work, in other words, applies an economic approach to those questions of "Japanese civilization" which, as we have seen, have been enthusiastically addressed by a number of prominent scholars in the past few years. On the other side, there may well be copies of *The Asia That Can Say "No,"* a volume written jointly by Malaysian prime minister Mahathir Mohamad and the Japanese nationalist writer Ishihara Shintarō, who argue that Asian societies operate according to a unique set of ethical principles (Mahathir and Ishihara 1994). This is just one of a recent outpouring of Japanese writings on the issues of "Asian values." To add to the complexity, a little farther down the aisle you are likely to find rows of books proclaiming the resurgence of more local identities and values: books which discuss the unique value systems of the indigenous Ainu people of northern Japan or proclaim the distinct identity of Okinawa and (in some cases) call for Okinawan independence from Japan.

As anthropologist Joel Kahn has recently pointed out, there is nothing new about such upsurges of interest in cultural identity. From at least the eighteenth century onward, enlightenment visions of the unity of humankind have been counterpointed by ideas emphasizing the radical diversity of human groups. Kahn suggests, though, that many contemporary debates about cultural identity—and these, of course, are debates which occur not just in Japan but worldwide—have roots which can be traced back specifically to the interwar period of the 1920s and 1930s. Like many other commentators, Kahn reflects on the paradox that present-day notions of cultural distinctiveness and identity should be so influential precisely at a time when the spread of global trade, investment, transport, and communications seems indeed to be creating a "borderless world" in which everywhere is becoming more and more like everywhere else. The same thing, he points out, happened in the interwar years: The worldwide spread of mining and plantation companies, and the expansion of the media and higher education, were accompanied by the rise of nationalism, often expressed in terms of a nostalgia for the disappearing traditions of rural folk culture (Kahn 1995).

These comments are certainly applicable to Japan, where debates about the meaning and nature of "Japanese culture" first began to take shape around the 1890s and reached a crescendo during the 1920s and 1930s. Japan's experience also seems to confirm Kahn's contention that incorporation into the global system and awareness of local cultural identity are parts of the same process, different sides of the same coin. In other words, as the social anthropologist Ulf Hannerz has put it, "there is now a world culture" but that culture is "marked by an organisation of diversity rather than by a replication of uniformity" (Hannerz 1990, 237). In the following pages, I trace the relationship between globalization and identity debates in Japan since the beginning of the twentieth century, and in doing so I hope to shed some light on contentious issues of cultural and ethnic identity in Japan today.

Global Knowledge and the Formatting of Difference

In the course of the nineteenth century, Japan's place in the world was redefined by the creation of a new, Western-dominated world order which subsumed and transformed the older, China-centered East Asian system. This new order was not simply a matter of political power and trade relations: It was also a global system of knowledge. As colonization extended into the Americas, Asia, and Africa, European explorers and scholars confronted a previously unimagined array of biological, geological, linguistic, social, and artistic variety. Their attempts to deal with this overwhelming vision of global diversity and complexity inspired the development of European scientific knowledge and promoted the increasing subdivision and refinement of scholarly specialization. The eighteenth-century French philosopher Antoine-Nicholas de Condorcet was one of the first to point out that ever-expanding human knowledge of the world makes it necessary to create increasingly abstract and generalized sets of rules to handle that knowledge (Condorcet 1933). This process, of course, gave rise to the modern academic disciplines. A second facet to the creation of a global knowledge system, then, was the worldwide export of European systems of organizing human knowledge and behavior. Japan began to be influenced by these new systems of thought during the seventeenth and eighteenth centuries, when aspects of European scientific ideas (including the Copernican system of astronomy) filtered into Japan via the Dutch trading post in Nagasaki; it was only from the middle of the nineteenth century that Japan's elite began to be exposed to the whole range of European scientific, social, political, and legal ideas and institutions.

A recent study by Jan Aart Scholte points out that a key element in the creation of the global system has been the establishment of international "norms" or "regimes": that is, globally accepted standardized forms of knowledge and behavior which provide the essential basis for international communication and interaction. These in turn can be divided into two categories: formal regimes, established by treaties or international organizations, and informal regimes which are essentially matters of practice and convention. Good examples of formal international regimes were the new frameworks of time and space: Greenwich Mean Time, which was accepted as the global norm in 1884, and the metric system or the system of inches, feet, and miles, both of which were adopted by many countries in the last decades of the nineteenth century (Scholte 1993, 68–80; see also Giddens 1987, 257–266).

The subtle but pervasive influence of these regimes is clear if we consider the case of time in Japan. In Japan before the second half of the nineteenth century, time was reckoned by dividing night from day. Most country people, of course, lived by the sun and had no need for clocks. In cities like Edo, however, the beating of a drum or the strik-ing of a temple bell at roughly equal intervals of the night and day marked the progress toward dusk or dawn. For this purpose, each period of night and day was subdivided into six "hours." This naturally meant that the length of an "hour" varied according to whether it was a daytime or a nighttime hour and whether it was summer or winter. When mechanical clocks were first introduced into Japan from Europe in the seventeenth century, Japanese artisans used immense patience and ingenuity to adapt their workings so that they could be adjusted to fit the flexible Japanese system of time. In some cases, for example, a sliding weight was moved up and down the pendulum twice a day to adjust its movement and ensure that the striking of the clock approxi-mated to the public measurement of time. With the coming of large-scale international trade, railways, and telegraph, however, this system rapidly became unsustainable, and the Western system of standard, unvarying hours was adopted in 1873, the year when Japan's first railway was opened (Morris-Suzuki 1994, 84).

The example of Greenwich Mean Time illustrates an important point about international regimes. What they created was not in fact absolute global *uniformity* but an agreed set of rules—a common for-mat—which made coordination between many subregimes possible. The basic rule regarding time, for example, was that hours were the same length everywhere and that time was calculated with reference to a fixed single starting point—Greenwich Mean Time. Once they ac-cepted these basic rules, countries had some latitude to adjust their own particular system to meet local needs. For example, they were free to adopt daylight savings time (a system first introduced by Germany during World War I) and to determine the number of time zones within their own borders. The key process was "formatting"—the creation of a single underlying common framework or set of rules which is used to coordinate local subregimes—and it is this process which continues to provide the *leitmotiv* of globalization to the present day.

Examining the process of formatting helps us to understand the paradoxical fact that the growing incorporation of societies into the global system was accompanied by growing consciousness of local cultural "uniqueness." As Scholte emphasizes, not all global regimes were imposed by international treaty. Many were implicit taxonomies of knowledge voluntarily adopted by governments as part of their poli-cies of modernization. Consider, for example, the case of scientific research. The formation of a global knowledge system involved the worldwide spread of a common set of basic ideas about scientific research: It was to be performed by specialist scientists in laboratories; it involved the establishment of hypotheses, the testing of hypotheses through controlled experiments, and the reporting of the results of experiments in written papers following a prescribed pattern. When the Japanese government began to create national research laboratories in the second half of the nineteenth century, it naturally followed this pattern, both because this appeared to open the path to technological success and industrial might and because it enabled Japan to participate in an international community of scientific ideas.

At the same time, though, Japanese scientific research did not turn out to be exactly the same as British or American scientific research. In the early stages, while the framework of research—the laboratory benches, the test tubes, the scientific formulae, the published papers— followed an increasingly global format, the content was often local. In other words, much scientific research in late nineteenth-century Japan involved recasting the existing technical traditions of lacquer-making, silk production, ceramics manufacture, and so on into the global language of modern science. Scientific formulae were worked out for glazes, lacquers, and dyestuffs which (in many cases) had been used for centuries, and experiments were run to compare the properties and effectiveness of various traditional techniques. Local content, in other words, was reformatted by being written into the globally standardized frame of modern science. This in turn provided the basis for incremental improvement of traditional techniques and ultimately for patentable innovations. Perhaps the most famous example of this process was the synthesizing of monosodium glutamate (MSG), achieved in 1908 by the Japanese scientist Ikeda Kikunae, who based his research on the chemical analysis of traditional Japanese forms of food flavoring using kombu seaweed (an achievement for which not everyone would thank him) (Yuasa 1961, 216–218).

The distinction between the *global format* of methods, theories, and taxonomies of knowledge (defined almost entirely in the West) and *local content* was an important one for early Japanese scientific researchers. As relative newcomers to the world of global science, with limited resources and little familiarity with scientific processes, Japanese scientists had at first few prospects of playing an important role in defining the global formats of scientific knowledge. But in certain areas they had great opportunities to gather local empirical information, which, reassessed in the light of imported scientific theories, could be used to refine and expand the store of global knowledge. Some of the earliest Japanese successes came in the fields of geology and seismology. Japan's volatile geological environment, with its frequent earthquakes and volcanic eruptions, made it the ideal place to study the most violent and unpredictable of geological phenomena, and by the 1920s Japanese researchers had been able to combine imported theories with local fieldwork to produce findings which were acknowledged worldwide.

By this time, however, Japanese scholars were beginning not simply to claim a place in the global scientific community but also to comment on the "unique" or "distinctive" characteristics of Japanese science itself. Often these comments were disparaging. Numerous newspaper and magazine articles deplored the backward state of Japanese science, the reliance on imported theory and the lack of indigenous creativity. But some writers saw things in a different light. As early as 1894, for example, the geographer and ardent nationalist Shiga Shigetaka was arguing that the Japanese environment, with its typhoons, volcanoes, and earthquakes, had produced a special relationship between humans and nature: a relationship evident not only in Japanese art and poetry but also in the Japanese approach to the natural sciences (Shiga 1968, 231–234).

During the interwar period, a number of intellectuals debated the specifically national qualities of Japanese research. The philosopher of science and technology Saigusa Hiroto, for example, argued that the fundamental progress of human knowledge was universal, but that knowledge of nature was structured somewhat differently in different cultural environments. Since the Renaissance, he suggested, European thought had been characterized by a desire to analyze the inner workings of things, whereas Japanese thought had focused more on an appreciation of the outer appearance of natural forms. This explained the relatively slow progress of modern scientific theorizing in Japan (Saigusa 1978b, 259–264). On the other hand, Saigusa also suggested that Japanese culture was characterized by diligence, manual skill, and a fundamental curiosity about the world, which had made it relatively easy for Japan to absorb Western scientific ideas (Saigusa 1978b, 168–171). The modern era, Saigusa suggested, was characterized by the spread of a single global model of scientific rationality, but the cultural heritage of each country helped to determine the particular course of scientific and technological modernization within its frontiers.

The example of scientific research can help us to understand why the spread of global knowledge formats was accompanied by a growing sense of national distinctiveness. The very fact that Japan's modern research laboratories were based on the same underlying rules of knowledge and behavior as Western laboratories made it all the *easier* to spot the differences between Japanese and (say) German or American systems of research. As Japanese scientists participated in international conferences and visited foreign universities and laboratories, they could readily make comparisons with their home institutions and draw conclusions about international differences in the scale and organization of research, the quality of the equipment, the fields of strength and weakness, and the training and intellectual orientation of scientists. Such comparisons are in many ways more difficult to make where there is no common ground about the underlying norms for studying natural phenomena. This function of formatting in highlighting difference is similar to the process that occurs when we look at symbols like the national flag: The fact that all flags follow the same basic format (they are rectangular and patterned with a simple, bold design usually in two or three contrasting colors) is precisely what makes it easy instantly to distinguish one flag from another.

The same basic pattern continues to the present: The more global formats of knowledge (schools, universities, bureaucracies, scientific papers, corporate management systems, newspapers, film, television programs, advertising, computer games) penetrate all facets of everyday life, the more people use differences in local content as a basis for defining distinct national, regional, or ethnic identities.

Formatting the Colonial State

It is probably no coincidence, therefore, that increasingly impassioned debates about the nature of Japanese ethnic and cultural identity began to take shape around the 1890s. The last decade of the nineteenth century was a time when new social and political institutions, based on global models, were beginning to have a profound impact on Japanese society. Japan's first parliament opened in 1890, though at this stage it was still based on a very limited franchise. The bureaucracy, which had initially consisted of a tiny elite drawn mainly from the ranks of the ex-samurai, grew rapidly as the role of government expanded. Between 1902 and 1923, the administrative ranks of the public service swelled from around 20,000 to over 160,000 people. The large Japanese corporations which came to be known as *zaibatsu* also established their hierarchical managerial structures between the 1890s and the 1920s, and the need for managerial and administrative skills stimulated the expansion of an educated urban middle class.

This is turn encouraged the expansion of the media, which served an increasingly literate population. By the 1890s, a number of major national newspapers had been established, and these were beginning to create links with international news agencies such as Reuters. Periodicals catering to the urban middle classes flourished from the late 1880s onward, with establishment of monthly or quarterly magazines like *Kokumin no tomo* (1887), *Nihonjin* (1888), and *Chūō Kōron* (1899), and by the 1920s several of the major newspapers were also beginning to publish weekly newsmagazines (Shishido 1995).

Until about the 1890s, while there had been much concern with questions of Westernization, modernization, and the pursuit of "civilization," issues of national identity had attracted little attention. From the end of the 1880s onward, however, a steady stream of studies attempted to locate and define the distinctive essence of "Japaneseness": among them Shiga Shigetaka's *Nihon fūkei ron* (Theory of the Japanese Landscape, 1894), Nitobe Inazo's *Bushido* (1900), and Haga Yaichi's *Kokuminsei jūron* (Ten Theses on National Character, 1908). In outlining the course of these debates, though, it is important to bear in mind two significant features of the nature of Japan's incorporation into the global knowledge system from the 1890s to the interwar years.

The first feature was the uneven impact of global knowledge regimes on Japanese society. The intellectual framework imposed by university education, scientific research, managerial hierarchies, and the national media affected only fairly restricted spheres of everyday life—particularly the public lives of the urban middle classes. Of course, other aspects of Japan's incorporation into the global system had more far-reaching effects. The new regimes of time and space, the disciplines of primary education, and the knowledge formats of local newspapers, for example, gradually and subtly permeated the lives even of farm families in remote villages. All the same, uneven exposure to the global regimes of the modern system created regional and social differences which were remarked upon by many contemporaries.

In trying to define a "uniquely Japanese" identity, therefore, many Japanese intellectuals followed a pattern rather like the pattern of scientific research discussed above. In other words, they drew the content of their analysis from those areas of local everyday life which had not been greatly affected by globalization and then recast that content into the framework of globalized knowledge formats: newspaper articles, philosophical or ethnographic texts, and so on. The U.S. scholar Marilyn Ivy provides an excellent illustration of this in her discussion of Yanagita Kunio's classic work *Tōno monogatari* (The Tales of Tono, 1910) (Yanagita 1963d). Perhaps the most famous of Yanagita's early writings, *The Tales of Tono* had an immense influence on twentieth-century debates about Japanese culture. The book purports to be a straightforward record of folktales, many of them concerning the supernatural, told by a storyteller in a remote rural area of northern Japan. The stories were widely seen by contemporary readers as embodying the essence of a traditional Japanese culture which was rapidly being eroded by the march of modernity. But, in fact, as Ivy emphasizes, the *Tales* were not actually a verbatim record of "tradition," but were carefully rewritten by Yanagita to express his vision of traditional Japan to the largely urban and middle-class readership who were to consume this best-seller (Ivy 1995). Yanagita's writing reflects his knowledge of Western ethnography and of modern literary debates and recasts the raw material of Japanese oral tradition into frameworks influenced by this intellectual background, so producing a modern vision of a distinctive traditional Japanese identity.

The second important feature of the early twentieth-century global system is that it was a system based on the colonial nation-state. When we looked at Jan Aart Scholte's notion of international regimes, we saw that these regimes did not create total global uniformity. Instead, they laid down a set of ground rules which made it possible to coordinate many slightly differing subregimes (educational systems, transport networks, scientific research systems, etc.) whose shape was usually determined by, and within the framework of, the nation-state.

This national system of subregimes, however, was complicated during the first half of the twentieth century by the fact that many nation-states, including Japan, were also colonial powers. Japan, indeed, began to create a colonial empire within decades of the start of the country's own fully fledged incorporation into the global system. Its national subregimes, therefore, were not simply molded to fit the formats of the global order but also exported, with certain modifications, to the colonies. Like other colonial systems the Japanese empire embodied essentially a two-tier structure. The institutions of the "Japan proper"—*Naichi*—provided the basic model for the colonies, but were adapted in various ways to maintain the control of the colonizer over the colonized. In general, colonial policy was at once highly assimilationist and highly discriminatory. Indeed, assimilation and discrimination were opposite sides of the same coin: In order to turn the often reluctant colonial subjects into "Japanese" it was necessary for the state to intervene in private lives and to restrict individual rights far more comprehensively in the colonies than it did in "Japan proper."

This dual regime helps explain some of the ambiguities which are obvious in interwar debates about Japanese identity. Throughout the early twentieth century, there was an essential ambivalence arising from the urge of Japanese intellectuals, on the one hand, to define Japan's *uniqueness,* as the only Asian great power, and, on the other, to identify the international *commonalities* which justified Japan's claim to impose its regimes on others and to create an empire in Asia. One approach to this dilemma was an appeal to ethnic history. As seen in Chapter 5, the Japanese ethnos (*minzoku*) was defined, on the one hand, as possessing distinct national characteristics. But, on the other, it was often pointed out that the Japanese were an ethnically mixed people: the product of many waves of migration from China, Siberia, Korea, the South Pacific, and elsewhere. This latter emphasis on the multicultural origins of the Japanese enabled proponents of Japanese expansionism to argue that Japan had successfully assimilated many ethnic groups in the past and would have little difficulty assimilating its new colonial subjects in the future.

An alternative solution to the problem was to define Japan's position in the world order not in terms of a distinct "Japanese" identity, but in terms of an "Asian" or "Oriental" identity. Ever since 1902, when the philosopher and art historian Okakura Tenshin opened a famous essay with the sentence "Asia is one," certain Japanese intellectuals had attempted to define Japan in terms of a wider Asian culture (Okakura 1963, 67). In the early stages, this generally involved contrasting Western materialism with Asian aesthetics and spirituality. By the 1930s and early 1940s, however, a growing number of writers were also attempting to define a distinctive "Asian mode of thought" which could be contrasted with the "Western mode of thought."

The scholar of Buddhism Takakusu Junjirō, for example, defined the essential division as being between Western "logic" or "reasoning" (*suirisei*), on the one hand, and Asian "immediacy" or "direct perception" (*chokkansei*), on the other. While Western scientific and technological success had been based on logical analysis of phenomena, he argued, Eastern culture was based on a direct, unmediated appreciation of reality in which all sense of subject and object disappeared, rather as it does in Zen meditation (Takakusu 1941). This echoes a distinction between "East" and "West" which can be found in many philosophical writings of the late 1930s and early 1940s.

Defining Japan's culture as intrinsically "Asian," however, did not in itself make sense of Japan's increasingly expansionist role in Asia. To do this, it was necessary to define Japan as a kind of "super-Asia"—the distilled essence of Asia—which therefore had a special cultural and political destiny in the region. Thus Takakusu wrote, "The greatest creation of India is Buddhism; but this Buddhism has been more completely developed in Japan than in India or China. The greatest product of China is Confucianism; but this Confucianism has been more fully studied and preserved in Japan than in China or Korea" (ibid., 27). Japan, he went on, also has its own special form of "direct perception" embodied in the native beliefs of Shintō. Besides, Japan has been successful in combining the best of Asian tradition with the more recently imported fruits of Western "logic." The implication was that Japanese culture embodied a uniquely advanced form of the essence of Asian culture and that this gave Japan a special position in Asia: a position epitomized in the person of the emperor, who was living incarnation of the properties of "direct perception" (ibid., 49).

Globalization and Identity in Postwar Japan

The decades which followed Japan's defeat in the Pacific War can be seen as a second phase of globalization, in which internationally standardized economic, political, technological, and media regimes made new inroads into the structures of everyday life. But, once again, this process was accompanied by a new wave of interest in analyzing and defining national identity. The globalization of the 1950s and 1960s differed from interwar trends in several key respects. During the occupation period from 1945 to 1952, many of the central institutions of Japanese society were reshaped. Universal suffrage was introduced, the power of the parliament enhanced, the constitution rewritten, farmland redistributed, and the education system overhauled.

Because of these reforms, and the high economic growth which followed, the standardized norms of the global order penetrated the daily life of most Japanese people far more deeply than they had done in the first half of the twentieth century. As the percentage of the workforce employed in farming fell from around 45 percent in 1950 to about 17 percent in 1970, a growing section of the population was exposed to the daily routines of factory labor or office work. Democratization and shifts in the employment structure encouraged an enormous growth in secondary and tertiary education: By 1970 about 80 percent of students were completing high school and almost 1.5 million were attending college or university.

Meanwhile, in Japan as in other industrialized countries, the age of mass consumption was both transforming and standardizing many aspects of daily life. More than 95 percent of Japanese households had a television by the end of the 1960s, and viewers were being exposed to a mixture of U.S. serials and Japanese dramas and game shows, loosely based upon U.S. models. The rapid diffusion of household consumer goods did not wholly "Westernize" Japanese family life, but resulted in a new pattern which blended global and local elements. The apartment blocks which sprouted up all over Japan's expanding cities embodied an internationally standardized frame, containing and structuring an inner content made up of a mix of old and new: refrigerators and rice cookers, televisions and tatami matting.

It was against this background that postwar images of Japanese uniqueness were developed by Ishida Eiichirō and other theorists of *Nihonjinron*. Here, I briefly sketch some characteristics shared by many of these postwar identity debates and distinguish them from the debates of the interwar period. Within the overarching divide of the Cold War, the global order of the 1950s and 1960s was, above all, the golden age of the nation-state. Japan had now lost its colonial empire, and throughout Asia former colonies had acquired national independence. Like other countries, Japan participated in the formal international organizations of the postwar order (the United Nations, the International Labour Organisation, the Organization for Economic Cooperation and Development, etc.) as a nation-state, usually via official government delegations. The expanding corporate and educational institutions of the 1950s and 1960s and the new media (such as television) also generally operated on a national basis. The subregimes of the global system, in other words, were largely national, and this appears to be reflected in the strongly national focus of Japanese identity debates in the postwar decades.

Shortly after the war, the prominent political theorist Maruyama Masao had suggested that Japan's defeat might produce a "decomposition" of national consciousness, so that individuals would return to the old, premodern ways of identifying themselves primarily with their village or local region (see Maruyama 1963, 150). But this prophecy was not to be fulfilled; instead, more than ever identity became an issue debated in national terms. Besides, though prehistorians continued to research the diverse origins of the Japanese people, notions of racial origins and ethnic diversity largely disappeared from the wider public debates about contemporary "Japaneseness," to be replaced by the popular assumption that the Japanese were (in the notorious words of former Prime Minister Yasuhiro Nakasone) an "ethnically homogeneous people" (*tan'itsu minzoku*).

During the 1950s, 1960s, and early 1970s, there were also relatively few attempts to analyze Japan's cultural or social peculiarities in terms of an overarching Asian identity. Rather, Japan tended to be seen as an entity unto itself: an approach embodied most notably in the outpouring of *Nihonjinron*. These theories, as we have seen, focused on the contrast between Japan and "the West," and in the relatively few cases where comparisons with other Asian societies were invoked (as in Nakane Chie's *Japanese Society*) this was done mainly to emphasize the cultural gulf, not just between Japan and the West, but also between Japan and the rest of Asia (Nakane 1970).

As issues of identity became more firmly enclosed within national boundaries, their content too underwent certain subtle shifts. While postwar writings drew on many of the images of uniqueness developed during the first half of the century, they used these images in new ways. With urbanization and the rapid transformation of rural life, ethnographic attempts to seek out and describe the rural roots of Japanese "tradition" in folklore or village festivals became less significant. Instead, many postwar writers looked for the essence of Japanese tradition behind the apparently globalized facades of institutions like the factory, the bureaucracy, and corporate management hierarchy. The argument was that, although Japan had adopted Western institutional formats, the inner workings of these organizations were shaped by older indigenous forms of behavior inherited from the traditional family and rural village. "Tradition" was now doubly enframed: Indigenous values and human relationship were seen as having been transposed into the framework of the modern corporate organization, which in turn was analyzed and described within the standardized framework of the sociological thesis or management textbook. Different writers approached the issue from different angles: Some emphasized the unique psychology of the Japanese; others focused on the survival of social behavior; still others stressed the incorporation of traditional values into Japan's modern management techniques: A key emphasis throughout, however, was on the relationship between the individual and the group within the various corporate structures comprising modern Japanese society.

Nihonjinron tended to define Japanese identity in positive terms, identifying the unique features of Japanese systems with social harmony and successful economic development. But it is important to emphasize that many critical scholars of postwar Japan also framed their theories within broadly similar parameters. Writers like Maruyama Masao presented a far more complex and nuanced picture of Japanese society than did the theorists of *Nihonjinron.* They saw national culture not as innate and unchanging, but as the product of specific national histories, and they were deeply aware of the costs to freedom and individual responsibility implicit in the apparent harmony of Japanese group structures. But they, too, responding to the circumstances of their time, perceived matters largely in terms of the relationship between national society and a global order framed (by and large) by Western norms. They therefore often focused upon the national peculiarities of Japan and saw those peculiarities above all in terms of the relationship between the individual and the group and of the survival of distinctive national patterns of behavior within the structure of modern and apparently universal social institutions (the corporation, the education system, the institutions of political democracy, etc.).

Globalization and Identity in the Age of Signs

On 1 January 1994, the *Asahi Shimbun* (one of Japan's leading national newspapers) greeted the new year with a special supplement entitled "Multinational Japan" (*Takokuseki Nippon*). The supplement dealt with the rapid growth of immigration, which, it said, had turned the central Tokyo entertainment district of Shinjuku into "the cross-roads of Asia." By the mid-1990s, Japan had over one million officially registered foreign residents, not including an estimated 300,000 "illegal" foreign workers—many from Southeast Asia, Korea, Iran, and the Indian subcontinent—employed without work permits or residents' rights (Tanaka 1995, 198–200). But the growing presence of foreigners, and particularly of the "visibly foreign," in Japanese society is only part of the emergence of multinational Japan or, in other words, of the third wave of Japan's twentieth-century globalization.

The influx of immigrants coincided with, and was encouraged by, an outflow of Japanese capital to the Asian region and beyond. Between 1977 and 1994, while U.S. direct investment in Asia increased approximately eightfold (from just under $6 billion to around $46 billion) Japanese investment in the region increased more than twelvefold (from a similar starting point to over $74 billion) (Hatch and Yamamura 1996, 5–6). This global spread of Japanese capital brought with it not only a growing range of Japanese brand-named goods, but also less visible accompaniments. By the second half of the 1980s, the distinctive Japanese management structures and practices celebrated by writers of *Nihonjinron* were being exported to many other parts of the globe, creating a worldwide process which Raphael Kaplinsky has termed "Easternisation" (Kaplinsky 1994).

Japan's cultural influence makes itself felt around the world in other ways too. Japanese companies are investing not just in foreign manufacturing, but also in the overseas production of music, film, and television, as indicated, for example, by Sony's tie-up with the U.S. film giant Columbia Pictures and the CBS network and by the growing role of the Japanese national broadcasting company NHK in Thailand (Lewis 1994). Japanese cartoons, both on television and in comic-book form, are widely distributed throughout Southeast Asia, and karaoke is now, of course, almost universal. By the end of 1992, the Japanese computer game manufacturer Nintendo had sold some 60 million of its game machines worldwide, and Japanese-designed computer games like "Mario Brothers" formed part of the collective fantasies of a whole worldwide generation of children.

But, in this age of information technology, the flows of influence are complex and intersecting. While Japan exports cartoon films, computer games, and broadcasting technology, it is also on the receiving end of new information systems devised and developed abroad. In the past few years, the most important of these has been the Internet. There were estimated to be around 4 to 5 million users of the Internet in Japan in 1995, and the number has grown exponentially since then. Yet Internet services remain dominated by English-speaking countries, particularly the United States, and many Japanese observers see the rapid worldwide diffusion of the net as a sign of the reassertion of U.S. cultural and economic dominance in the last decade of the twentieth century (Nishi 1995, 45–48). Another area of concern has been the attempt by Australian-born media entrepreneur Rupert Murdoch to obtain a major stake in Japanese satellite television: an attempt which provoked headlines announcing (with echoes of Pacific War terminology) "the decisive media battle for the Japanese mainland" (see *Forbes Japan,* December 1996, 112–113).

Despite these fears, one of the unmistakable characteristics of the new wave of globalization is the multinational origin of its underlying codes and norms. While the global regimes of the early twentieth century were based largely on Western norms, the new regimes of transnational corporate management and global information flows involve (as Kaplinsky suggests) not just a one way process of "Westernization" but more complex and multidirectional negotiation of global formats.

A second feature of contemporary globalization is its pervasiveness. It affects not just the public sphere of the workplace but the most intimate corners of daily life. Leisure is structured around the global formats of video, computer games, and package tourism. Advertising and international fashion shape the clothes we wear, the food we eat, and the way we keep our bodies in shape in health clubs and gyms. An important part of this process, in fact, seems to be an erosion of the boundaries which once separated the public and private spheres of life. Information technology makes it easier for employees to do part of their work at home, while the new and increasingly intrusive techniques of corporate management (many of them pioneered by Japanese companies) make the physical fitness and human relationships of workers an integral part of company life.

The result is a situation which has been highlighted by a number of analysts of contemporary society, among them the prominent Japanese sociologist Yamanouchi Yasushi (Yamanouchi 1996b; see also Melucci 1989; Lash and Urry 1994). The world economy today needs highly educated workers capable of processing information, making independent judgments and reflecting upon their own position in the social system. But, at the same time, the implicit rules of corporate hierarchies, the format of information systems like satellite TV or computer networks, and the protocols of international organizations create increasingly standardized frameworks which implicitly restrict and channel human action and ideas. The result is that people find their lives constrained less by the oppressive power of identifiable human authorities than by anonymous codes which seem to be built into the very systems within which we live.

As in earlier waves of globalization, the creation of internationally standardized norms or regimes does not simply produce worldwide uniformity but, rather, creates a framework in which various sub-regimes can be coordinated and compared. The key characteristic of the contemporary wave, though, is that its subregimes are no longer entirely, or even mainly, built around the nation-state. It is true that nation-states continue to maintain tight control over aspects of the global order, such as the international migration of people, but other aspects follow a quite different geographic logic. Satellite television, for example, involves a standardized format of programming which allows for local variations in content. The local variations, though, are not normally *national,* but are based on larger geographical "foot-prints": East Asia in the case of the Hong Kong–based Star TV or of the Japanese satellite stations BS1 and BS2; the Indian subcontinent in the case of Zee TV.

At the same time, the end of the Cold War and the liberalization of economic regulations have created scope for other regional groupings which cross national boundaries. At one end of the Japanese archipel-ago, for example, the southernmost prefecture of Okinawa has begun to recreate those trading links which, in the sixteenth century, connected the Ryūkyū Kingdom to the Chinese province of Fujian and to the Southeast Asian countries beyond. A growing number of medium-sized Okinawan companies are developing complex ties with their neighbors to the south—for example, importing partially finished goods from Fu-jian or Taiwan for final processing in Okinawa—and proposals have been put forward for the creation of an "Okinawa-Fujian Economic Zone" (Yoshikawa and Ogata 1996). At the opposite end of the coun-try, the disappearance of Cold War tensions has created scope for the creation of new links between the island Hokkaidō and its northern neighbor, the Russian province of Sakhalin. The Hokkaidō local government has established its own representative office in the provincial capital of Yuzhno-Sakhalinsk, and many of the forty or so Japanese companies which have invested in Sakhalin are based on Hokkaidō. While national negotiations over the disputed territory of the Kurile Islands remain unresolved, at a local level, cross-border links are steadily developing through trade, investment, and educational exchanges, all of which contribute to a process which has been described as the perforation of national sovereignty (Duchacek et al. 1988). Many of the subregimes of the contemporary system, however, do not simply cross international frontiers: They are no longer grounded in geographical space at all. The Internet, for example, links communities that are connected by social status (mostly young, professional, and male) and shared beliefs or interests, rather than by the country or region where they live. (Surveys suggest that 73 percent of all Japanese Internet users are in their twenties or thirties, and 96 percent are male) (Nihon Intānetto Kyōkai 1996).

It is perhaps predictable, then, that this latest wave of globalization should have been accompanied by a new upsurge of identity debates in Japan; and predictable, too, that these debates should no longer be played out on a purely national stage. Now images of national, supernational, and subnational identity increasingly coexist and jostle against one another. At one level, the nature of the new wave of globalization helps to explain the shift from theories about "Japanese culture" to theories of "Japanese civilization." The images of Japan presented in books like Sakakibara's, and in the comparative civilization theories discussed in Chapter 7, echo familiar themes: the special Japanese relationship between humans and nature; the Japanese tradition of absorbing and assimilating foreign influences; the unique structure of interaction between individual and group. By replacing the word "culture" with the word "civilization," however, these works imply that the distinctive features of Japanese society are no longer merely national issues, but offer a pattern for others to follow, just as the patterns of Egyptian, Greek, or Roman civilization once shaped the development of wide realms of world history.

For many, however, these civilizations no longer can be seen in national terms, but must be understood as part of a wider Asian system of values. Indeed, it is almost startling to observe the ease with which the "uniquely Japanese" values of the 1960s and 1970s have become the "Asian values" of the 1990s. This is perhaps most strikingly evident in the writings of the novelist-turned-nationalist politician Ishihara Shintarō, where the "uniquely Japanese" diligence, self-sacrifice, and moral restraint of *The Japan That Can Say "No"* (coauthored by Ishihara and Morita Akio) are effortlessly transformed into the distinctively Asian values of diligence, self-sacrifice, and moral restraint of *The Asia That Can Say "No"* (1994, coauthored by Ishihara and Malaysian prime minister Mahathir Mohamad) (Mahathir and Ishihara 1994, 128–165). What is also striking about these writings, however, is their extremely generalized, fleeting, and brief characterizations of a common "Asian culture." Where prewar Japanese Asianism focused on aesthetics and philosophy, trying to define a distinctly Asian mode of thought, contemporary "Asianism" tends to content itself with an amalgam of generalized comments about work practices, group structures, and political ideals. In fact, its descriptions of the failures of "Western" modernity are often much longer, more detailed, and more vivid than its rather hazy outlines of an Asian alternative. In many new Asianist writings Asia itself appears less as a clearly defined reality than as the goal of an inchoate longing which combines nostalgia for lost values and traditions with the dream of a yet-undefined alternative model of modernity (for example, Ogura 1993; for a good discussion of this, see McCormack 1996). As Japanese critics have pointed out, interest in "Asian values" is undoubtedly connected to the rise of a mobile Asian middle class, whose multinational networks increasingly bring together managers and technicians from Japan, Taiwan, Korea, and the Southeast Asian newly industrialized countries (Nakajima et al. 1995). The notion of "Asian values" represents one way in which sections of this middle class attempt to carve out a distinct identity for themselves amid the pressures of U.S. and European competition, on the one hand, and domestic demands for the redistribution of wealth and power, on the other.

Even more striking than a revived interest in an "Asian identity," however, is the recent emergence within Japan of subnational and regional identities. The most obvious case is Okinawa. At one level, the issue in Okinawa is the presence of U.S. military bases. But the evolution of the Okinawan issue since 1995 indicates that other deep-seated issues are also at work here.

The history of Okinawa during the twentieth century has ensured that a distinctive Okinawan identity, rather than disappearing into the common sense of Japanese nationhood, has survived and been reinterpreted by successive generations. As seen earlier, many members of the Okinawan social elite in the Meiji period were articulate advocates of cultural assimilation. Yet, despite the presence of a strongly assimilationist education system, social differences between the archipelago and other parts of Japan survived. In the interwar years Okinawa's cash-crop economy (based on sugar production) suffered particularly severely from the world recession, and large numbers of islanders emigrated, many of them going to seek their fortunes in South America (Onga 1996, 127).

In the closing stages of the Pacific War, Okinawa became the only part of Japan to experience the full force of an Allied land and sea invasion, and its population suffered horrific casualties: About one in four Okinawans died in the war. Then, as a result of the postwar settlement, the archipelago was separated from Japan and placed under direct U.S. military control, a situation which lasted until 1972. As one of the most important U.S. military bases in the Pacific, Okinawa experienced all the social disruptions which beset militarized economies. New urban centers, clustered around the U.S. bases, sprang up almost overnight. After unsuccessful attempts to lease land for military purposes, the United States resorted to compulsory land acquisition, backed up with the full force of their massive armed presence. At the same time, Japanese assimilation policies of the past were replaced by often heavy-handed efforts by the U.S. authorities to persuade "Ryukyuans" (as they were now called) that they were *not* part of Japan (Rabson 1996). Citizens' protests over the scale and nature of the U.S. military presence on the islands were frequent and intensified during the late 1960s, when Okinawa became a major base for U.S. military operations in Vietnam. At this stage, however, most demonstrations against U.S. bases were linked to demands that Okinawa be returned to Japan. The rhetoric of these protests, therefore, rejected U.S. attempts to impose a separate identity, emphasizing the "Japaneseness" of Okinawans and their desire to be reunited with the "mainland" (*hondo*). Reunification with Japan, it was felt, would lead to the gradual demilitarization of Okinawa, the creation of a more balanced civilian economy, and relief from the incessant pressures of imported goods, fashions, music, and ideas.

In the twenty-five years since the return of Okinawa to Japan, however, these hopes have been dashed. U.S. bases continue to dominate the islands, and many of the benefits of nonmilitary economic growth are seen as having flowed to large firms from the "mainland." A younger generation of Okinawan activists has increasingly sought to revitalize their region's own distinct artistic traditions, and many have come to define themselves primarily as *Uchinanchu* (Okinawans) and only secondarily as "Japanese" (Nakandakari 1996, 97). Okinawa in this sense became the site for an early and particularly dramatic manifestation of a revival of "local consciousness" which has recently started to become evident in many other regions of Japan. During the 1990s, therefore, opposition to the U.S. presence in Okinawa has quickly expanded into protests about the prefecture's marginalized position in the Japanese state, and even into calls for Okinawan independence.

Another less dramatic, but still significant, resurgence of subnational identity is evident in the indigenous Ainu community of northern Japan. As seen in Chapter 1, the very pressures of assimilationist policies directed against the Ainu community had from the first paradoxically marked out the Ainu as "different" from other Japanese citizens. Deprived of access to the rivers and forests which sustained their lives and compensated only with tiny and infertile plots of farmland, many Ainu moved into poorly paid work in fisheries, timber, or the construction industry. Meanwhile, the spread of compulsory education to Ainu communities became a means of implementing the policy of eradicating Ainu language and customs. From 1901 onward a network of "native schools" (*dojin gakkō*) were set up across Hokkaidō, combining basic education with heavy doses of nationalist "ethics." By the mid-1930s, these schools were felt to have fulfilled their aims so successfully that Ainu children could be merged into the regular school system. The repressive hand of assimilation policy, however, did not entirely destroy a sense of distinct identity. The very fact that they had been incorporated into Japanese society on inherently unequal terms, and that they continued to be subject to discrimination in employment and marriage, encouraged many people of Ainu ancestry to hold onto a sense of distinct history. In many cases this was a quiet form of resistance to assimilation, expressed through the stories passed on from parents to children and in the maintenance of Ainu songs, dances, and celebrations. From the 1920s onward, though, more visible forms of resistance began to appear.

One remarkable example was a petition composed by Kaizawa Hisanosuke, an Ainu villager from Biratori, and addressed to the local government of Hokkaidō, demanding the right for Ainu and other indigenous people of the colony of Karafuto to be represented at a major government-sponsored Congress of Asian Peoples (Ajia Minzoku Taikai) to be held in Nagasaki in 1926. Kaizawa defined himself as "a member of the Japanese ethnic group [*Nihon minzoku*] and a member of the people of the world" but also "as a member of the Ainu tribe [*Ainu zoku*]," and called for the participation of indigenous representatives on the grounds of the equal human rights of all peoples (*Hokkai Taimusu,* 26 July 1926; reprinted in Hokkaidō Utari Kyōkai 1989, 865). Another key figure in this resistance was the poet Iboshi Hokuto (1901–1929), whose writings attacked the devastation wrought by industrial development on the Ainu homeland and expressed the pain inherent in the survival of identity in the midst of assimilation:

> Standing up for the dying Ainu
> With shining eyes—
> Iboshi Hokuto, Ainu.

> Adjusting my necktie, I glance at my face
> The mirror tells me
> You are Ainu after all.
>   (Quoted in Siddle 1996, 130)

Both Kaizawa and Iboshi, in different ways, rejected the notions that "being Japanese" required amnesia about their own history and that adjustment to the realities of life in a modern nation-state implied renouncement of their self-awareness as Ainu. Their assertions of identity, in other words, quietly but radically challenged the predominant bracketing of *kokumin kokka* (nation-state) with *minzoku kokka* (ethnic state) and pointed to the possibility of a nation which contained multiple origins and memories of the past.

In the postwar period, the Hokkaidō Utari Association (established as the Hokkaidō Ainu Association in 1930) has continued for fight to the rights and living conditions of Ainu people. An important upsurge of identity politics occurred in the early 1970s, inspired partly by the civil rights movement in the United States and by student movements in other parts of Japan. A younger generation of Ainu activists attacked discrimination and the stereotyping of Ainu culture in the Japanese education system and were particularly critical of the role of certain non-Ainu historians and anthropologists in the production of knowledge about Ainu society ("Shisam o mezashite" 1994, 47; Siddle 1996, 155–179). At the same time, activists like Kayano Shigeru sought to record and preserve Ainu knowledge, which was rapidly being lost as the numbers of native speakers of the Ainu language dwindled. Kayano recalls how, at the time of his father's death in 1956, an elderly friend spoke of his envy at the good fortune of the dying man: "You're so lucky to be able to go first. Who will send me off when I die?" (Kayano 1994, 108). Moved by events like this, Kayano and others have worked to create museums and cultural centers which preserve both Ainu artifacts and a living knowledge of Ainu language, legends, arts, and skills.

This continuous history of resistance provided the basis for the resurgence of Ainu identity politics during the 1980s and 1990s. Most estimates of the number of Ainu in Japan today vary from around 24,000 to around 80,000: variations which suggest the complexity of allocating and claiming identities in a society which has for decades sought to eradicate subnational senses of being. Despite the relatively small number of people involved, however, the rising tide of Ainu activism since the 1980s has forced the Japanese government to enact a new Ainu law, to replace the grossly outdated "Former Natives Protection of Act" of 1899, which (with certain amendments) remained on the statute book for ninety-eight years. The new Ainu Cultural Promotion Law passed in May 1997 remains controversial. The Hokkaidō Utari Association welcomed the introduction of the law but argued that its recommendations do not go far enough to recognize the distinct rights of the Ainu as indigenous people. While providing support for the maintenance and dissemination of Ainu culture, the legislation fails to address calls for an "Independence Fund" (*Minzoku Jiritsuka Kikin*) to promote economic self-reliance, and for guaranteed seats in parliament and local government. All the same, the new law, with its specific recognition of cultural diversity and the oppressiveness of past policies, marks a small step forward in a gradual rediscovery of Japan as an ethnically and culturally diverse nation. This rediscovery differs from the prewar acknowledgment of Japan's multicultural origins, for, rather than being used to assert the value of a continuing process of assimilation, it is now being used by many writers to defend the maintenance of cultural diversity.

What is clear is that both Okinawan and Ainu protests are also, in their way, products of the new age of globalization. Demands for

Okinawan autonomy are related (as we have seen) to the revival of cross-border links, at the level of local government, small business, educational exchange, and so on between Okinawa and its southern neighbors. The resurgence of Ainu identity, on the other hand, has been greatly encouraged by the creation of connections to other indigenous groups in Asia, North America, and elsewhere. Links with indigenous groups in other parts of the world have been established both by the Hokkaidō Utari Association and by individual activists, among them Kayano Shigeru, the first Ainu member of Japan's upper house of parliament, and the feminist Ainu writer Chikap Mieko (see Kayano 1993, 55–58; Chikap 1991). Many of the recent expressions of Ainu identity reflect the influence of these connections. To give just one example, the successful Ainu artistic group "Moshir" draws its distinctive dance and musical styles partly from Ainu tradition, but partly also from the traditions of Canadian, American, and Siberian indigenous cultures.

The aim of this chapter has been to explore the continuing interplay between local traditions and global ways of framing knowledge in modern Japan. To understand shifts and conflicts in public definitions of identity, it is important to consider not just events within Japan itself, but changes in the international order and in Japan's position within that order. Looking at the issue in terms of the relationship between global knowledge formats and local traditions can help us to understand changes, both in the imagery through which identity is defined and in the level at which it is defined: whether, for example, people at any given moment see themselves primarily as "Asians," "Japanese," or "Okinawans." These identities, however, do not exist in isolation from one another. The present wave of globalization is not simply a phase of shifting identity debates, but also an era in which many individuals find it more than ever necessary to live with multiple identities. The implications of this multiplicity, and its relationship to concepts of national identity in Japan, are the main themes of the final chapter.

9

Citizenship

In 1791 the German philosopher and historian Johann Gottfried von Herder wrote the twentieth and final volume of his most famous work, *Reflections on the Philosophy of the History of Mankind* (Ideen zur Philosophie der Geschichte der Menschheit). This vast and rambling text depicted a world of almost endless cultural diversity: a world divided into communities shaped both by natural environment and by language and traditions, so that "each bears in itself the standard of its perfection, totally independent of comparison with that of all others" (von Herder 1968, 98).

Three years later, Herder's French contemporary the marquis de Condorcet completed a much shorter study entitled *Sketch for a Historical Picture of the Progress of the Human Mind* (Equisse d'un tableau historique des progres de l'esprit humain), in which, among other things, he welcomed the French Revolution as the dawn of a coming human utopia. Within weeks of finishing this study, Condorcet himself had been arrested by the forces of that Revolution and would die in prison soon afterward, probably by his own hand. While Herder had interpreted human difference above all in terms of space—of the unique characteristics distinct "peoples" (*Völker*)—Condorcet interpreted it above all in terms of time—of differing stages on a single human stairway of social evolution. Thus "all peoples whose history is recorded fall somewhere between our present degree of civilization and that which we still see among primitive tribes" (Condorcet 1933).

Herder and Condorcet are sometimes seen as representing two antithetical approaches to the modern understanding of society: one based on space, the other on time; one German, the other French; one relying on concepts of "culture," the other on notions of "civilization" (Nishikawa 1992). But an alternative way of looking at their writings suggests that they represent not so much opposites as complementary and interdependent aspects of the intellectual effort to deal with the emerging implications of the nation-state and of citizenship. After all, Herder and Condorcet not only lived in the same era of revolutionary change but also shared similar attitudes to that change: "both are anti-despotic and libertarian, in favor of commerce and the mercantile ideal, antimilitary and antiaristocratic, if not completely egalitarian" (Manuel 1968, xxii).

The modern nation-state, whose idealized image fueled the ideological fires of the French Revolution, embodies a number of fundamental paradoxes. Although legally based upon the equality of citizens (an initially limited, but expanding proportion of its population), in practice it embodies a hierarchy of social and economic power relations. Although formally a member of an international community of equal states (a community which was at first limited in geographical scope, but which expanded greatly in the course of the twentieth century), the nation itself is also incorporated into a hierarchy of unequal power relationships. At one level, the nation-state is a highly rational entity based on laws, contracts, and constitutions, but at the same time the declining capacity of religion to ensure loyalty to the ruler impels national governments to devise new ways of creating a spiritual sense of belonging and of distinguishing members of the nation from outsiders and sojourners.

To deal with these paradoxes, national governments have deployed both spatial and temporal senses of difference. Temporal difference—ideas of "progress" and "backwardness"—could be used to justify inequalities of power and status and to provide a rationale for the assimilation of colonized or conquered peoples. Spatial difference—notions of "racial," "ethnic," or "cultural" diversity—could be used, on the other hand, to justify exclusion and segregation, to sanctify rivalries between nation-states of roughly equal power, and to support challenges by less powerful states against hegemonic definitions of universal "progress" and "civilization." The spatial concepts of "race," "ethnicity," and "culture" were also mobilized to deal with those aspects of difference which repeatedly escaped from the grand organizing frameworks of universalist ideas of progress. As a result, the temporal and spatial dimensions of difference have formed closely intertwined strands in the ideologies of nationhood and nationality, even though the relative emphasis placed on time or space varied according to the circumstances of the individual nation, its position in the international hierarchy, and the structure of the international system itself.

This book has shown how both dimensions of difference were incorporated into Japanese debates on nationhood. Temporal ideas of "civilization" (in the singular), of a universal historical trajectory, were used to support the assimilation of the people of frontier regions, to justify Japan's expansion into Korea and China, and as an intellectual defense of assimilationism in the colonies. Spatial ideas of culture and ethnicity, meanwhile, were used to question the universal validity of imported images of progress, to create a vision of "Asia" as opposed to "the West," but also at times to maintain the exclusion of colonized people from the rights and privileges of the colonizer. More recent comparative civilization theories (discussed in Chapter 7) combine both spatial and temporal dimensions to create an image of a distinct Japanese civilization which bears the seeds of the next stage in a global historical trajectory.

The interplay between ideas of time and space was connected to an interplay between notions of universality and particularism. Ideas of progress, for example, could be used to define "Japaneseness" as representing a universal standard from which the more "backward" people of the frontiers and colonies differed. Concepts of culture and ethnicity, on the other hand, were often used to distinguish "Japan" not only from Asian colonies and neighbors but also from a self-proclaimed universal "West." This final chapter considers how the legacy of these ideas has shaped notions of Japanese citizenship and then goes on to explore alternative approaches to the understanding of belonging and difference in contemporary Japan.

Jinmin, Shinmin, Kokumin: Citizens in Modern Japan

The ideals of human rights and citizenship which had sustained the American and French Revolutions were central to the political philosophies imported and adapted by Meiji intellectuals. These ideals resonated with older notions of the right of rebellion against unjust rulers (articulated, for example, by some Tokugawa-period peasant uprisings), and the combination of imported ideologies and indigenous traditions inspired much of the democratic theory of the Meiji era (Bowen 1980, 200–201). The climax of democratic activism in nineteenth-century Japan was the People's Rights movement of the 1880s—in fact a confluence of disparate movements revolving around demands for the creation of a national constitution. A number of leading figures in the movement, such as Ueki Emori, composed their own draft constitutions: Ueki proposed a federal Japan where a large share of political power would be devolved to the regions and where the Japanese people would enjoy wide-ranging rights, including the right to freedom of speech, freedom of religion, and freedom of assembly. Ueki defined "the Japanese people" rather circuitously as "those people who exist within the political society of Japan," but also proposed a clause which stated (with commendable succinctness), "Japan will allow the naturalization of foreigners" (Ueki 1965, 77 and 89).

In the end, though, a combination of suppression and internal dissension led to the collapse of the People's Rights movement, and the ideas of citizenship enshrined in the Meiji constitution of 1889 proved very different from those proposed by activists like Ueki. For one thing, while Ueki's proposed constitution had referred throughout to "the Japanese people" (*Nihon jinmin*), the Meiji constitution spoke instead of "Japanese subjects" (*Nihon shinmin*). This choice of words symbolized an official philosophy in which members of the national community were seen not as possessing inherent natural rights, but as enjoying only the benefits conferred on them by a benign sovereign in return for their loyalty and obedience. A corollary of this approach was that the Meiji constitution placed at least as much emphasis on the *duties* of the subject as on the *privileges* which flowed from membership in the national family.

The most important of all duties, of course, was the obligation to defend the state by military service—and since this obligation did not extend to women or (until the very last months of the Pacific War) to colonial subjects, it provided a basis for the exclusion of women and the colonized from the rights extended to other subjects. One interesting exception to this logic was that, from 1920 onward, Korean or Taiwanese colonial subjects who lived in "Japan proper" (*naichi*) were recognized as having the right to vote (since voter registration was based on place of residence) although they were not liable to conscription (which was based on the family registration—*koseki*—system, and thus on one's place of origin). In the early years, these voting rights meant little because the franchise was restricted to those in the top tax brackets. But after universal male suffrage was introduced in 1925, the number of eligible voters rose rapidly: In 1936, for example, there were more than 40,000 registered Korean voters in Japan (Matsuda 1995, 37).

The Meiji constitution left open the question of defining precisely who was and who was not a "Japanese subject": This issue was not settled until the passing of Japan's first Nationality Law in 1899. Early drafts of the law suggest that Japanese officials were thinking of a relatively generous definition, including people of foreign ancestry born in Japan as well as children of Japanese parents. But when the law was eventually enacted, shortly after the Sino–Japanese War ended and at a time when fears of large-scale Chinese migration were sweeping the Pacific region, it adopted a restrictive approach based on *ius sanguinis* (that is, citizenship derived from descent or "blood line") rather than on place of birth or residence. Although the 1899 law included provisions for naturalization, these were cumbersome and seldom used: Between 1900 and 1949 just 298 people (including 161 Chinese and 39 British citizens) became naturalized Japanese (Haniwa 1980, 316).

People of the colonies, on the other hand, were defined as Japanese nationals: automatically in the case of Koreans, though the residents of Taiwan were given a choice of accepting Japanese nationality or leaving the island once it became a Japanese colony. Despite apparent equality of nationality, a clear dividing between "Japanese proper" (*naichijin*) and "colonial subjects" could be maintained because of the existence of the family registration (*koseki*) system, which separated individuals into groups defined by place of origin—those with *naichi* family residence, Korean family residence, Taiwanese family residence, etc.—groups which served almost as "subnationalities" within the larger community of "Japanese imperial subjects."

The boundaries of nationality were also complicated by the fact that, in the first half of the twentieth century, more than 700,000 Japanese emigrated to countries outside the Japanese empire, the largest share going to North and South America. Japan's "blood line" approach to citizenship created difficulties for many of these emigrants. Until World War I, Japan continued to claim them as its own citizens, so preventing them, in many cases, from seeking naturalization in their new homes. It was only as a result of pressure from emigrant groups that the Nationality Law was revised (in 1916 and 1923) to make it easier for emigrants to renounce their Japanese citizenship. Even then, however, the government attempted to maintain a firm line between "foreigners" and "Japanese" by imposing tight restrictions on the holding of dual nationality.

After Japan's defeat in the Pacific War, the legal and philosophical basis of citizenship was radically reconstructed. Under the postwar constitution, which came into effect in 1947, the Japanese people were no longer "subjects" (*shinmin*) but "nationals" (*kokumin*), and their status was no longer seen as bestowed by the emperor but, rather, as founded upon natural human rights. This extension of the political basis of citizenship, however, coincided with a restriction of its geographic basis. Former colonial subjects from Korea and Taiwan, even those who were permanent residents in Japan, lost their Japanese citizenship and their right to vote in Japanese elections. The new, postwar Nationality Act of 1950 (revised in 1952 and 1984) continues to be based on the principle of *ius sanguinis,* the holding of dual nationality is tightly restricted, and naturalization continues to be a privilege granted on the basis of bureaucratic discretion. Until the 1980s, that discretion commonly included "advice" by officials to applicants that they should adopt "Japanese-sounding" names. These restrictions, combined with the nationalism of the newly independent colonies, made it difficult for former colonial subjects to become Japanese citizens. Korean residents in Japan were encouraged by their community organizations—the South Korean–backed Mindan and the North Korean–backed Chōsen Sōren—to maintain their distinct Korean identities and nationalities. Since the 1980s, some of the assimilationist elements of naturalization processes have been abandoned, and growing numbers of long-term residents have adopted Japanese citizenship: Between 1952 and 1991, 212,095 people became naturalized citizens, 11,146 in 1994 alone. Japan's levels of naturalization are still low by international standards, however, and most descendants of prewar or wartime Korean immigrants to Japan are still officially "foreigners" (Kondō 1996, 104).

In the past two decades, existing patterns of exclusion, inclusion, and marginalization have been challenged, in Japan as elsewhere, by the shift from a world order of nation-states to an increasingly globalized order. During the golden age of the nation-state, the most visible global economic divisions existed between nations: between "developed" and "underdeveloped," "first" and "third" worlds. Today, at least in the Asia-Pacific region, centers of industrial and financial dynamism are widely distributed through many countries, and economic

and social inequalities are increasingly created within, rather than between, nations: rich financial centers with highly paid workers existing
side by side with impoverished communities engaged in casual manual
or service work. It is not so much that the "third world" has ceased to
exist but rather that it has become ubiquitous, tucked into the back
streets or crumbling housing projects of cities throughout the world. In
older industrialized countries like Japan, and increasingly also in
newly industrialized countries like Taiwan and Malaysia, a key element of this "internal third world" consists of migrant workers. As
seen in Chapter 8, the shift to a global world order has been accompanied in Japan by a rapid growth of the immigrant workforce.

Typically, this process of immigration has been seen at first as a
temporary phenomenon. "Migrant workers" (the very name is revealing) are expected to come, perform a job, earn some money, and leave:
They are "labor power," whose social existence as whole human beings can be ignored. But, as in Europe, so also in Japan, authorities
have witnessed the gradual erosion of this illusion by the relentless
force of reality. Migrants put down roots; they develop social networks; even if they themselves expect their stay to be a short one, they
often find their calculations disrupted by the difficulties of saving
money or by the social pressures of the host society; they get sick; they
marry; they have children: in playwrite Max Frisch's words, "We
asked for labor, and what we got was people."

So far, the Japanese government has failed to confront the key question of immigration policy, continuing to maintain a highly restrictive
system while turning a blind eye to the presence of many illegal immigrant workers. But since the early 1980s it has been persuaded to
extend the range of social rights—rights to public housing, social secu-
rity, etc.—available to foreign residents. The next step may be local
voting rights. In 1995 the Supreme Court ruled that it was constitutionally possible for foreign residents to be given voting rights in local
elections, though the government has yet to pass the laws necessary to
make this possibility a reality (Kajita 1996a).

A number of Japanese commentators are now beginning to argue
that civic rights can no longer be seen as being tied to "citizenship" in
the sense of formal "Japanese nationality." In the present global system, they argue, it is necessary to understand the rights of individuals,
in terms of their status not only as "citizens" or "nationals" (*kokumin*)
but also as "residents" or "denizens" (*jūmin*): people whose long-term

residence in a particular community gives them a right to share in the social and political life of that community, whatever their official nationality (Kondō 1996; Kajita 1996a). The concept of *jūminken* (the rights of residents) as opposed to *kokuminken* (the rights of nationals), however, raises profound questions, not simply about legal issues such as voting qualifications, but also about our understandings of the relationship between national society and those notions of "culture" and "ethnicity" which have been recurring themes of this book.

Multicultural Citizenship

Acknowledgment of the cultural diversity of nation-states is now very widespread. Indeed, Joëlle Bahloul describes the very word "multicultural" as semantically redundant: "Culture is a mestizo universe par excellence, and all human societies are offsprings of cultural and biological interbreeding. In other words, culture is 'multi,' or rather 'inter,' by its very nature" (quoted in Segal and Handler 1995). Even in Japan, where ideologies of ethnic homogeneity have maintained a powerful grasp on the popular imagination for much of the postwar period, ideas of multiculturalism are now attracting growing attention. It seems almost as though the arrival of a new wave of migrants has "reminded" many Japanese commentators of a cultural diversity which had always been present, but had temporarily sunk from the surface of public consciousness. Debates about the expanding numbers of foreign residents in Japan are commonly linked to references to the Ainu and Okinawan communities and to the older established Korean and Chinese resident populations in Japan, and sometimes (though less often) also to the issue of discrimination against the *hisabetsu buraku* communities. Sone Shinichi, for example, presents an optimistic picture of multiculturalism, particularly of multicultural education, as a palliative for problems of discrimination against foreign residents in Japan and against groups like the *hisabetsu burakumin*. Mushakoji Kinhide even points to phenomena like U.S. multiculturalism and the UN's Decade of Indigenous Peoples as evidence of an emerging "new constitutional world order" which will help to reconcile the competing claims of nation-states and ethnic minorities (Sone 1996, 148–189; Mushakōji 1996, 14–18).

Japan, however, entered the multiculturalism debate at a relatively late stage, when early optimism about the future of multicultural societies in the United States, Canada, Australia, and Western Europe was giving way to more cautious and critical reassessments. One aspect of this process has been a straightforward backlash from those sections of the population that feel that they have lost power or status in the national pursuit of multiculturalism and yearn for a return to the simpler certainties of assimilationism. Another, however, has been the emergence of critical voices which acknowledge the achievements of multiculturalism while questioning aspects of its theory and practice.

In the United States, for example, David Hollinger observes that multiculturalism, while enriching and diversifying U.S. culture, tends to lock individuals into a "racial pentagon" made up of simplistic official ethnic categories—Euro-American, African American, Asian American, indigenous (Native American), and Latino—and he argues that "the defenders of cultural diversity need to take a step beyond multiculturalism, toward a perspective I call 'postethnic' " (Hollinger 1995, 2–3). In using the word "postethnic," Hollinger implies a world where individuals feel free to choose and enjoy affiliation with many identity groups, rather than with just one: a world which would be better attuned to the realities of increasing hybridity. Hollinger, however, also argues for an approach where a major emphasis would be placed on civic, rather than ethnic, identity and which would therefore reinforce the place of a supraethnic national citizenship as a focus of belonging. From a slightly different point of view, Canadian-based academic Sneja Gunew has tried to unpack the hidden assumptions of multiculturalism, revealing the concept as "a kind of floating signifier which gains both meaning and strategic capabilities only in a specific context. It can be used by any faction and has no privileged or unchanging meaning" (Gunew 1994, 17).

Joining the discussion, as it were, in mid-stream, Japanese commentators have incorporated some of these criticisms into their search for more open and egalitarian forms of "cultural citizenship" in Japan. A number of writers, for example, echo Sneja Gunew's observations on the hazy and shifting definitions of "multiculturalism" (Sekine 1996; Kajita 1996b). Others reflect Hollinger's concern for the creation of a more open "cosmopolitanism" based upon a shared sense of civic responsibility or remind their readers (as some British critics of multiculturalism have) that defining disadvantage in terms of the "soft" notion of cultural difference can obscure the decisive role of that more intractable phenomenon, racism (Kajita 1996b; see also Rex 1991).

Here I focus on just two recent studies of the issue which help illumin-
ate some crucial questions of human equality in a globalizing world.

The Internationalization Within

In the mid-1980s, when the term "internationalization" (*kokusaika*)
was the Japanese media's favorite buzzword, Kobe University academic Hatsuse Ryūhei coined the expression "the internationalization
within" (*uchi naru kokusaika*) (Hatsuse 1985). By using this phrase,
Hatsuse hoped to draw attention to some aspects of Japan's internationalization which were being overlooked in the current enthusiasm
for foreign investment, foreign travel, and other more visible (and
profitable) aspects of the phenomenon. "The internationalization
within"—a phrase soon taken up by the media and even by the government itself—referred to the subtle global influences which were alter-
ing everyday life, values, and the nature of Japanese "civil society."
One of the most important of those influences was the growing presence of immigrants in Japan (Hatsuse 1985; Hatsuse 1996, 205–206).

Since the 1980s, Hatsuse has developed these reflections into a more
detailed discussion of multiculturalism. The success of "the internationalization within" will, he argues, depend upon Japan's ability to accept
a more diverse society, particularly to accommodate immigrants from
other parts of Asia (who constitute by far the largest share of the migrant inflow) (Hatsuse 1996, 228). In setting out these ideas, Hatsuse
traces a history surveyed here in earlier chapters. He observes that
modern Japan took shape through the absorption of frontier societies to
its north and south and that its twentieth-century growth was fueled by
migration from the colonies and, more recently, from other parts of
Asia. So "Japanese society" today is not a homogeneous and neatly
bounded entity. Instead, it is made up of many communities divided by
the multiple boundaries of ethnicity, citizenship, and place of residence.
It contains not just people of Japanese descent living in Japan (*zainichi
nikkeijin*), but also Ainu, Okinawans, Japanese living abroad, and people of foreign ancestry living in Japan (Hatsuse 1996, 213).

In its approach to this diversity, the state can choose between policies of assimilation and those of multiculturalism. Hatsuse does not
condemn assimilationism out of hand but, rather, suggests that each
approach has its own strengths and weaknesses: Assimilationism en-
courages national integration and offers the universal value of equality,

while multiculturalism allows the maintenance of distinct identities and helps create a society which can adapt flexibly to the outside world (Hatsuse 1996, 215). Multiculturalism itself, however, can take on different forms. Hatsuse, like other Japanese commentators, draws on M.M. Gordon's theories of pluralism to suggest a basic distinction between two models of multiculturalism: a liberal model and a corporatist model (Gordon 1988, 157–166). In the liberal model, the emphasis is on the individual's human right to practice his or her own culture in private. The public sphere is seen essentially as a "culture-free zone," in which the state seeks only to maintain equality of opportunity; cultural diversity is confined largely to the private sphere of the household, where individuals are free to practice their own religion, eat their own food, listen to their own music, and so on. In corporate multiculturalism, on the other hand, culture invades the public sphere, and equality is seen in terms of outcome rather than of opportunity. The state is expected, therefore, not just to allow cultural freedom to the individual, but also to provide active support, enabling ethnic groups to maintain their own public celebrations and festivals, teach their own languages and histories in schools, and so forth.

Proposals for a "multicultural Japan" often combine aspects of both models. Hatsuse points out, for example, that a multicultural manifesto published by the magazine *Aruta* in 1992 included both "liberal" elements such as demands that foreign residents be given voting rights and the right to government employment and "corporatist" elements such as demands for indigenous autonomy and the inclusion of minority issues in school textbooks (Hatsuse 1996, 224). His own (debatable) conclusion is that Japan is close to realizing the "liberal" version of multiculturalism. However, he also concludes that, to fully achieve "the internationalization within," the state needs to move forward toward implementing some aspects of the "corporatist" model, such as the inclusion of other Asian languages in the school and college curriculum. At the same time, though, Hatsuse warns that this will be a difficult process, involving re-examination of the basic structures of Japanese education. He also emphasizes the need to avoid the "negative" aspects of corporate multiculturalism, which include the creation of a divisive social system and the artificial preservation of "premodern" aspects of minority cultures (Hatsuse 1996, 223–228).

Hatsuse's proposals are interesting, not only because of their image of the Japanese future but also because they confront some of the key questions of culture, development, and assimilation which are recurring themes in this book. As in many writings on multiculturalism, the underlying image here is of a world where each individual belongs to a distinct cultural/ethnic group and where cultural groups are integrated and enduring entities which sit, like pieces of a mosaic, side by side within the boundaries of the nation-state. Hatsuse observes that culture is neither pure nor unchanging. Modernization, he suggests, produces a growing global "assimilation" in which people accept the same universal values of human rights and equality, as well as the same tastes in rock music, fashions, and fast food. Nevertheless, "culture" survives in the private sphere of the family through the maintenance of minority languages, religion, dietary patterns, holidays, and festivals. (Hatsuse 1996, 217–220). Culture, in other words, becomes a sort of eternal residual: an amalgam of all those social elements which constantly fall through the net of "modernity." Although the political implications are radically different from those of the civilization theories explored in earlier chapters, the underlying model of culture is quite similar. Here again, the assumption is that nations choose between a "multiculturalism" where a variety of cultures is tolerated and an "assimilationism" where everyone becomes the same. But, as we have seen in Chapter 7, this image is open to question.

Consider, for example, the case of Korean citizens in Japan. The majority of the second and third generation speak Japanese as their first language, have been brought up in the Japanese education system, and know as much about Japanese history and society as any other resident of Japan. Koreans in Japan are not in any way "racially" identifiable from their Japanese neighbors, and a taste for Korean food (for example) is hardly an identifying characteristic in a world where Korean restaurants proliferate and are patronized by people of many nationalities. "Difference" here is not (as it is so often assumed to be in multicultural theory) a matter of a set of describable peculiarities of behavior or belief which separate the "minority" from the "majority." Rather, it is a matter of symbolic forms of identification, most conspicuously the use of recognizably "Korean" names, which become (in the eyes of both the individual and the wider society) a statement of relationship between self and nation. Ultimately the defining characteristic of Koreans in Japan is that (in many different ways according to personal circumstances) they identify themselves and are identified by others as "Korean." These forms of identification are not merely the outcome of individual choice, but are also influenced and reinforced by organizational structures created both by the state and by identity communities themselves. The issue, then, is not a simple question of whether "the minority" should become *the same as* "the majority" or should be allowed to remain *different.* It is a question of the way in which boundaries (which are usually the legacy of past colonization, exploitation, or exclusion) are maintained, shifted, and reinterpreted in the process of struggles over the nature of the state.

The Multiculturalism Within

This point is vividly illustrated in the writings of Chong Yong Hye, whose approach to identity draws on postcolonial theories of hybridity (such as the writings of Julia Kristeva, Gayatri Chakravorty Spivak, and Sneja Gunew). Chong highlights the absurdity of the very label which is generally imposed upon Japanese residents of Korean descent: "South Koreans and/or North Koreans Resident in Japan" (*zainichi kankoku chōsenjin*). What sort of an "identity group," she asks, includes in its title the copula "and/or," represented in Japanese by an ambiguous back dot? Are the 200,000–odd Koreans who have become naturalized Japanese citizens, and the children of marriages between Korean and Japanese couples, still "South Koreans and/or North Koreans Resident in Japan"? Are *zainichi kankoku chōsenjin* still "South Koreans and/or North Koreans Resident in Japan" when they go to live in other countries (Chong 1996, 15–16)?

Chong's point is not a denial of her Korean ancestry. On the contrary, she sees the reclaiming of suppressed or marginalized identities as a crucial first step toward freedom. But to place oneself too firmly within the predefined category of "ethnic minority" is, she argues, in effect to validate existing stereotypes about the homogeneity and purity of the majority. Defining herself as "purely Korean" would be to allow others to define themselves as "purely Japanese." The more challenging stance, she proposes, is to define oneself as *impurely* "Japanese" (*fujun Nihonjin*) and by implication also as impurely "Korean" (Chong 1996, 17–18).

Chong's reflections take the issue of "multicultural citizenship" one step further than the conventional rhetoric of "tolerance." "Up to the present," she writes, "the 'coexistence with difference' which has been emphasized in the struggle against discrimination has always referred to a difference external to 'myself.' On the contrary, coexistence with difference within 'myself' has been denied as undesirable" (Chong 1996, 28). But Chong's pursuit of identity begins from this fact of internal diversity, this sense of living in the "borderlands."

Her approach (like Sakai Naoki's analysis, discussed in Chapter 7) points to a way of understanding tradition and identity which goes beyond the reified images of "national/ethnic culture" discussed in this book. In contemporary society, after all, people are likely not only to have multiple ethnic origins but also belong to a whole range of cross-cutting communities (family, neighborhood, workplace, professional association, religion, political movement), each of which, in some sense, can become a focus of identity. Besides, since our "culture" is also the product of the information we receive, we participate in a diverse array of transnational cultural communities created by the shared consumption of Bruce Lee movies, CNN news, Michael Jackson's music, and so forth. In this process, it is not possible to sift out the "modern (= noncultural)" from the residuum of enduring "ethnic culture." On the contrary, as we saw in earlier discussion of the formatting of difference, local and global traditions become inseparably intertwined and irrevocably and continuously transform one another. It is not, in other words, simply that immigration is turning Japan (and other nation-states) into a "multicultural" society, but that the emergence of a global system has created a growing complexity in the cultural resources which shape the identity of every individual— members of the "majority" or "mainstream" just as much as members of "minorities." In other words, it has created a growing "multiculturalism within."

To borrow a non-Japanese metaphor, I find it useful to refer to the image of indigenous Australian society presented in seminars given by the Aboriginal educator Mary Graham. Graham describes Aboriginal society as shaped around a powerful and complex kinship structure which can be likened to a mesh or grid. For each individual, kinship is not a matter of lineal descent from a single "family tree," but of cross-cutting relationships which—via mother and father, grandparents, aunts and uncles—provides links to many different families, language groups, and territories. Each of these links, in turn, carries its own traditions and stories (Graham 1993). The individual, therefore, occupies a unique intersection in a vast network: a network rich with possibilities because each person will not be able to maintain all their kinship links equally, but will develop and maintain some while others (through choice or chance) lapse into oblivion. In the same way, we can imagine the individual in the contemporary world as standing at the intersection of many flows of knowledge, created by family, education, religion, nationality, place of residence, work, and so on: flows which potentially link each individual to a multitude of groups in many places. So a common sense of the nature of kinship may link most Australian Aboriginal people to one another in a shared Aboriginal identity, while a belief in Presbyterian Christianity, a passion for judo or science fiction, or a concern for indigenous land rights may provide potential links of identity between particular Aboriginal individuals and people in many other parts of the world, including Japan.

To make better sense of this multiculturalism within, it may be useful to adapt Pierre Bourdieu's idea of *prises de position* ("position takings"). Bourdieu uses the term as part of his literary theory to refer to the way in which writers position themselves within the literary world. The decision to work in a particular genre (e.g., novel or poetry) or subgenre (e.g., romantic fiction, the satirical novel) is a choice of position, where "every position, even the dominant one, depends for its very existence . . . on the other positions constituting the field" (Bourdieu 1993, 30). In Bourdieu's theory, though, the positions are external ones, like the positions of shifting pieces on a giant chessboard. The "position takings" to which I am referring, on the contrary, are internal ones, which relate to the definition of identity within the intersecting network of knowledge resources to which we have access. Human beings do not usually possess a single identity—as "Japanese," "Christian," or "middle class"—but adopt various positions in different social circumstances. Sometimes I am conscious of myself as an Australian; sometimes as a mother; sometimes as a person whose ethnic roots lie in England, Scotland, and Ireland; sometimes as a person who has married into a Japanese family; sometimes as someone whose social values were formed in the 1960s (a convenient euphemism for middle age). As Bourdieu notes, however, the way in which I mobilize these identities is always influenced by an awareness of "the other identities constituting the field." Identities flash between polar points of positive and negative, shaped by both the need to be "one with" and the need to be "distinct from."

In using this approach, I am trying to move away from the determinist visions of culture and ethnicity embodied in the writings of

Nihonjinron and of more recent civilization theorists. But at the same time I also have doubts about the simple voluntarism of writers like Orlando Patterson, who sees ethnicities as something we can step into and out of, almost like a suit of clothes, to maximize economic advantage (Patterson 1975). Instead, we might adapt from Paul DiMaggio (who also clearly owes a debt to Bourdieu) and suggest that the raw material of our identity is derived from our "cultural resources." Because the word "culture" is so difficult to separate from the image of an organic whole (as in Kroeber's and Ishida's definitions of the term), here I alter DiMaggio's expression slightly and speak of "symbolic resources" (though I should emphasize that these are different from Bourdieu's notion of "symbolic capital"). Symbolic resources, in this sense, are "any form of symbolic mastery . . . used in a specific relational context" (DiMaggio 1991, 134). They are both physical and mental, and include our bodily appearance, our posture, the way we move and dress as well as the language we speak, the skills in which we are trained, and the knowledge we possess about nature, history, or politics. Some of these resources are inherited, and a large share are acquired in childhood, though as adults we continue to add to our store of resources: We gain new knowledge and may choose to dye our hair or even change our sex.

But our choice of identities is also constrained by the particular range of identity positions which we find mapped out in the society around us. Identity positions are defined not by the whole mass of symbolic resources shared by a particular social group, but by a small number of *symbolic markers* which, through a process of conflict and compromise, come to be defined as the badges of a given identity. These symbolic markers are profoundly political, created out of continuing social contests over the control of meaning. They therefore change with shifts in power within the identity group. Changes in the markers of one position in turn provoke shifts in the markers of others: Thus the spread of feminism in the 1970s and 1980s provoked intensely debated redefinitions of masculinity in the early 1990s. The depth and rigidity of identity positions is determined both by the intrinsic nature of symbolic resources and by the choice of symbolic markers to define a particular identity. For example, the ease with which people can move between nationalities or combine national and other identities depends on whether the symbolic markers of nationality are defined in terms of physical appearance or family history (which are largely inherited), language competency (which can be acquired in early life), or legal citizenship (which can be acquired in adulthood).

To be able to move easily between a range of identity positions, in which we can use our cultural resources to the full, is perhaps one of the most essential of human rights. In the words of a young Ogasawaran (Bonin) Islander—a descendant of the group whose history was touched on in Chapter 2—"it's convenient and fun to have . . . many different faces" (Arima 1990, 274). But the history of the Ogasawaran Islanders also illustrates the pain that has at times been caused by the definition of the markers of national identity in Japanese history. Although intermarried with Japanese migrants and possessors of Japanese citizenship, descendants of the original islanders were in the prewar period commonly distinguished from other Japanese as "the naturalized people" (*kikajin*). At the same time, though, they failed to conform to prevailing images of "Western" wealth and power, and Japanese official and popular imagery therefore tended to define them as "South Sea Islanders"—an expression which carried mingled over-tones of romanticism and condescension, much like those conveyed by European representations of "the South Seas." After World War II, the problems of identity were given a further twist when the U.S. forces (which occupied the islands from 1945 to 1968) allowed only those islanders with some non-Japanese ancestry to return to the archipelago and gave them an English-language education complete with daily raising of the Stars and Stripes and frequent showings of Hollywood movies, but, for various political reasons, denied them the right to become U.S. citizens (Arima 1990, 58–71; Shepardson 1977). They therefore had to face a new process of reintegration into Japanese society when the islands were returned to Japan in the late 1960s.

Symbolic Markers and the Nation-State

The state plays a crucial role in defining the range of identity positions available to its citizens. For it is the state which has the greatest capac-ity (through policy statements, education systems, and the visible sym-bols of flag, anthem, and public celebration) to define the markers of the imagined national community and so to determine which people, among those who live within its boundaries, are able to share an iden-tity as "citizen" without renouncing crucial parts of their symbolic heritage (Anderson 1991). And since national identity occupies such a central place in the constellation of identity positions, the markers which define citizenship exert a powerful influence on the markers with which other groups (religions, political movements, ethnic minorities, etc.) draw their own communal boundaries.

In some countries (such as France) the revolutionary origins of the nation-state gave a distinctive cast to the symbolic markers of nationhood, which have come to be understood in terms of a particular set of political imagery: terms such as "liberty" or "revolution" have been endlessly reinterpreted and contested by generations of political elites. This does not mean an absence of discrimination, of course, merely that discrimination is cast in terms of symbolic markers—such as the wearing of the veil by Islamic women—which can be interpreted in ideological terms as contrary to the secular, egalitarian "culture of the 'land of the Rights of Man' " (Balibar 1991, 24). Elsewhere, nationalist struggles or wars of revolution against imperialist powers provide the sources of the symbolic markers of nationhood.

Nationality, in other words, is never just a matter of legal definitions, documentation, and papers; it also involves efforts by the state to inculcate that sense of belonging—those "habits of the heart"—which bind the individual irrevocably to the nation (Bellah et al. 1985). It is the common practice of states to mistrust their citizens. In the language of national identity, there is a profound and almost unquestioned image of society as fragile entity which, without a powerful center of gravity, is liable to fly apart into chaos. The ordinary processes of political participation, public discourse, and daily life, it is assumed, are not enough to counter the potential perfidy of the people. Without a focus of suprarational cohesive force, they are always liable to betray the cause, to sleep with the enemy. National elites therefore reassure themselves by creating symbols of unity and images of cohesion which become touchstones to gauge the trustworthiness of its citizens.

One archetypal example of such a touchstone was the Tokugawa ritual of requiring subjects to act out their rejection of subversive beliefs by treading on the *fumie* (see Chapter 5). The modern state has similar rituals, though backed up by less drastic sanctions. From 1890 to the end of the Pacific War, for example, Japanese schools and colleges performed a didactic drama of national loyalty on major public holidays, when students were required to bow their heads before a portrait of the emperor as they listened to a solemn public reading of the Imperial Rescript on Education, reminding them that the purpose of learning was to enhance the individual's ability to serve the nation. Even today, in Japan as in many other nations, the practice of making people stand for the national anthem performs a similar function.

Such ceremonies mark the boundaries of the nation and therefore (like the Japanization policies imposed upon the northernmost Ainu communities in the Tokugawa period) tend to be enforced most enthusiastically in the areas where the dangers of disloyalty are believed to be greatest. So the colonial government of Korea (but not the colonial government of Taiwan, whose people were regarded as less hostile to Japanese rule) demanded the repeated public recitation of the "Oath of Imperial Subjects," which stated:

> 1. We are the subjects of the imperial nation; we will repay His Majesty as well as the country with loyalty and sincerity.
> 2. We the subjects of the imperial nation shall trust, love and help one another so that we can strengthen our unity.
> 3. We the subjects of the imperial nation shall endure hardship, train ourselves, and cultivate strength so that we can exalt the imperial way. (Quoted in Chou 1996, 43)

The unequal imposition of boundary markers has been common in the history of many nations. During the Pacific War, for example, the United States imposed a complex set of "loyalty tests" on Americans of Japanese descent (though not on those of German or Italian origin): one version of the test (in a conscious or unconscious replication of the Tokugawa ritual of the *fumie*) required these U.S. citizens to trample on a portrait of the Japanese emperor (Murakawa 1996, 198).

In modern nationalism, however, the tests of belonging are not confined to the conscious performance of rituals. Inspired by ideologies of culture and race, they also involve a continuous "testing" of the implicit and embodied markers of appearance, name, pronunciation, and so on. Modern states tend to possess, to a greater or lesser degree, an ambivalent tolerance of groups of people who do not conform to official images of nationality. On the one hand, the alien is seen as potentially destabilizing, and the impulses of assimilationism are strong; on the other, groups that are defined as different can be all the more readily isolated, subordinated, and turned into potential targets for economic exploitation.

But the functions of identifiable "minorities" are not purely economic. It is useful for the national population to encompass small groups that fail the tests of belonging because it is only through the visible failure of defined "minorities" that the state can repeatedly reassure itself of the invisible homogeneity and loyalty of the "majority." The coherence of the nation, in other words, can be imagined only by drawing a line around its boundary, and that line can be drawn not just by political rituals but also by symbols of ethnic or cultural difference. Politics and ethnicity often become superimposed, so that signs of difference are automatically identified as signs of subversion and vice versa: In prewar Japan, citizens who questioned the role of the emperor were liable to become "nonnationals" (*hikokumin*), while the identifiable markers of ethnic difference (use of Korean names or the Korean language, for example) became automatically identified as markers of disloyalty, reflected in the ubiquitous term *futei Senjin* (Korean malcontents).

In the Japanese case, in other words, the imagery of modern nationality which emerged in the prewar period came to be expressed, above all, in the concept of an organically integrated "family-state" centered on the emperor. This imagery was open to varying interpretations. Some saw it in clearly "racial" terms, others in terms of a metaphorical family which transcended biological bounds. In either case, however, loyalty to the emperor and assimilation to the norms of proper "family behavior," embodied above all in self-identification with the version of history told by the "main branch" of the family (the Japanese state), were inseparably fused. Central to this process of identity creation was the emergence of the chameleon term *minzoku,* which, by fusing overtones of ethnicity, shared history, culture, and nationhood, could effortlessly adapt to subtle shifts of emphasis in ideologies of "Japaneseness."

In the postwar period, the notion of a "Japanese culture" which was unproblematically associated with "Japanese ethnicity" was gradually reworked by both conservative and liberal thinkers into the central definer of citizenship. Of course, the precise content of this "Japanese culture" was the subject of debate. Some saw it as transhistorical; others interpreted it as the product of continuing social change. Some (like the ideologues of *Nihonjinron*) interpreted it in terms of benign images of diligence and social harmony; others wrote more critically of weak individualism and subservience to authority. In either case, however, the implicit equation of Japanese citizenship with ethnic markers (appearance, names, language), and of these ethnic markers with cultural characteristics (group consciousness, social order), has had profound consequences for the negotiation of citizenship in postwar Japan. For one thing, it makes notions of diversity particularly threatening to established definitions of Japanese citizenship. For another, commonly accepted equations, such as "Japanese ethnicity = Japanese citizenship = social harmony" all too readily produce parallel equations: "non-Japanese appearance or name = foreign = social disruption."

So, during the course of the twentieth century, notions such as the family state, the imperial system, the *minzoku,* and "Japanese culture" have all played their role as key touchstones of national unity, and at various times the visible "failure" of Ainu, Okinawans, Bonin Islanders, *han-Nihonjin, hikokumin, futei Senjin, hisabetsu burakumin,* "South Koreans and/or North Koreans resident in Japan," "migrant workers," and so on to conform to officially defined symbolic markers of "Japaneseness" repeatedly reinforced the comforting illusion that those who *do* conform are bound together by a single political allegiance and a single cultural soul (see Sakai 1996b, 44).

The Nation in Time

As Elizabeth Colson has remarked, "the societies we study are a stream of time, rather than a stable environment whose dimensions can be securely plotted . . . once and for all" (Colson 1984, 1). Modern nation-states represent an attempt to channel the stream, to plot the dimensions, to create a stable environment.

The nation has always been a compound entity, in which a multiplicity of functions have been imposed one on the other. It claims the authority to serve simultaneously as a focus of (1) sovereignty—autonomous political action; (2) citizenship—the rights associated with membership of the national community; (3) traditions—the national heritage of knowledge, including the symbolic resources necessary to put civic rights to use; (4) culture—distinctive patterns of value and behavior; (5) identity—the sense of belonging through which individuals define their place in the world; (6) allegiance—submission to the underlying rules of the political order. The relationship between these overlapping dimensions of the state has in practice often been strained. In colonial empires, for example, the intersection of nationhood and imperialism created continuous friction, contradiction, and inconsistency within concepts of "citizenship," "culture," and "identity."

In the present wave of globalization, similar tensions are re-emerging in a slightly different way. The nation-state is no longer the only locus of political sovereignty; it is forced to share its power with international, and sometimes also with subnational, institutions. By the same token, civic rights are no longer guaranteed purely through "citizenship," that is, membership in the nation-state. Increasingly, the international community also provides overarching guarantees of human rights which apply (for example) to those who live in countries of which they are not formal citizens. These trends have been widely recognized, and the gradual separation of civil rights from formal citizenship has been debated by many scholars. But it is also just as important to look critically at the relationship between the more nebulous dimensions of nationhood: traditions, culture, identity, and allegiance.

Chapter 8 considered the emergence of a global knowledge system and the creation of subregimes within that system. As long as the nation-state remains an important locus of political power, it will also be an important subsystem of the wider global knowledge system. In other words, to function as political entities, nations need their members to share certain common knowledge—knowledge of the national language or languages and a reasonable understanding of national social and economic subregimes and their historical evolution. This historical understanding matters because the language of public debate is never a transparent language of dictionary-definition words, but is always full of allusions to past events, famous individuals, or resonant phrases. In this sense it is important for members of the nation to share certain "traditions," that is, certain symbolic resources which makes the practice of citizenship possible. It should also be emphasized, though, that these resources can be acquired during an individual's lifetime. These is nothing, in other words, to exclude outsiders from joining the knowledge community of the nation. Japanese history itself is full of examples of this process. Within twenty-two years of the Japanese colonization of Korea, for example, twelve Korean-born candidates had stood in a Japanese general election, and one had been elected to parliament; today (to give just one contemporary instance) the local council of the little Japanese town of Yugawara includes among its elected members a naturalized immigrant from Finland (Matsuda 1995, 102; Kajita 1996a, 110).

One of the main problems which has bedeviled debates about nationhood and national identity has been the tendency to equate this sharing of symbolic resources with an organic image of "culture" and to see this "culture" in turn as the key to individual identity. Too often it is assumed that a knowledge of Japanese language, history, intellectual traditions, and so on must be linked to the possession of a single nationally shared core of fundamental values, behavior, and "ethnicity." This common culture, which the conservative philosopher Watanabe Shōichi has described as being "imprinted" on the minds of infants from ancient times to the present day, is then seen as the source of a common "identity" (Watanabe 1990, 66). But, as argued here in earlier chapters, this notion of an eternal cultural soul or "paideuma" is a pseudo-scientific myth. There is no reason why people who share certain knowledge in common should not interpret that knowledge in radically different ways. In other words, it is both possible and crucial to distinguish among three concepts: the sharing of symbolic resources; sameness of fundamental belief and behavior; and a sense of personal identification with the nation or ethnic group.

It is not necessary for people who share a common "identity" to share a common "culture" in Ishida Eiichirō's or Watanabe Shōichi's sense of the word. James Clifford provides an interesting illustration of this point in his book *The Predicament of Culture,* where he recounts the story of a 1976 lawsuit in which the Native American residents of the town of Mashpee, Massachusetts, sued for ownership of a tract of land around the town. In order to claim ownership, the Mashpee people had to prove that they had constituted an "Indian tribe" continuously since the beginning of European colonization. The case therefore revolved around the attempt to prove that there was a common tribal culture with which members had continuously identified. But, while the Mashpee witnesses insisted that they had no doubts about their own tribal identity, there was no unanimity about the source of that identity: For some, it had to do with ancestry; for others, it was a matter of participation in ceremonies or use of traditional healing practices; still others "just knew." The jury therefore concluded that even in the case of the three hundred-odd native inhabitants of Mashpee, it was impossible to discover any single observable set of characteristics defining membership of the "tribe" since the beginning of colonization or encompassing all those who saw themselves as "tribal" members in 1976, and the Mashpees lost their case (Clifford 1988). In the instance of the Mashpees, in other words, individual identity as a tribe member was not fixed to a single core of beliefs with which every member identified, but was created from the mobilization of a cross-cutting and evolving network of symbolic resources, of which some were relevant to some members and some to others.

In the same way, it is possible for a large number of people to identify themselves as "Japanese" without sharing a single discernible "culture" in the sense of agreeing *what it is that makes them "Japanese."* For some, it may simply be a matter of passport or place of residence, for others, a sense of kinship or attachment to their place of birth; for some, the ties of language may be significant, for others, the heritage of poetry, art, and music produced within Japan; for some, it may still be loyalty to the emperor, for others, it is attachment to the postwar Japanese constitution. Just as "culture" is not a *thing* which societies carry with them intact through time, but only an endless and fractured process of the reworking of multiple traditions, so "identity" is not a *thing* which individuals carry with them through life, like a scar on the soul. Instead, it is something that we make in the present moment out of an interweaving of our cultural resources, as we talk to others, listen, write, or read the final pages of a book.

Growing ethnic diversity in contemporary Japan, then, is not important just because it creates a "multiculturalism" where imported Korean, Chinese, or Filipino cultures, or indigenous Okinawan and Ainu cultures, are recognized as having their place alongside "mainstream Japanese" culture. Rather, it performs the much more challenging role of turning the spotlight onto the notion of "culture" itself, forcing us to reconsider the soothing images of homogeneity and harmony which the word conveys. In the process it becomes necessary to recognize the multiple identities in which all individuals participate. The issue is not simply the recognition and "tolerance" of the difference of Ainu or Koreans, but a recognition of the difference which has *always* existed within the category "Japanese." And this difference in turn exists not just because there are *Tōhoku-kei Nihonjin* and *Kyūshū-kei Nihonjin* (Japanese of varied regional ancestry) as well as *Okinawa-kei Nihonjin* or *Kankoku-kei Nihonjin* (Japanese of Okinawan ancestry or Korean ancestry), but because individuals are not containable within bounded cultural groups which ensure "sameness." The individual, rather, is a point where many flows of knowledge and many dimensions of identity intersect. Cultural citizenship and cultural democracy depend not on the "majority's" tolerance of the "minorities," but on everyone's ability to question the categorization which produces the imperious image of "majority" and "minorities."

This questioning is no simple matter, for the categories of the past have been absorbed into the very words we use to discuss these matters. Every time we speak of "culture," "race," *minzoku,* "femininity," or even "Japan," we are haunted by the ghosts of dead theories. It is only gradually, by confronting those ghosts, that we can start to loosen their invisible grip on the language with which we describe our world. As the boundaries around the functions of the nation become more porous, and the nature of national society as "a flow of time" becomes more obvious, so this rethinking of national "culture" may provide a starting point for a redefinition of the markers with which the nation stakes its claim to identity.

Bibliography

Adams, F.O. 1870. *Third Report by Mr. Adams on Silk Culture in Japan.* London: Harrison and Sons.

Aida, Yūji. 1972. *Nihonjin no ishiki kōzō.* Tokyo: Kōdansha.

Amamiya, Gijin. 1954. *Tanaka Shōzō no hito to shōgai.* Tokyo: Meikeidō.

Amino, Yoshihiko. 1990. *Nihonron no shiza: Rettō no shakai to kokka.* Tokyo: Shōgakukan.

————. 1992. "Deconstructing: 'Japan' " (trans. G. McCormack). *East Asian History,* no. 3, (June): 121–142.

————. 1994. "Emperor, Rice and Commoners" (trans. G. McCormack). *Japanese Studies* 14, no. 2 (September): 1–12.

Amino, Yoshihiko, et al., eds. 1992. *Rekishigaku to minzokugaku.* Tokyo: Furukawa Kōbunkan.

Anderson, Benedict. 1991. *Imagined Communities: Reflections on the Origin and Spread of Nationalism,* 2nd ed. London: Verso.

Anon. 1981. "Ryūkyū kaigo." (1850). In *Edoki Ryūkyū mono shiryō shūran,* vol. 4. Tokyo: Honpō Shoseki.

Anthias, Floya, and Yuval-Davis Nira. 1992. *Racialized Boundaries: Race, Nation, Gender, Colour and Class and the Anti-Racist Struggle.* London: Routledge.

Aoki, Tamotsu. 1988. *Bunka no hiteisei.* Tokyo: Chūō Kōronsha.

Aoki, Yayoi. 1986. *Feminizumu to ekorojī.* Tokyo: Shinhyōron.

Arai, Hakuseki. 1979. "Ezo shi" (1720). Reprinted in *Hoppō mikōkai kobunsho shūsei,* vol. 1: 39–54. Tokyo: Sōbunsha.

Arima, Midori. 1990. "An Ethnographic and Historical Study of Ogasawara/The Bonin Islands, Japan." Ph.D. dissertation, Stanford University.

Arnason, Johann P. 1988. "Social Theory and the Concept of Civilization." *Thesis Eleven* 20: 87–105.

Baldry, H.C. 1965. *The Unity of Mankind in Greek Thought.* Cambridge: Cambridge University Press.

Balibar, Etienne. 1991. "Is There a Neo-Racism." In *Race, Nation, Class: Ambiguous Identities,* ed. Etienne Balibar and Immanuel Wallerstein, 17–27. London: Verso.

Bambrick, Susan, ed. 1994. *The Cambridge Encyclopedia of Australia.* Cambridge: Cambridge University Press.

Barrett, Michelle. 1991. *The Politics of Truth: From Marx to Foucault.* London: Polity Press.

Befu, Harumi. 1987. *Ideorogī toshite no Nihon bunkaron.* Tokyo: Shisō no Kagakusha.

Bellah, Robert N., et al. 1985. *Habits of the Heart: Individualism and Commitment in American Life.* Berkeley: University of California Press.

Benedict, Ruth. 1946. *The Chrysanthemum and the Sword.* Boston: Houghton Mifflin.

Bitō, Masahide. 1956. "Edo jidai chūki ni okeru honzōgaku: Kindai kagaku no seisei to kanren suru men yori." In *Tokyo Daigaku kyōikubu jinbun kagaku kiyō,* Part 11, History and Culture 2. Historical Research Report 5.

Bourdieu, Pierre. 1993. *The Field of Cultural Production.* Cambridge: Polity Press.

Bowen, Roger W. 1980. *Rebellion and Democracy in Meiji Japan.* Berkeley: University of California Press.

Braudel, Fernand. 1994. *A History of Civilizations* (trans. Richard Mayne). London: Allen Lane.

Brown, Delmer M. 1955. *Nationalism in Japan: An Introductory Historical Analysis.* Berkeley: University of California Press.

Buckley, Sandra. 1994. "A Short History of the Feminist Movement in Japan." In *Women of Japan and Korea: Continuity and Change,* ed. J. Gelb and M.L. Palley, 150–186. Philadelphia: Temple University Press.

———. 1997. *Broken Silence: Voices of Japanese Feminism.* Berkeley: University of California Press.

Buffon, Louis Georges Comte de. 1866. *A Natural History, General and Particular,* vol. 1 (trans. William Smellie). London: Thomas Kelly and Co.

Caxton, William. [1840] 1988. *The Description of Britain.* Ed. Marie Collins. Reprint, New York: Weidenfeld and Nicolson.

Chan, Wing-Sit. 1968. "The Story of Chinese Philosophy." In *The Chinese Mind,* ed. Charles A. Moore. Honolulu: University of Hawaii Press.

Chatterjee, Partha. 1986. *Nationalist Thought in the Colonial World: A Derivative Discourse?* London: Zed Books.

Chikap, Mieko. 1991. *Kaze no megumi: Ainu minzoku no bunka to jinken.* Tokyo: Ochanomizu Shobō.

Childe, Vere Gordon. 1936. *Man Makes Himself.* London: Watts and Co.

Chiri, Mashiho. 1974. "Ainugo nyūmon" (1956). In *Chiri Mashiho Chosakushū,* vol. 4, 229–412. Tokyo: Heibonsha.

Chong, Yong Hye. 1996. "Aidentiti o koete." In *Sabetsu to kyōsei no shakaigaku,* ed. Inoue Shun et al., 1–33. Tokyo: Iwanami Shoten.

Chou, Wan-yao. 1996. "The Kōminka Movement in Taiwan and Korea: Comparisons and Interpretations." In *The Japanese Wartime Empire 1931–1945,* ed. Peter Duus, Raymon H. Myers, and Mark R. Peattie. Princeton: Princeton University Press.

Christy, Alan S. 1993. "The Making of Imperial Subjects in Okinawa." *Positions: East Asia Cultures Critique* 1, no. 3 (Winter): 607–639.

Clayre, A., ed. 1977. *Nature and Industrialisation.* Oxford: Oxford University Press.

Clifford, James. 1988. *The Predicament of Culture.* Cambridge, MA: Harvard University Press.

Cole, Robert E. 1979. *Work, Mobility and Participation: A Comparative Study of American and Japanese Industry.* Berkeley: University of California Press.

Colson, Elizabeth. 1984. "The Reordering of Experience: Anthropological Involvement with Time." *Journal of Anthropological Research* 40: 1–13.

Condorcet, Antoine-Nicolas de. [1794] 1933. *Equisse d'un tableau historique des progres de l'esprit humain,* ed. O.H. Prior. Reprint, Paris: Boivin et Cie.

Dale, Peter. 1986. *The Myth of Japanese Uniqueness.* London: Croom Helm.

de Bary, W.T., and I. Bloom, eds. 1979. *Principle and Practicality: Essays in Neo-Confucian and Practical Learning.* New York: Columbia University Press.

DiMaggio, Paul. 1991. "Social Structure, Institutions, and Cultural Goods: The Case of the United States." In *Social Theory for a Changing Society,* ed. P. Bourdieu and J.S. Coleman. Boulder: Westview Press.

Doak, Kevin M. 1997. "Culture, Ethnicity and the State in Early 20th Century Japan." In *Competing Modernities: Re-evaluating Taisho Democracy,* ed. Sharon Minichiello. Honolulu: Hawaii University Press (forthcoming).

Doi, Takeo. 1973. *The Anatomy of Dependence* (trans. John Bester), 2d ed. Tokyo: Kōdansha.

Dower, John. 1986. *War Without Mercy: Race and Power in the Pacific War.* London: Faber and Faber.

D'Souza, Dinesh. 1995. *The End of Racism: Principles for a Multiracial Society.* New York: Free Press.

Duchacek, I.D., et al. 1988. *Perforated Sovereignties and International Relations.* New York: Greenwood Press.

Ehara, Yumiko. 1990. "Feminizumu no 70 nendai to 80 nendai." In *Feminizumu ronsō: 70 nendai kara 90 nendai e,* ed. Ehara Yumiko, 2–46. Tokyo: Keisō Shobō.

Eisenstadt, S.N. 1994. "The Japanese Attitude to Nature: A Framework of Basic Ontological Conceptions." In *Asian Perceptions of Nature: A Critical Approach,* ed. O. Bruun and A. Kalland, 189–214. London: Curzon Press.

Eliot, T.S. 1948. *Notes Towards the Definition of Culture.* London: Faber and Faber.

Elvin, Mark. 1993. "Three Thousand Years of Unsustainable Development: China's Environment from Archaic Times to the Present." *East Asian History,* no. 6 (December): 7–46.

Fabian, Johannes. 1983. *Time and the Other: How Anthropology Makes Its Object.* New York: Columbia University Press.

Fried, Morton. 1975. *The Notion of Tribe.* Menlo Park, CA: Cummings Publishing.

Frobenius, Leo. [1921] 1953. *Paideuma: Umrisse einer Kultur- und Seelenlehre.* Reprint, Düsseldorf: Eugen Diederichs Verlag.

Fujine, Iwao. 1983. *NHK dorama gaido Oshin.* Tokyo: Nihon Hōsō Shuppan Kyōkai.

Fujisawa, Chikao. 1938. *Tairiku keirin no shidō genri.* Tokyo: Daiichi Shuppan.

Fujitani, Takashi. 1996. *Splendid Monarchy: Power and Pageantry in Modern Japan.* Berkeley: University of California Press.

Fukasawa, Yuriko. 1995. "Ainu Archaeology as Ethnohistory: Iron Technology among the Saru Ainu of Hokkaidō in the 17th Century." Ph.D. dissertation, Cambridge University.

Fukuda, Tsuneari, ed. 1965. *Hankindai no shisō.* Tokyo: Iwanami Shoten.

Fukuoka, Yasunori. 1996. "Sabetsu kenkyū no genjo to kadai." In *Sabetsu to kyōsei no Shakaigaku,* ed. Inoue Shun et al., 223–248. Tokyo: Iwanami Shoten.

Fukuta, Ajio. 1992. "Shoki Yanagita Kunio no kenkyū to gendai minzokugaku." In *Rekishigaku to minzokugaku,* ed. Amino Yoshihiko et al., 135–160. Tokyo: Furukawa Kōbunkan.

Fukuzawa, Yukichi. 1926. "Sekai kunizukushi." Reproduced in *Fukuzawa Yukichi zenshū*, Vol. 2. Tokyo: Kōmin Tosho.

———. [1876] 1973. *An Outline of a History of Civilization* (trans. David A. Dilworth and G. Cameron Hurst). Reprint, Tokyo: Sophia University Press.

Furukawa, Tetsushi. 1961. "Watsuji Tetsurō, the Man and His Work." In *A Climate* (trans. G. Bownas), ed. T. Watsuji , 209–255. Tokyo: Japanese Government Printing Bureau.

Gamst, F.C., and E. Norbeck. 1976. *Ideas of Culture: Sources and Uses.* New York: Holt, Reinhart and Winston.

"Getting Back Our Islands." 1993. *Ampo* 24, no. 3: 7–9.

Giddens, Anthony. 1987. *The Nation-State and Violence.* Berkeley: University of California Press.

Gluck, Carol. 1985. *Japan's Modern Myths.* Princeton: Princeton University Press.

Goodman, Grant K. 1986. *Japan: The Dutch Experience.* London: Athlone Press.

Gordon, Milton M. 1988. *The Scope of Sociology.* Oxford: Oxford University Press.

Graham, Mary. 1993. Seminar on Cross-Cultural Understanding (oral presentation). Australian National University, 20 March.

Guizot, F. [1828–30] 1851. *Histoire de la Civilization en Europe Depuis la Chute de L'Empire Romain.* Paris: Victor Masson.

Gunew, Sneja. 1994. "Multicultural Critical Theory: Beyond the Binaries of Race and Ethnicity." Paper presented at the Conference on Identity, Ethnicity and Nationality, La Trobe University, Melbourne, July.

Haga, Yaichi. 1977. "Kokuminsei jūron" (1907). In *Nihonjin ron,* ed. Ikimatsu Keizō. Tokyo: Toyamabō.

Hall, Robert K., ed. 1949. *Kokutai no Hongi: Cardinal Principles of the National Entity of Japan.* Cambridge, MA: Harvard University Press.

Hamaguchi, Eshun, et al. 1992. *Japanese Systems: An Alternative Civilization.* Tokyo: Sekotac.

Hanazaki, Kōhei. 1993. *Shizukana taichi.* Tokyo: Iwanami Shoten.

Hane, Mikiso. 1988. *Reflections on the Way to the Gallows: Rebel Women in Prewar Japan.* Berkeley: University of California Press.

Haniwa, Satoru. 1980. "Meiji 32–nen no kokusekihō seiritsu ni itaru katei." In *Nihon shakaishi kenkyū,* ed. Haga Kōshirō Sensei Koki Kinenkai, 301–322. Tokyo: Kasama Shoin.

Hannerz, Ulf. 1990. "Cosmopolitans and Locals in World Culture." In *Global Culture: Nationalism, Globalisation and Modernity,* ed. Mike Featherstone. London: Sage Books.

Hargrove, Eugene C. 1989. "Foreword." In *Nature in Asian Traditions of Thought: Essays in Environmental Philosophy,* ed. J. Baird Callicott and Roger T. Ames. Albany: State University of New York Press.

Harootunian, H.D. 1974. "The Problem of Taisho." In *Japan in Crisis: Essays on Taishō Democracy,* ed. Bernard S. Silberman and H.D. Harootunian. Princeton: Princeton University Press.

———. 1988. *Things Seen and Unseen: Discourse and Ideology in Tokugawa Nativism.* London: University of Chicago Press.

Harvey, Paul A.S. 1995. "Interpreting *Oshin:* War, History and Women in Modern Japan." In *Women, Media and Consumption in Japan*, ed. Lise Skov and Brian Moeran. London: Curzon Press.

Hashida, Sugako. 1984. *Oshin* (screenplay), 4 vols. Tokyo: Nihon Hōsō Shuppan Kyōkai.

Hastings, Sally Ann. 1996. "Women Legislators in the Postwar Diet." In *Re-Imaging Japanese Women*, ed. Anne E. Imamura, 271–300. Berkeley: University of California Press.

Hatch, Walter, and Kozo Yamamura. 1996. *Asia in Japan's Embrace*. Cambridge: Cambridge University Press.

Hatsuse, Ryūhei, ed. 1985. *Uchi naru kokusaika*. Tokyo: Sanryō Shobō.

———. 1996. "Nihon no kokusaika to tabunkashugi." In *Esunishiti to tabunkashugi*, ed. Hatsuse Ryūhei, 205–230. Tokyo: Dōbunkan.

Hayashi, Shihei. 1979. *Hayashi Shihei zenshū*, vol. 2. Tokyo: Daiichi Shobō.

Hayashi, Yoshishige. 1969. *Ainu no nōkō bunka*. Tokyo: Keiyūsha.

Hayes, Louis D. 1992. *Introduction to Japanese Politics*. New York: Paragon House.

Higashionna, Kanjun. 1966. *Ryūkyū no rekishi*. Tokyo: Kyōbundō.

Hokkaidō Utari Kyōkai, ed. *1989. Ainu shi: Shiryō hen 4: Kingendai shiryō*, Part 2. Sapporo: Hokkaidō Utari Kyōkai .

———. ed. 1990. *Ainu shi: Shiryō hen 3: Kingendai shiryō*, Part 1. Sapporo: Hokkaidō Utari Kyōkai.

———. ed. 1996. *"Ainu Shimpō" seitei yōbō*. Discussion paper. Sapporo: Hokkaidō Utari Kyōkai.

Hollinger, David. 1995. *Postethnic America*. New York: Basic Books.

Howell, David. 1994. "Ainu Ethnicity and the Boundaries of the Early Modern Japanese State." *Past and Present*, no. 142 (February): 69–93.

Huntington, Samuel. 1993. "Clash of Civilizations?" *Foreign Affairs*, 72, no. 3. (Summer).

———. 1996. *The Clash of Civilizations and the Remaking of World Order*. New York: Simon and Schuster.

Iesaka, Kazushi. 1980. *Nihonjin no jinshukan*. Tokyo: Kōbunsha.

Iketani, Kankai. 1904. "Han-Nihonjin." *Nihonjin*, no. 223 (November): 462–464.

Imamura, Anne E. 1987. *Urban Japanese Housewives: At Home and in the Community*. Honolulu: University of Hawaii Press.

Inoue, Tetsujirō. 1928. "Naichi zakkyo ron." In *Meiji bunka zenshū*, ed. Yoshino Sakuzō, vol. 6, 472–488. Tokyo: Nihon Hyōronsha.

Ishida, Eiichirō. 1956. *Momotarō no haha*. Tokyo: Hōsei Daigaku Shuppankai.

———. 1972. "Nihon bunka no jaken to kankōsei: aru henkyō bunka no takushitsu." In *Nihon bunka no kōzō*, ed. Umesao Tadao and Tada Michitarō. Tokyo: Kōdansha.

———. 1974. *Japanese Culture: A Study of Origins and Characteristics*. Tokyo: University of Tokyo Press.

———. 1977a. "Bunka to wa nani ka." In *Ishida Eiichirō zenshū*, vol. 1. Tokyo: Chikuma Shobō.

———. 1977b. "Bunka jinruigaku josetsu" (1959). In *Ishida Eiichirō zenshū*, vol. 1. Tokyo: Chikuma Shobō.

Itazawa, Takeo. 1960. *Shiiboruto*. Tokyo: Yoshikawa Kōbunkan.

Itō, Shuntarō. 1990. *Hikaku bunmei to Nihon*. Tokyo: Chūō Kōronsha.

Ivy, Marilyn. 1995. *Discourses of the Vanishing: Modernity, Phantasm, Japan.* Chicago: University of Chicago Press.

Iwamoto, Yoshiteru. 1990. *Yanagita Kunio o yominaosu.* Tokyo: Sekai Shisōsha.

Iwasaki, Minoru. 1995. "Poiēshisuteki metashutai no yokubō." In *Sōryokusen to gendaika,* ed. Yamanouchi Yasushi et al., 185–209. Tokyo: Kashiwa Shobō.

Jōfuku, Isamu. 1986. *Hiraga Gennai.* Tokyo: Furukawa Kōbunkan.

Johnson, Chalmers. 1965. *An Instance of Treason: The Story of the Tokyo Spy Ring.* London: Heinemann.

Jones, S.H. 1968. "Scholar. Scientist, Popular Author: Hiraga Gennai 1728–1780." Ph.D. dissertation, Columbia University.

Kada, Tetsuji. 1938. *Nihon kokkashugi no hatten.* Tokyo: Keiō Shobō.

———. 1939. *Gendai no shokuminchi seisaku.* Tokyo: Keiō Shobō.

———. 1940a. *Jinshu, minzoku, sensō.* Tokyo: Keiō Shobō.

———. 1940b. *Seiji, keizai, minzoku.* Tokyo: Keiō Shobō

———. 1962. *Nihon shakai keizai shisōshi.* Tokyo: Keiō Shobō.

Kahn, Joel S. 1995. *Culture, Multiculture, Postculture.* London: Sage Publications.

Kaiho, Mineo. 1979. *Kinsei no Hokkaidō.* Tokyo: Kyōikusha.

Kajita, Takamichi. 1996a. "Gaikokujin sanseiken: Seiō no keiken to Nihon ni okeru kanōsei." In *Gaikokujin rōdōsha kara shimin e: chiiki shakai no shiten to kadai kara,* ed. Miyajima Takashi and Kajita Takamichi, 99–122. Tokyo: Yūhikaku.

———. 1996b. "'Tabunkashugi' o meguru ronsōten: Gainen no meikakuka no tame ni." In *Esunishiti to tabunkashugi,* ed. Hatsuse Ryūhei, 67–101. Tokyo: Dōbunkan.

Kalland, Arne. 1994. "Culture in Japanese Nature." In *Asian Perceptions of Nature: A Critical Approach,* ed. O. Bruun and A. Kalland, 243–257. London: Curzon Press.

Kamiya, Nobuyuki. 1990. *Bakuhansei kokka no Ryūkyū shihai.* Tokyo: Kokura Shobō.

Kanagawa, Ken. [1916] 1966. "Kawasaki hōmen no kōgyō." Reprint, *Keizai to bōeki 88.*

Kaneko, Fumiko. 1991. *The Prison Memoirs of a Japanese Woman* (trans. J. Inglis). Armonk, NY: M.E. Sharpe.

Kaner, Simon. 1996. "Beyond Ethnicity and Emergence in Japanese Archaeology." In *Multicultural Japan: Palaeolithic to Postmodern,* ed. D. Denoon et al. 46–59. Cambridge: Cambridge University Press.

Kang, Sang Jung. 1996. "Naiteki kokkyō to radikaru demokurashī." *Shisō* (September): 25–37.

Kang, Sang Jung, and Murai Osamu. 1993. "Ranhansha suru orietarizumu." *Gendai shisō* 21, no. 5: 182–197.

Kanō, Mikiyo, ed. 1979. *Josei to tennōsei.* Tokyo: Shisō no Kagakusha.

Kaplan, David, and Robert Manners. 1972. *Cultural Theory.* Englewood Cliffs, NJ: Prentice Hall.

Kaplinsky, Raphael. 1994. *Easternisation: The Spread of Japanese Management Practices to Developing Countries.* Ilford and Portland: F. Cass.

Kawada, Minoru. 1993. *The Orgins of Ethnography in Japan: Yanagita Kunio and His Times* (trans. T. Kishida-Ellis). London and New York: Kegan Paul International.

Kawai, Hayao. 1976. *Bosei shakai Nihon no byōri*. Tokyo: Chūō Kōronsha.
———. 1984. *Nihonjin to aidentiti*. Tokyo: Sōgensha.
Kawakatsu, Heita. 1977. "Meiji zenki ni okeru naigai men kankeihin no hinshitsu." *Waseda seiji keizaigaku zasshi*, 250–251: 184–211.
———. 1991. *Nihon bunmei to kindai Seiyō*. Tokyo: Nihon Hōsō Shuppan Kyōkai.
———. 1992a. "'Shakai no bussan fukugō' toshite no bunmei." *Mugendai* 91: 37–45.
———. 1992b. "Aratanaru 'Nihonron' no tame ni." *Chūō Kōron* (February).
———. 1993. "Shakai kagaku no datsuryōikika." In *Shakai kagaku no hōhō*, vol 1. Tokyo: Iwanami Shoten.
———. 1995. *Fukoku utokuron*. Tokyo: Kinokuniya Shoten.
Kawamura, Nozomu. 1988. "The Concept of Modernisation Re-examined from the Japanese Experience." In *The Japanese Trajectory: Modernisation and Beyond*, ed. G. McCormack and Y. Sugimoto. Cambridge: Cambridge University Press.
Kawatō, Akio. 1995. "'Ajiateki kachi' o koete." *Chūō Kōron* (December): 45–53.
Kayano, Shigeru. 1993. *Kokkai de charanke: Nibutani ni Ainu toshite ikiru*. Tokyo: Shakai Shimpō Bukkuretto.
———. 1994. *Our Land Was a Forest: An Ainu Memoir* (trans. Kyoko Selden and Lili Selden). Boulder: Westview Press.
Kikuchi, Isao. 1988. "Kinsei ni okeru Ezokan to 'Nihon Fūzoku.'" In *Kita kara no Nihonshi*, ed. Hokkaidō Tōhoku Shi Kenkyū Kai, 206–229. Tokyo: Sanseidō.
———. 1991. *Hoppōshi no naka no kinsei Nihon*. Tokyo: Kokura Shobō.
———. 1992. "Kyokai to minzoku." In *Ajia no naka no Nihonshi*, vol. 4, ed. Arano Teiji et al., 55–80. Tokyo: Tokyo Daigaku Shuppankai.
Kikuchi, Toshiyoshi. 1988. *Zufu Edo Jidai no Gijutsu*, vol. 1. Tokyo: Kōwa Shuppan.
Kimiya, Yasuhiko. 1955. *Nikka bunka kōryūshi*. Tokyo: Toyamabō.
Kita, Sadakichi. 1918. "'Minzoku to rekishi' hakkan shuisho." *Minzoku to rekishi* 1, no. 1: 1–8.
———. 1978. "Nihon minzokushi gaisetsu." (1929). In *Nihon minzoku bunka taikei 5: Kita Sadakichi*, ed. M. Ueda. Tokyo: Kōdansha.
Koga, Jūjirō. 1969. *Maruyama yūjo to tōkō mōjin*, vol. 2. Nagasaki: Nagasaki Gakkai.
Kokusai Bunka Shinkōkai. 1939. *Academic and Cultural Organizations in Japan*. Tokyo: Kokusai Bunka Shinkōkai.
Kondō, Atsushi. 1996. *Gaikokujin sanseiken to kokuseki*. Tokyo. Akashi Shoten.
Kondo, Dorinne K. 1990. *Crafting Selves: Power, Gender, and Discourses of Identity in a Japanese Workplace*. London: University of Chicago Press.
Kōsaka, Masaaki. 1966. *Shiken kitai sareru ningenzō*. Tokyo: Chikuma Shobō.
Kōseishō Kenkyūjo Jinkō Minzokubu. [1943] 1981. *Yamato minzoku o chūkaku to suru sekai seisaku no kentō*, 6 vols. Reprint, Tokyo: Bunsei Shoin.
Koshiro, Yukiko. 1995. "Japan's Racial Discourse in the U.S. Occupation of Japan." In *Racial Identities in East Asia*, ed. B. Sautman, 311–331. Hong Kong: Hong Kong University of Science and Technology.

Kristeva, Julia. 1993. *Nations Without Nationalism* (trans. L.S. Roudiez). New York: Columbia University Press.

Kroeber, A.L. 1952a. "The Superorganic" (1917). In *The Nature of Culture.* Chicago: University of Chicago Press.

———. 1952b. "So-Called Social Science" (1936). In *The Nature of Culture.* Chicago: University of Chicago Press.

———. 1957. *Style and Civilizations.* Ithaca: Cornell University Press.

Kroeber, A.L., and C. Kluckhohn. 1963. *Culture: A Critical Review of Concepts and Definitions.* New York: Vintage Books.

Kumazawa, Banzan. 1971. "Shūgi washo" (1672). Reprinted in *Nihon shisō taikei,* vol. 30. Tokyo: Iwanami Shoten.

Kurihara, Akira. 1993. "Shimin shakai no haikyo kara." *Sekai* (October): 45–58.

Laclau, Ernesto, and Chantal Mouffe. 1985. *Hegemony and Socialist Strategy.* London: Verso Press.

LaFleur, William R. 1989. "Saigyō and the Buddhist View of Nature." In *Nature in Asian Traditions of Thought: Essays in Environmental Philosophy,* ed. J. Baird Callicott and Roger T. Ames. Albany: State University of New York Press.

Lash, Scott, and John Urry. 1994. *Economies of Signs and Space.* London: Sage Publications.

Lehmann, Jean-Pierre. 1978. *The Image of Japan: From Feudal Isolation to World Power—1850–1905.* London: George Allen and Unwin.

Lewis, Glen. 1994. "Communication Strategies for Thailand and Australia in an Age of Pacific Globalism." In *Information Superhighways and Cultural Diversity,* ed. Malee Boonsiripunth. Bangkok: Faculty of Journalism and Mass Communication, Thammasat University.

Li, Dun Jen. 1975. *The Civilization of China.* New York: Charles Scribner.

Liu, James T.C. 1959. *Reform in Sung China: Wang An-Shih (1021–1086) and his New Policies.* Cambridge, MA: Harvard University Press.

Lock, Margaret. 1993. *Encounters with Aging: Mythologies of Menopause in Japan and North America.* Berkeley: University of California Press.

Low, Morris. 1996. "The Body of the Emperor and the Japanese Soldier." Paper presented at the Biennial Conference of the Asian Studies Association of Australia, La Trobe University, Melbourne, July.

———. 1998. "The Japanese Nation in Evolution: W.E. Griffis, Hybridity and the Whiteness of the Japanese Race." *History and Anthropology* (forthcoming).

Lull, James. 1991. *China Turned On: Television, Reform and Resistance.* London: Routledge.

Macaulay, Thomas Babington. [1848–61] 1986. *The History of England,* ed. and abr. Hugh Trevor-Roper. Reprint, London: Penguin.

McCormack, Gavan. 1991. "Manchukuo: Constructing the Past." *East Asian History,* no. 2 (December): 105–124.

———. 1996. *The Emptiness of Japanese Affluence.* Armonk, NY, and Sydney: M.E. Sharpe/Allen and Unwin.

McKibben, Bill. 1990. *The End of Nature.* London: Viking.

Mackie, Vera. 1995. "Engaging with the State: Socialist Women in Imperial Japan." In *Feminism and the State in Modern Japan,* ed. Vera Mackie, 16–30. Melbourne: Papers of the Japanese Studies Centre, no. 22.

MacMaster, Robert E. 1967. *Danilevsky: A Russian Totalitarian Philosopher.* Cambridge, MA: Harvard University Press.

Maes. 1970. *Hiraga Gennai et son temps.* Paris: Ecole Française d'Extrême Orient.

Mahathir, Mohamad, and Ishihara Shintarō. 1994. *"No" to ieru Ajia.* Tokyo: Kōbunsha.

Mamiya, Rinzō. 1972. "Kita Ezo zusetsu" (1855). Reprinted in *Hokumon sōsho,* vol. 5, ed. Ōtomo, Kisaku. Tokyo: Kokusho Kankōkai.

Manuel, Frank E. 1968. "Editor's Introduction." In *Reflections on the Philosophy of the History of Mankind,* by von Herder, Johann Gottfried. Reprint, Chicago: Chicago University Press.

Marshall, Byron K. 1994. *Learning to Be Modern: Japanese Political Discourse on Education.* Boulder: Westview Press.

Maruyama, Masao. 1996. "Minshushugi no rekishiteki haikei." Reprinted in *Maruyama Masao shū,* vol. 8, 87–95. Tokyo: Iwanami Shoten.

———. 1963. *Thought and Behaviour in Modern Japanese Politics.* London: Oxford University Press.

Matsuda, Toshihiko. 1995. *Senzenki no zainichi Chōsenjin to sanseiken.* Tokyo: Akashi Shoten.

Matsumoto, Shigeru. 1970. *Motoori Norinaga: 1730–1801.* Cambridge, MA: Harvard University Press.

Melucci, Alberto. 1989. *Nomads of the Present: Social Movements and Individual Needs in Contemporary Society.* London: Hutchinson Radius.

Merchant, Carolyn. 1980. *The Death of Nature.* London: Wildwood House.

Miyake, Setsurei. 1977. "Shin zen bi Nihonjin" (1891). In *Nihonjin ron,* ed. Ikimatsu Keizō. Tokyo: Toyamabō.

Miyazaki, Yasusada. 1972. "Nōgyō zensho" (1697). Reprinted in *Kinsei kagaku shisō,* vol. 1. Tokyo: Iwanami Shoten.

Mogami, Tokunai. 1972. "Ezo sōshi" In *Hokumon sōsho,* vol. 1, 310–410. Tokyo: Kokusho Kankōkai.

Montagu, Ashley. 1945. *Man's Most Dangerous Myth: The Fallacy of Race.* New York: Columbia University Press.

Moore, C.A., ed. 1967. *The Japanese Mind: Essentials of Japanese Philosophy and Culture.* Honolulu: University of Hawaii Press.

———. ed. 1968. *The Chinese Mind.* Honolulu: University of Hawaii Press.

Morris-Suzuki, Tessa. 1994. "Creating the Frontier: Border, Identity and History in Japan's Far North." *East Asian History,* no. 7 (June): 1–23.

———. 1994. *The Technological Transformation of Japan.* Cambridge: Cambridge University Press.

Morse, R.A. 1990. *Yanagita Kunio and the Folklore Movement.* New York and London: Garland.

Motoori, Norinaga. 1983. "Isonokami no sasamegoto" (1763). Reprinted in *Motoori Norinaga shū,* ed. Hino Tatsuo, 251–504. Tokyo: Shinchōsha.

Mouer, Ross, and Sugimoto Yoshio. 1986. *Images of Japanese Society.* London: Kegan Paul International.

Murai, Osamu. 1992. *Nantō ideorogī no hassei: Yanagita Kunio shokuminchishugi.* Tokyo: Fukutake Shoten.

Murakawa, Yōko. 1996. "Chūsei o tou koto, towareru koto." In *Nihon shakai to imin,* ed. Iyotani Toshio and Sugihara Tōru. Tokyo: Akashi Shoten.

Muroga, Nobuo. 1978. "Atarashii sekai no ninshiki: Nanban sekaizu byōbu." In *Daikōkai jidai no Nihon 5: Nihon kara mita ikoku,* 93–102. Tokyo: Shōgakukan.
Mushakōji, Kinhide. 1996. "Kokusai seiji ni okeru esunikku shūdan." In *Esunishiti to tabunkashugi,* ed. Hatsuse Ryūhei, 5–18. Tokyo: Dōbunkan.
Myers, R.H., and M.R. Peattie, eds. 1984. *The Japanese Colonial Empire 1895–1945.* Princeton: Princeton University Press.
Najita, T. 1987. *Visions of Virtue in Tokugawa Japan.* Chicago: University of Chicago Press.
Najita, T., and H.D. Harootunian. 1988. "Japanese Revolt against the West: Political and Cultural Criticism in the Twentieth Century." In *The Cambridge Encyclopedia of Japan: Volume 6, The Twentieth Century,* ed. P. Duus. Cambridge: Cambridge University Press.
Nakajima, Mineo, et al. 1995. "Ajia bunmei no rinkēji" (A discussion between Nakajima Mineo, Watanabe Toshio, Hamashita Takeshi, Tsuboi Yoshiharu and Sonoda Shigeto). *Sekai,* no. 616 (December): 83–101.
Nakandakari, Kiyoshi. 1996. "Okinawa shinsedai ron." *Jōkyo* (January): 94–97.
Nakane, Chie. 1967. *Tate shakai no ningen kankei.* Tokyo: Kōdansha.
————. 1973. *Japanese Society.* London: Pelican Books.
Namikawa, Kenji. 1992. *Kinsei Nihon to hoppō shakai.* Tokyo. Sanseidō.
Narita, Ryūichi. 1995. "Haha no kuni no onnatachi." In *Sōryokusen to Gendaika,* ed. Yamanouchi Yasushi, 163–184. Tokyo: Kashiwa Shobō.
Nihon Bunka Kyōkai, ed. 1939. *Nihon bunka,* 33 vols. Tokyo: Nihon Bunka Kyōkai.
Nihon Intānetto Kyōkai. 1996. *Intānetto hakusho 1996.* Tokyo: Inpuresu.
Nishi, K. 1995. "Nihonjin ga miotoshita maruchimedia no YTT." *Daiyamondo* 23 (December).
Nishida, Kitarō. 1965a. "Mu no jikakuteki gentei" (1932). In *Nishida Kitarō zenshū,* vol. 6. Tokyo: Iwanami Shoten.
————. 1965b. "Bashoteki ronri to shūkyōteki sekaikan" (1944). In *Nishida Kitarō zenshū,* vol. 11, Tokyo: Iwanami Shoten.
————. 1965c. "Ronri to sūri" (1944). In *Nishida Kitarō zenshū,* vol. 11. Tokyo: Iwanami Shoten.
————. 1966. "Nihon bunka no mondai" (1940). In *Nishida Kitarō zenshū,* vol. 12. Tokyo. Iwanami Shoten.
Nishikawa, Nagao. 1992. *Kokkyō no kōekata.* Tokyo: Chikuma Shobō.
————. 1996. "Two Interpretations of Japanese Culture" (trans. M. Murata and G. McCormack). In *Multicultural Japan: Paleolithic to Postmodern,* ed. D. Denoon et al., 245–264. Cambridge: Cambridge University Press.
Nitobe, Inazo. 1931. "Two Exotic Currents in Japanese Civilization." In *Western Influences in Modern Japan.* Chicago: University of Chicago Press.
————. 1905. *Bushido.* London: G.P. Puttnam's Sons.
Norman, E.H. 1949. *Andō Shōeki and the Anatomy of Japanese Feudalism.* Tokyo: Asiatic Society of Japan.
Ogawa, Sanae. 1986. "Ningen toshite ikiru tame no tatakai." In *Hokkaidō to shosū minzoku,* ed. Sapporo Gakuin Daigaku Jinbun Gakubu, 155–178. Sapporo: Sapporo Gakuin Daigaku.
Ogi, Shinzō, et al. 1986. *Tōkyō kūkan. 1868–1930.* Tokyo: Chikuma Shobō.
Ōgoshi, Aiko. 1994. "Kindai Nihon no feminizumu no kadai: 'sabetsu,' 'kankyō,' 'Ajia.' " *Femirōgu* 5: 153–175.

Oguma, Eiji. 1995. *Tanitsu mizoku shinwa no kigen.* Tokyo: Shinyōsha.

Ogura, Kazuo 1993. " 'Ajia fukken' no tame ni." *Chūō Kōron* (July): 60–73.

Ohmae, Kenichi. 1990. *The Borderless World: Power and Strategy in the Inter-linked Economy.* London: Fontana.

Okakura, Tenshin. 1963. "Tōyō no shisō" (1902). Reprinted in *Gendai Nihon shisō taikei* 9: Ajiashugi, ed. Takeuchi Yoshimi. Tokyo: Chikuma Shobō.

Okinawa, Ken, ed. 1977. *Okinawa Ken Shi.* Tokyo: Gannandō Shoten.

Ōkubo, Toshimichi. 1964. "Ōkubo Toshimichi bunsho." Reprinted in *Nihon kagaku gijutsu shi taikei,* vol. 1, ed. Nihon Kagakushi Kyōkai. Tokyo: Daiichi Hōki Shuppan.

Olson, Edward A. 1975. "Man and Nature: East Asia and the West." *Asian Profile* 3, no. 6 (December).

Onga, Takashi. 1996. "Okinawa no rekishi o yomu." *Jōkyō* (January): 109–143.

Ōta, Masahide. 1969. *Minikui Nihonjin: Nihon no Okinawa ishiki.* Tokyo: Simul Press.

Ouchi, W.G. 1981. *Theory Z: How American Business Can Meet the Japanese Challenge.* New York: Avon Books.

Pascale, R.T., and A.G. Athos. 1981. *The Art of Japanese Management.* New York: Simon and Schuster.

Patterson, Orlando. 1975. "Context and Choice in Ethnic Allegiance: A Theoretical Framework and Caribbean Case Study." In *Ethnicity: Theory and Experience,* ed. N. Glazer and D. Moynihan. Cambridge, MA: Harvard University Press.

——— . 1982. *Slavery and Social Death.* Cambridge, MA: Harvard University Press.

Pearson, Richard. 1996. "The Place of Okinawa in Japanese Historical Identity." In *Multicultural Japan: Palaeolithic to Postmodern,* ed. D. Denoon et al., 95–116. Cambridge: Cambridge University Press.

Pettman, Jan Jindy. 1996. *Working Women.* St Leonards: Allen & Unwin.

Preiswerk, R., and D. Perrot. 1978. *Ethnocentrism and History: Africa, Asia and Indian America in Western Textbooks.* New York and Lagos: Nok Publishers.

Rabson, Steve. 1996. *Assimilation Policy in Okinawa: Promotion, Resistance and Reconstruction.* Cardiff, CA: Japan Policy Research Institute Occasional Paper.

Reader, Ian. 1990. "The Animism Renaissance Reconsidered: An Urgent Response to Dr. Yasuda." *Nichibunken Newsletter,* no. 6 (May).

Rex, John. 1991. "Multiculturalism, Anti-Racism and Equality of Opportunity in Britain." In *Immigration and the Politics of Ethnicity and Race in Australia and Britain,* ed. R. Nile. London: Sir Robert Menzies Centre for Australian Studies.

Robertson Scott, J.W. 1922. *The Foundations of Japan.* London: John Murray.

Robinson, Michael. 1997. "Broadcasting in Korea 1924–1937: Colonial Modernity and Cultural Hegemony." In *Competing Modernities: Re-evaluating Taisho Democracy,* ed. Sharon Minichiello. Honolulu: Hawaii University Press (forthcoming).

Ronan, Colin, A., and Joseph Needham. 1978. *The Shorter Science and Civilisation in China,* vol. 1. Cambridge: Cambridge University Press.

Russell, John G. 1995. *Henken to sabetsu wa dono yō ni tsukurareru ka.* Tokyo: Akashi Shoten.

Ryang, Sonia. 1997. "Love and Colonialism in Takamure Itsue's Feminism." *Feminist Review* (forthcoming).

Said, Edward W. 1978. *Orientalism*. London: Routledge and Kegan Paul.

Saigusa, Hiroto. 1973. "Nihon no chisei to gijutsu" (1939). Reprinted in *Saigusa Hiroto Chosaku Shū*, vol. 10. Tokyo: Chūō Kōronsha.

———. 1978a. "Gijutsu no shisō" (1941). Reprinted in *Saigusa Hiroto chosakushū*, vol. 7. Tokyo: Chūō Kōronsha.

———. 1978b. "Nihon no shisō bunka" (1937). Reprinted in *Saigusa Hiroto chosakushū*, vol. 5. Tokyo: Chūō Kōronsha.

———. 1978c. "Josei to sono 'kaihō'" (1946). In *Saigusa Hiroto chosakushū*, vol. 7, 285–290. Tokyo: Chūō Kōronsha.

Sakai, Naoki. 1996a. *Shisan sareru Nihongo, Nihonjin*. Tokyo: Shinyōsha.

———. 1996b. "Nashonariti to bo(koku)go no seiji." In *Nashonariti no datsukōchiku*, ed. Sakai Naoki et al., 9–53. Tokyo: Kashiwa Shobō.

Sakakibara, Eisuke. 1995. "The End of Progressivism." *Foreign Affairs* 74, no. 5 (September): 8–14.

———. 1996. *Beyond Capitalism: The Japanese Model of Market Economics*. Lanham, MD: University Press of America.

Sakakura, Genjirō. 1979. "Ezo zuihitsu" (1739). Reprinted in *Hoppō mikōkai kobunsho shūsei*, vol. 1. Tokyo: Sōbunsha.

Sakamoto, Yoshikazu. 1997. "Sōtaika no jidai: shimin no seiki o mezashite." *Sekai*. (January): 35–67.

Sakatani, Shiroshi. 1976. "Descending from Heaven" (1875). In *Meiroku Zasshi: Journal of the Japanese Enlightenment*, ed. W.R. Braisted. Tokyo: University of Tokyo Press.

Sakihara, Mitsugu. 1987. *A Brief History of Early Okinawa Based on the Omoro Sōshi*. Tokyo: Honpō Shoseki Press.

Satō, Nobuhiro. 1925. "Sonka zateki ron." Reprinted in *Satō Nobuhiro kagaku zenshū*, vol. 2. Tokyo: Iwanami Shoten.

———. 1977a. "Tenchūki" (1825). Reprinted in *Nihon shisō taikei*, vol. 45. Tokyo: Iwanami Shoten.

———. 1977b. "Keizai yōryaku" (1822). Reprinted in *Nihon shisō taikei*, vol. 45. Tokyo: Iwanami Shoten.

———. 1977c. "Suitō hiroku." Reprinted in *Nihon shisō taikei*, vol. 45. Tokyo: Iwanami Shoten.

———. 1977d. "Kondo hisaku." Reprinted in *Nihon shisō taikei*, vol. 45. Tokyo: Iwanami Shoten.

Scholte, J.A. 1993. *International Relations of Social Change*. Buckingham: Open University Press.

Screech, Timon. 1995. "Race and Gender? Human Categorisation in Japan." In *Disrupted Borders: An Intervention in Definitions of Boundaries*, ed. Sunil Gupta. London: Rivers Oram Press.

Segal, Daniel A., and Richard Handler. 1995. "U.S. Multiculturalism and the Concept of Culture." *Identities: Global Studies in Culture and Power* 1, no. 4 (April): 391–407.

Sekine, Masami. 1996. "Kokumin kokka to tabunkashugi." In *Esunishiti to tabunkashugi*, ed. Hatsuse Ryūhei, 41–66. Tokyo: Dōbunkan.

"Shisam o mezashite" editorial group, ed. 1994. *"Senjū minzoku no 10–nen" to Ainu minzoku rentai.* Sapporo: Gendai Shakai Kenkyūkai.

Shepardson, Mary. 1977. "Pawns of Power: The Bonin Islanders." In *The Anthropology of Power: Ethnographic Studies from Asia, Oceania and the New World,* eds R.D. Fogelson and R.N. Adams. New York: Academic Press.

Shiga, Shigetaka. 1968. "Nihon Fūkeiron." Extract in *Kagaku gijutsushi taikei,* vol. 6, ed. Nihon Kagakushi Kaigi. Tokyo: Dai-Ichi Hōki Shuppan.

Shinmei, Masamichi. 1939. *Tōa Kyōdōtai no risō.* Tokyo: Nihon Seinen Gaikō Kyōkai Shuppanbu.

Shinmei, Masamichi. 1980a. Author's introduction in *Shinmei Masamichi chosakushū,* vol. 8. Tokyo: Seishin Shobō.

———. 1980b. "Jinshu to shakai" (1940). In *Shinmei Masamichi chosakushū,* vol. 8. Tokyo: Seishin Shobō.

———. 1980c. "Minzoku no rekishiteki kigen" (1940). In *Shinmei Masamichi chosakushū,* vol. 8. Tokyo: Seishin Shobō.

———. 1980d. "Shiteki minzoku riron" (1948). In *Shinmei Masamichi chosakushū,* vol. 8. Tokyo: Seishin Shobō.

Shinya, Gyō. 1977. *Ainu minzoku to tennōsei kokka.* Tokyo: San-Ichi Shobō.

Shirai, Mitsutaro. 1926. "A Brief History of Botany in Old Japan." In *Scientific Japan: Past and Present.* Tokyo: Pan-Pacific Science Congress.

Shishido, Keiichi, ed. 1995. *Nihon shimbun hattatsu shi—Meiji, Taishō.* Tokyo: Taru Shobō.

Shoji, Kichiro, and Sugai Masuro. 1992. "The Ashio Copper Mine Pollution Case." In *Industrial Pollution in Japan,* ed. Ui Jun, 18–63. Tokyo: United Nations University Press.

Siddle, Richard. 1996. *Race, Resistance and the Ainu of Japan.* London: Routledge.

Sievers, Sharon. 1983. *Flowers in Salt: The Beginnings of Feminist Consciousness in Modern Japan.* Stanford: Stanford University Press.

Sloan, Phillip. 1995. "The Gaze of Natural History." In *Inventing Human Science: Eighteenth-Century Domains,* ed. C. Fox et al. Berkeley: University of California Press.

Smethurst, Richard J. 1974. *A Social Basis for Prewar Japanese Militarism: The Army and the Rural Community.* Berkeley: University of California Press.

Smith, Robert J., and Ella Lurie Wiswell. 1982. *The Women of Suye Mura.* Chicago: University of Chicago Press.

Sone, Shinichi. 1996. *Jinken mondai to tabunka shakai: Jiritsu to kyōsei no shiten kara.* Tokyo: Akashi Shoten.

Song, Yingxing. 1969. *Tenkō kaibutsu* (trans. Yabuuchi Kiyoshi). Tokyo: Heibonsha.

Steward, Julian H. 1973. *Alfred Kroeber.* New York and London: Columbia University Press.

Strong, Kenneth. 1977. *Ox Against the Storm: A Biography of Tanaka Shozo, Japan's Conservationist Pioneer.* Tenterden: Paul Norbury.

Suehiro, Ichio. 1943. *Nippon minzoku no yūsei ni kansuru kihon kenkyū.* Tokyo: privately published.

Sugimoto, Masayoshi, and David L. Swain. 1989. *Science and Culture in Traditional Japan*. Rutland, VT: Charles E. Tuttle.

Sun, E-tu Zen, and Sun Shiou Chuan, eds. 1966. *Chinese Technology in the Seventeenth Century* (English translation of the *Tiangong kaiwu*). University Park: Pennsylvania State University Press.

Suzuki, Michio. 1973. "Hikaku minzokugaku to bunka jinruigaku: Yanagita Kunio to Ishida Eiichirō no aida." In *Shimpojumu Yanagita Kunio*, ed. Kamishima Jirō and Itō Mikiharu. Tokyo: Nihon Hōsō Kyōkai.

Suzuki, Shūji. 1981. *Bunmei no kotoba*. Tokyo: Bunka Hyōron Shuppan.

Suzuki, Tōru. 1977. *Nishida Kitarō no sekai*. Tokyo: Toyamabō.

Suzuki, Yūko. 1989. "Hirohito shi to 'Shōwa' shi to onna." In *Onna, tennōsei, sensō*, ed. Suzuki Yūko, 7–37. Tokyo: Orijin Sentā.

———. 1992. *Jūgun ianfu, naisen kekkon: sei no shinryaku, sengo sekinin o kangaeru*. Tokyo: Miraisha.

Tachi, Kaoru. 1995. "Women's Suffrage and the State: Gender and Politics in Pre-War Japan." In *Feminism and the State in Modern Japan*, ed. Vera Mackie, 16–30. Melbourne: Papers of the Japanese Studies Centre, no. 22.

Takada, Yasuma. 1939. *Tōa minzoku ron*. Tokyo: Iwanami Shoten.

Takakura, Shinichirō. 1972. *Shinpan Ainu seisakushi*. Tokyo: San-ichi Shobō.

Takakusu, Junjirō. 1941. "Gaikoku bunka no inyū to sono hatten." In *Nihon bunka no hattatsu*, ed. Takakusu Junjirō et al. 2–70. Tokyo: Keimeikai.

Tanaka, Hiroshi. 1995. *Zainichi gaikokujin*, rev. ed. Tokyo: Iwanami Shoten.

Tanaka, Stefan. 1993. *Japan's Orient: Rendering Pasts into History*. Berkeley: University of California Press.

Taniguchi, Konen. 1942. *Tōyō minzoku no taishitsu*. Tokyo: Sangabō.

Terajima Yōan. [1712] 1929. *Wakan sansai zue*, vol. 1. Reprint, Tokyo: Nihon Zuihitsu Taisei Kankōkai.

Thongchai, Winichakul. 1994. *Siam Mapped: A History of the Geo-Body of a Nation*. Honolulu: University of Hawaii Press.

Toby, Ronald P. 1984. *State and Diplomacy in Early Modern Japan*. Princeton: Princeton University Press.

———. 1994. "The 'Indianness' of Iberia and Changing Japanese Iconographies of Other." In *Implicit Understandings: Observing, Reporting and Reflecting on Encounters Between Europeans and Other Peoples in the Early Modern Era*, ed. S.B. Schwartz, 323–351. Cambridge: Cambridge University Press.

Tōkyō Fu, ed. 1929. *Ogasawarato Sōran*. Tokyo: Tōkyō Fu.

Torii, Ryūzō. 1976. "Aru rōgakuto no shuki." In *Torii Ryūzō zenshū*, vol.12. Tokyo: Asahi Shimbunsha.

———. 1926. *Kyokutō Minzoku*, vol. 1. Tokyo: Bunka Seikatsu Kenkyūkai.

Totman, Conrad. 1989. *The Green Archipelago*. Berkeley: University of California Press.

Tsunoda, R., W.T. de Bary, and D. Keene, eds. 1958. *Sources of Japanese Tradition*. New York: Columbia University Press.

Twine, Nannette. 1991. *Language and the Modern State: The Reform of Written Japanese*. London and New York: Routledge.

Tylor, E.B. 1871. *Primitive Culture*. London: J. Murray.

Uchimura, Kanzō. 1955. "Ninomiya Sontoku: A Peasant Saint." In *Ninomiya Sontoku: His Life and "Evening Talks,"* ed. T. Ishiguro. Tokyo: Kenkyūsha.

Ueki, Emori. 1965. "Nihonkoku kokken an" (1881). Reprinted in *Gendai Nihon Shisō Taikei 3: Minshūshugi*, 74–90. Tokyo: Chikuma Shobō.

Uemura, Hideaki. 1990. *Kita no umi no kōekishatachi. Ainu shakai keizaishi*. Tokyo: Dōbunkan.

———. 1996. "Ainu Shinpō e no kewashii michi." *Sekai* (October): 93–100.

Ueno, Chizkuo. 1986. *Onna wa chikyū o sukueru ka*. Tokyo: Keisō Shobō.

———. 1996. "Modern Patriarchy and the Formation of the Japanese Nation State." In *Multicultural Japan: Palaeolithic to Postmodern*, ed. D. Denoon et al., 213–223. Cambridge: Cambridge University Press.

Ueyama, Shumpei, ed. 1990a. *Nihon bunmeishi no kōsō*, 7 vols. Tokyo: Kadokawa Shoten.

———. 1990b. *Juyō to sōzō no kiseki*. Vol. 1 of Ueyama Shumpei, ed., *Nihon bunmeishi no kōsō*. Tokyo: Kadokawa Shoten.

Umehara, Takeshi. 1991. *Mori no shisō wa jinrui o sukuu*. Tokyo: Shōgakukan.

Umehara, Takeshi, and Fujimura Hisakazu, eds. 1990. *Ainugaku no yoake*. Tokyo: Shōgakukan.

Umesao, Tadao. 1989. "Bunmei no seitai shikan" (1957). In *Umesao Tadao chosakushū*, vol. 5, 1–269. Tokyo: Chūō Kōronsha.

Utari Taisaku no Arikata ni Kansuru Yūshikisha Kondankai. 1996. *Hōkokusho*. Tokyo (April).

Vaporis, Constantine N. 1989. "Caveat Viator: Advice to Travellers in the Edo Period." *Monumenta Nipponica* 44, no. 4: 461–483.

Vasishth, Andrea. 1997. "A Model Minority: The Chinese Community in Japan." In *Japan's Minorities: The Illusions of Homogeneity*, ed. M. Weiner, 108–139. London: Routledge.

Véliz, Claudio. 1994. *The New World of the Gothic Fox: Culture and Economy in English and Spanish America*. Berkeley and Los Angeles: University of California Press.

von Herder, Johann Gottfried. [1784–91] 1968. *Reflections on the Philosophy of the History of Mankind*. Abridged and ed. by Frank E. Manuel. Reprint, Chicago: University of Chicago Press.

von Krusenstern, A.J. 1968. *Voyage Round the World in the Years 1803, 1804, 1805, and 1806*, vol. 2. Amsterdam and New York: N. Israel/Da Capo Press.

Wagatsuma, Hiroshi, and Yoneyama Toshio. 1967. *Henken no kōzō: Nihonjin no jinshukan*. Tokyo: Nihon Hōsō Shuppan Kyōkai.

Wakabayashi, Tadashi. B. 1986. *Anti-Foreignism and Western Learning in Early-Modern Japan: The New Theses of 1825*. Cambridge, MA, and London: Harvard University Press.

Walbank, F.W. 1981. *The Hellenistic World*. London: Fontana Press.

Wallerstein, I. 1990. "Culture as the Ideological Battleground of the Modern World-System." *Theory, Culture and Society* 7.

———. 1991a. "The Invention of TimeSpace Realities." In *Unthinking Social Science: The Limits of Nineteenth Century Paradigms*, ed. I. Wallerstein. London: Polity Press.

———. 1991b. "The Construction of Peoplehood: Racism, Nationalism and Ethnicity." In *Race, Nation, Class: Ambiguous Identities*, ed. Etienne Balibar and Immanuel Wallerstein, 71–85. London: Verso.

Watanabe, Shōichi. 1990. *Hi wa mada noboru*. Tokyo. Shōdensha.

Watsuji, Tetsurō. 1963. "Fūdo" (1943). Reprinted in *Gendai Nihon shisō taikei 28: Watsuji Tetsurō,* 143–297. Tokyo: Iwanami Shoten.

Weiner, Michael. 1994. *Race and Migration in Imperial Japan.* London: Routledge.

———. 1995. "Discourses of Race, Nation and Empire in Pre-1945 Japan." *Ethnic and Racial Studies* 18, no. 3 (July): 433–456.

White, Lynn. 1967. "The Historical Roots of Our Ecological Crisis." *Science* 155, 1203–1207.

Yabuuchi, Kiyoshi. 1982. *Kagakushi kara mita Chūgoku bunmei.* Tokyo: NHK Books.

Yamagata, Ishinosuke. 1906. *Ogasawaratō shi.* Tokyo: Tōyōdō .

Yamaguchi, Masao. 1979. *Nihon minzoku bunka taikei. Vol. 8: Ishida Eiichirō.* Tokyo: Kōdansha.

Yamamoto, Noritsuna. 1983. *Tōjin yashiki.* Tokyo: Kenkōsha.

Yamanouchi, Yasushi. 1996. *Shisutemu shakai no gendaiteki isō.* Tokyo: Iwanami Shoten.

Yamaori, Tetsuo. 1995. "Shūkyō o wasureta sengo seijigaku, rekishigaku". *Chūō Kōron* (September): 78–90.

Yanagita, Kunio. 1963a. "Yamabito gaiden shiryō" (1917). In *Teihon Yanagita Kunio shū,* vol. 4. Tokyo: Chikuma Shobō.

———. 1963b. "Katatsumuri kō" (1964). In *Teihon Yanagita Kunio shū,* vol. 18. Tokyo: Chikuma Shobō.

———. 1963c. "Saijitsu kō" (1946). In *Teihon Yanagita Kunio shū,* vol. 11. Tokyo: Chikuma Shobō.

———. 1963d. "Tōno monogatari" (1910). In *Teihon Yanagita Kunio shū,* vol. 4. Tokyo: Chikuma Shobō.

———. 1964a. "Tanoshii seikatsu" (1941). In *Teihon Yanagita Kunio shū,* vol. 30. Tokyo: Chikuma Shobō.

———. 1964b. "Josei to bunka" (1942). In *Teihon Yanagita Kunio shū,* vol. 30. Tokyo: Chikuma Shobō.

———. 1964c. "Minkan denshōron" (1934). In *Teihon Yanagita Kunio shū,* vol. 25. Tokyo: Chikuma Shobō.

———. 1964d. "Kyōdo seikatsu no kenkyūhō" (1935). In *Teihon Yanagita Kunio shū,* vol. 25. Tokyo: Chikuma Shobō.

Yasuda, Yoshinori. 1990. "Animism Renaissance." *Nichibunken Newsletter,* no. 5 (January).

———. 1989. "Passivity and Activity of Japanese Studies." *Nichibunken Newsletter,* no. 3 (July).

Yoshida, Heijirō. 1989. "Kōgyō shinkōron" (1885). Reprinted in *Kagaku to Gijutsu,* vol. 14 of *Nihon kindai shisō taikei.* Tokyo: Iwanami Shoten.

Yoshikawa, Hiroya, and Ogata Osamu. 1996. *Okinawa: Daikōeki runessansu.* Tokyo: Shakai Hyōronsha.

Yoshino, Kosaku. 1992. *Cultural Nationalism in Contemporary Japan.* London and New York: Routledge.

Yü, Ying-shi. 1991. "Clio's New Cultural Turn and the Rediscovery of Tradition in Asia." Keynote address presented to the Twelfth Conference of the International Association of Historians of Asia, June.

Yuasa, Mitsutomo. 1961. *Kagaku shi.* Tokyo: Tōyō Keizai Shimbunsha.

Index

Tessa Morris-Suzuki holds a chair in Japanese history in the Research School of Pacific and Asian Studies, Australian National University. Her research focuses on the social effects of technological change, and on issues of national identity in modern Japan. Her books include *Showa: An Inside History of Hirohito's Japan* (1984), *Beyond Computopia* (1988); *A History of Japanese Economic Thought* (1989) and *The Technological Transformation of Japan* (1994).